FIRST EDITION

INTER– CULTURAL COMPETENCY

LEARNING, COMMUNICATING, AND SERVING

Edited by Robert S. Littlefield, Jenna Currie-Mueller, Noor Ghazal-Aswad, and Nadene N. Vevea

North Dakota State University

D1445486

Bassim Hamadeh, CEO and Publisher
Michael Simpson, Vice President of Acquisitions and Sales
Jamie Giganti, Senior Managing Editor
Jess Busch, Senior Graphic Designer
Mark Combes, Senior Field Acquisitions Editor
Mirasol Enriquez, Senior Project Editor
Luiz Ferreira, Senior Licensing Specialist
Claire Yee, Interior Designer

First published in the United States of America in 2016 by Cognella, Inc.

Cover image copyright © 2012 Depositphotos/Irmairma.
      copyright © 2013 Depositphotos/malven.
      copyright © 2014 Depositphotos/AppleEyesStudio.
      copyright © 2012 Depositphotos/soleg.
      copyright © 2014 Depositphotos/AChubykin.
      copyright © 2013 Depositphotos/alessandro0770.
      copyright © 2012 Depositphotos/Mudryuk.
      copyright © 2013 Depositphotos/Irmairma.
      copyright © 2013 Depositphotos/aodaodaodaod.
      copyright © 2010 Depositphotos/Imagecom.
      copyright © 2014 Depositphotos/kenfotos.
      copyright © 2011 Depositphotos/piccaya.
      source: http://commons.wikimedia.org/wiki/File:K%C4%97daini%C5%B3_minaretas,_%C4%AFra%C5%A1as.JPG. Copyright in the Public Domain.
      copyright © 2013 Depositphotos/homydesign.
      copyright © 2013 Depositphotos/Dr.Art.
      copyright © 2010 Depositphotos/LaschonRichard.
      copyright © 2014 Depositphotos/Mongpro.
      copyright © 2013 Depositphotos/boggy22.
      copyright © 2014 Depositphotos/AndreyKr.

Printed in the United States of America

ISBN: 978-1-63487-466-3 (pbk)/ 978-1-63487-467-0 (br)

www.cognella.com   800-200-3908

CONTENTS

A NOTE FROM THE EDITORS

HOW TO USE THIS BOOK

Hello! Welcome to *Intercultural Competency: Learning, Communicating, and Serving*. Whether you have studied or interacted with cultures different than your own prior to owning this book, our hope is that this reader will aid you in your journey toward becoming a culturally competent communicator. This book is a collection filled with popular, scholarly, and useful readings located in one convenient place for you, the reader, as you embark on your journey.

This book is a great supplemental resource to your in-class instruction. In each chapter, several readings hand-selected by the editors are included to help you to better understand the concepts being introduced in the course. These readings present essential and relevant concepts related to intercultural communication.

At the beginning of each chapter, you will find three study objectives. These objectives will help you pinpoint the primary information you should take away from each chapter. Within most chapters, a section entitled, "Moving Forward," precedes each selected reading. These sections are designed to give you, the reader, an overview of the selection that follows, linking the reading to the topic and including concepts and questions you should be focusing on as you read. At the end of every chapter, you will find discussion questions that focus on key concepts within the chapter. These discussion questions are designed to put your new-found knowledge to the test.

As you begin reading this book, and continue to move through it, apply your critical thinking skills to the concepts presented in each reading. Make sure to question what you read, wrestle with the concepts and different approaches discussed throughout the book, and engage in your classroom discussions. Most of all, have fun while learning about intercultural communication and enjoy your journey toward becoming a culturally competent communicator.

—Editors,
R. Littlefield, J. Currie-Mueller, N. Vevea, & N. Ghazal-Aswad

INTRODUCTION TO INTERCULTURAL COMMUNICATION
CHAPTER 1

STUDY OBJECTIVES

After completing this chapter, you will be able to:
- Describe and define intercultural communication.
- Identify and explain why studying intercultural communication is important.
- Identify key moments in the development of the field of intercultural communication.

INTRODUCTION

We live in a connected world with opportunities to communicate immediately with other individuals regardless of distance that separates us. This connectedness has, in many ways, brought the world closer enabling different cultures to interact with one another on a daily basis. Here, in the United States, our cultural landscape is shifting as individuals from around the world move to this country to create new lives for themselves and their families. This has increased the need for culturally competent communicators in the United States and around the globe

There are several reasons why learning about intercultural communication should be useful to you. Perhaps you are entering the medical field and you would like to communicate more effectively with patients who are of a different culture than you. Maybe you will be entering the business world and will join a multinational organization. Perhaps you are from a family that represents several ethnicities, or you are a student about to embark on a study abroad trip. Whatever reason you may have for learning about intercultural communication, know that your journey toward becoming a culturally competent communicator may begin with this book, but your study will be a lifelong journey that you will continue long after this class is finished. Throughout your journey, be open to listening to others' experiences and the details of their journeys. Understand that everyone is at a different stage in becoming a culturally competent communicator and that sometimes interacting with those who are at different stages can be frustrating. Throughout this process, remember not to give up. Becoming a culturally competent communicator is a difficult and challenging process. However, congratulations on taking the first step on your journey!

In this chapter, we have a selection of readings that cover three main areas of intercultural communication: (1) defining intercultural communication; (2) explaining why you should study intercultural communication; and (3) providing the history and development of intercultural communication. In the first section, you will explore the components of intercultural communication. When striving to become a culturally competent communicator, it is important to create your own definition of what it means to be interculturally competent. The reading in this section will help you create your definition. In the second section we examine why studying intercultural communication is important. Here the readings discuss globalization and increasing diversity in the United States and around the world. Finally, our last section includes two readings that provide an understanding of the field of intercultural communication, how it developed, and some key moments in its timeline.

At the end of the chapter are several discussion questions. These questions will aid you in applying your knowledge about intercultural communication to different situations. Make sure to contemplate and answer each question carefully before progressing to the next chapter.

Moving Forward

Before we delve into learning about intercultural communication, take a moment to conceptualize what you think is meant by the topic of intercultural communication. Considering what you already know, how might you define intercultural communication? In order to become culturally competent communicators, we must first be able to define what we mean by intercultural communication. This first section explores just that: what intercultural communication is. This is done by briefly overviewing interpersonal communication and culture, before moving into a definition of intercultural communication. As you read this first section, see if the definition provided below matches the definition of intercultural communication you were just asked to consider.

DEFINITION AND BOUNDARIES

Scholars in the area generally agree that one element distinguishing intercultural communication from the rest of the communication field is the relatively high degree of difference in the cultural experiential backgrounds of the communicators. Intercultural communication, thus, is commonly defined as the communication process in which individual participants of *differing cultural backgrounds* come into direct contact and interaction with one another. The term *culture* is employed as a label for the collective life experiences of commonly recognizable large groups, such as national and ethnic/racial groups. It is also applied to other smaller, subcultural social groups with discernible life patterns (e.g., groups based on gender, sexual orientation, geographic area, or physical dis/ability). This inclusive conception of culture allows for the viewing of all communication encounters as potentially "intercultural," with varying degrees of "interculturalness" or heterogeneity in the experiential backgrounds of interactants (see Dodd, 1998; Ellingsworth, 1977; Martin & Nakayama, 1997; Samovar, Porter, & Stefani, 1998; Sarbaugh, 1988). Gudykunst and Kim (1997), for example, have employed the concept of "stranger" (Simmel, 1908/1950; see also Rogers, 1999) to integrate various types of intercultural situations (including intergroup and interethnic) into a continuum of interculturalness, with differing degrees of cultural difference, unfamiliarity, and psychological distance involved in specific communication encouners.

Integral to the domain of intercultural communication are the subdomains of cultural communication (which focuses on understanding communication in particular cultural or subcultural communities) and cross-cultural communication (which compares communication in two or more cultural or subcultural communities). Cultural and cross-cultural communication studies have been a vital part of the theorizing and research activities in the area. On the other hand, it is generally agreed that the domain excludes studies of mass-mediated and other technological forms of communication within and across different cultural and subcultural systems. These mediated communication activities are the objects of inquiry primarily in areas such as international communication, comparative mass communication, and media cultural studies. Also excluded are studies of development communication, which address various issues associated with modernization and sociocultural change in traditional societies.

Following Langer (1942), we believe that communication in its most fundamental form is intrapersonal. Communication begins as an attempt by human beings to come to know their environment through symbols. This occurs through a gradual recognition by the child that symbols, objects, and ideas, and internal mental representations of them, can be related to each other in a meaningful fashion. To paraphrase Langer, children first use communication to bring objects into their minds, not into their hands. Once children learn that this is possible, then symbol-object-mind relationships are possible. Only after such relationships are learned can communication evolve to a social stage where people recognize that others also make similar symbol-object-mind inferences, and that these related networks of inferences can be used to interact with others. At the social stage, communication can be used for social tasks, such as making requests or transmitting cultural information. In all stages of human development, communication involves the assignment of meaning by the individual to external stimuli, including symbolically encoded messages from other persons. Communication is inherently a meaning assignment process within the individual. Since meaning is assigned to messages based on the beliefs, attitudes, and values of the individual, and since persons from different cultures often have different beliefs, attitudes, and values, the normal human misunderstandings which occur in same-culture interactions are often magnified by the wider differences in cultural assumptions and belief systems inherent in cross-cultural interactions.

Culture

The diversity of the concept "culture" is illustrated by Kluckhohn's (1949) 12 meanings for the term, from the way of life of a people, their social legacy, pooled learning, way of thinking, feeling, and believing, through their mechanism for normative regulation of behavior and techniques for adjusting to the environment and other people, to theories about the way these people behave. Citing Max Weber as inspiration, Geertz (1973, p. 5) holds that "man is an animal suspended in webs of significance he himself has spun, I take culture to be those webs, and the analysis of it to be therefore not an experimental science in search of law but an interpretative one in search of meaning."

We conceive of culture in its broadest sense as the accumulated knowledge and beliefs of specific portions of humanity. Thus defined, the fundamental nature of culture is phenomenological: culture exists fundamentally in the hearts and minds of people. Cultural artifacts such as paintings, sculpture, machinery, and construction projects are products of the knowledge and beliefs that constitute culture. While cultural artifacts provide clues to culture, culture itself can be passed on to other persons and future generations only through communication. No study of culture's artifacts, no matter how deep or extensive, can describe, explain, predict, or even transmit culture from one person or generation to another without communication about cultural meaning. Intercultural communication involves communication between people from different cultures, leading to several questions: What constitutes a "different" culture? Do intercultural differences necessarily involve different languages? Different ways of thinking? Different world-views? Different beliefs, attitudes, and values?

Intercultural Communication

While there is little disagreement that communication between a Karen hill tribesman in northern Thailand and an American college student involves intercultural differences, might ask if communication between any two persons with different attitudes, beliefs, and values also involves intercultural differences. For example, while the value system espoused by a given corporation is commonly referred to as corporate culture, does that mean that communication between workers at IBM and Microsoft necessarily involves intercultural differences? Perhaps. Between someone at IBM and a farm worker? Possibly. To study such interactions from an intercultural perspective might raise different questions and produce different answers from those found in a more standard organizational communication analysis. But rather than attempt to give final answers, we prefer to discuss the central thrust of intercultural communication, as opposed to attempting to delineate intercultural communication's absolute boundaries.

Thus, we regard the study of intercultural communication as the study of communication between people with different mind-sets and ways of looking at and perceiving the world that go beyond the differences normally found among people who regard themselves as culturally similar. Since communication occurs through cognitive processing, we might ask whether Eastern and Western ways of thinking are different. Does such a notion imply different cognitive structures or communication processes, or, can the observations which lead people to infer a different way of thinking be explained simply through different content in beliefs, attitudes, and values within the cultures? Though commonly applied to communication between persons who are each embedded in a different cultural group, intercultural communication also has heuristic utility when applied to the examination of two persons, ostensibly from the same culture, gender, age, ethnic group, and socioeconomic status, whose assumptions about the nature of the world and ways of relating to it are sufficiently divergent to produce the forms of misunderstanding commonly found in intercultural analysis. *The central thrust of intercultural communication is in the analysis of meaning assignment in interactions between persons whose attitudes, beliefs, and values differ due to a corresponding difference in their cultural or co-cultural backgrounds.* These attitudes, beliefs, and values represent, in part, the individual's theories of what others in the same culture believe, as well as how this differentiates persons of that culture from persons of other cultures.

Thomas M. Steinfatt and Diane M. Millette, Excerpt from: "Intercultural Communication," *An Integrated Approach to Communication Theory and Research, ed. Don W. Stacks and Michael B. Salwen,* pp. 299–300. Copyright © 2009 by Taylor & Francis Group. Reprinted with permission.

Moving Forward

Now that you have an idea of what intercultural communication looks like and are familiar with its definition, we move forward the rationale for studying intercultural communication. This section is divided into two areas: globalization and diversity. These two areas are critical in helping you to understand why intercultural communication is important as an area of study and why culturally competent communicators are needed in our fast-paced and changing society. As you move throughout this section, consider the examples given in the readings. Have you witnessed any of these examples locally? Regionally? Nationally? Are there any other reasons you can think of for studying intercultural communication?

GLOBALIZATION

Today, we live in a world where Marshall McLuhan's term "the global village" has rich significance for many people. Technology has already radically changed the shape of interaction on this planet. Every day, unprecedented numbers of people from different groups and cultures are drawn into contact, inviting promise (and also potential conflict) into our world. Such relationships can be particularly problematic if we consider their potential for *mis*communication. Having been socialized in different cultures, participants often bring to interactions radically diverse ways of communicating and understanding communication. Thus, because of both the promises and the difficulties involved in intercultural communication, scholars have taken a keen interest in the process and have developed numerous training techniques intended to help individuals interact effectively regardless of their differences. Indeed, intercultural training has long been advocated as a means of facilitating favorable and productive intercultural interactions (Brislin, 1981; Harris & Moran, 1979; Mendenhall & Oddou, 1986; Tung, 1981;

Worchel & Mitchell, 1972). Those in nonacademic circles, too, have celebrated the presumed benefits (e.g., Caudron, 1991; Derderian, 1993) and have helped encourage the widespread use of training seen today.

Aaron Castelan Cargile and Howard Giles, Excerpt from: "Intercultural Communication Training: Review, Critique, and a New Theoretical Framework," Communication Yearbook, vol. 19, ed. Brant R. Burleson, pp. 385-386. Copyright © 1996 by Taylor & Francis Group. Reprinted with permission.

As we grow increasingly aware of the global interdependence of people and cultures, we confront ever shifting cultural, ecological, economic, and technological realities that define the shrinking world of the twenty-first century. The development of new ways of living in the world together is pivotal to further human progress; we must learn how to see things through the eyes of others and add their knowledge to our personal repertoires. Such a global mind-set can result only from competent communication among peoples form diverse cultures.

Intercultural Communication Competence: Why?

The citizens of the twenty-first century must learn to see through the eyes, hearts, and minds of people from cultures other than their own. Several important trends of the late twentieth century have transformed the world into a global village: technology development, globalization of the economy, widespread population migrations, the development of multiculturalism, and the demise of the nation-state in favor of sub- and supranational identifications. In order to live meaningfully and productively in this world, individuals must develop their intercultural communication competence.

Technology Development

The development of communication and transportation technology linking every part of the world has served to interconnect almost every aspect of life at the onset of the twenty-first century (Frederick, 1993; Porter & Samovar, 1994). Today the flow of ideas and information increasingly transcends national boundaries. People can also travel to anywhere in the world much more quickly than ever before. The faster travel speeds wrought by transportation technology have introduced increasing face-to-face communication among people from different cultures.

Globalization of the Economy

The progress of communication and transportation technology has rendered global markets more accessible and the business world more interrelated and international than in the past. Regional trade alliances have become the "new world order." The trend toward a global economy is bringing people from different cultures together. It requires representatives from multinational corporations to communicate with those in other parts of the world to retain a competitive space in the global economic arena. The interdependence among international economies reflects the important role that intercultural communication plays now and will play increasingly in the next century. The development of greater intercultural understanding has become an essential element of global business (Adler, 1991; Mead, 1990).

DIVERSITY

Widespread Population Migrations

As cultural interconnectedness has increased as a result of technology development, we have also witnessed remarkable population migrations across national borders. The United States especially has felt the impacts of this trend. In 1990, the U.S. Census revealed that the first-generation foreign-born population in the United States had reached almost 20 million. About 8.7 million immigrants entered the United States between 1980 and 1990. At least 32 million persons residing in the United States speak a first language other than English, and 14 million of these do not speak English fluently. These figures indicate that the increasing numbers of immigrants have restructured the fabric of American society. The United States has become much more culturally diverse than it has been in the past.

This multiethnic structure makes intercultural contact among co-cultures inevitable. Members of the various co-cultures and ethnic groups residing in the United States must learn to adjust to one another's identities. This trend demands that individuals learn to communicate in ways that are effective in such a diversifying society (Nieto, 1992).

The Development of Multiculturalism

The changing demographics described above stand to affect every aspect of life in the United States. Johnston and Packer (1987), for example, predict that the increasing diversity of workforce and social life in the United States will dramatically affect organizational life in the twenty-first century. The new workforce will comprise persons who are diverse in race, culture, age, gender, and language. Cultural diversity, or multiculturalism, will become the norm rather than the exception in American life. Thus, intercultural communication scholars need to address those issues that will help people learn to work and live together without being deterred by the differences they may bring to their encounters. The development of greater intercultural understanding and intercultural communication competence is an essential part of human life in the contemporary age.

De-Emphasis on the Nation-State

As new immigrants arrive and co-cultures make headway in achieving fuller participation in U.S. society, the very idea of national identity will surely change. Increasingly, the United States is pulled into regional alliances, such as NATO or NAFTA, that are larger than the nation. In addition, we see the reassertion of ethnic and gender differences within the nation; for instance, women have begun to talk as women, African Americans as African Americans, and Native Americans as Native Americans. The ability to negotiate the meanings and priorities of diverse identities has become a prerequisite of attaining interpersonal competence in modern society (Collier & Thomas, 1988).

Moving Forward

Now that we have an understanding of what intercultural communication is, and why we should study intercultural communication, let us move to exploring the history and development of the field of intercultural communication. These next two readings describe how intercultural communication came to be, highlighting important research along the way. In becoming culturally competent communicators, knowing the origins of intercultural communication will help you understand where intercultural communication is headed in the future. As you move throughout this section, try to visualize key moments that encouraged the development of this field of study.

ORIGINS OF INTERCULTURAL COMMUNICATION

Since the 1960s, when this relatively young area took shape, intercultural communication has enjoyed rapid growth and an increasing presence within and outside the field of communication. Within the field, we have witnessed a gradual mainstreaming of intercultural communication. Conference programs of the International Communication Association and other communication associations feature many sessions and individual papers that address issues of culture and intercultural interface in various contexts. In addition, intercultural communication theories and research findings have been increasingly incorporated into communication textbooks (e.g., Beebe & Masterson, 1997; Gudykunst, Ting-Toomey, Sudweeks, & Stewart, 1995; Infante, Rancer, & Womack, 1996). Facilitating this growth have been publications dedicated to theoretical and research development in intercultural communication, including handbooks of international and/or intercultural communication (Asante & Gudykunst, 1989; Asante, Newmark, & Blake, 1979; Gudykunst & Mody, in press) and the International and Intercultural Communication Annual book series (e.g., Tanno & Gonzalez, 1998; Wiseman, 1995; Wiseman & Shuter, 1994). As is the case in most other areas of communication, the intellectual roots of intercultural communication cut across the traditions of various older social science disciplines. In particular, intercultural communication owes its development significantly to the works of anthropologists (e.g., Hall, 1976), psychologists (e.g., Berry, 1980; Hofstede, 1980; Triandis, 1988), sociologists (e.g., Simmel, 1908/1950), and linguists (e.g., Whorf, 1952), among others.

In the 1970s, there began to emerge among communication and speech scholars the realization that if their disciplines were to have any impact upon the ever increasing problems experienced in human interactions, the use of a variety of approaches and methodologies would be necessary (Delia, 1977). Yet even the term *communication* seemed to defy attempts to come up with one commonly accepted definition (Dance, 1970). Finally, it became clear that the development of even one communication theory, responsive to all of the insights and needs of scholars in the field, was also not an attainable goal (Littlejohn, 1983). During that period, when the model for scholars and researchers in most of the social sciences was the one provided by physics, it did not seem to occur to anyone that coming up with *a theory of communication* was akin to coming up with *a comprehensive theory of physics*. Such a variety of needs, applications, interests, and approaches had been brought together under the umbrella term of *communication* that it became impossible to develop one single definition or methodological approach. That this confusion of symbolic activity with observable reality or identifiable processes was not understood more quickly was not one of the finest hours of communication scholars in general, or of intercultural communication scholars in particular, as the latter followed the imperfect examples set by their predecessors.

Under these circumstances, intercultural communication was predictably condemned to experience developmental phases, growing pains, and problems very similar to those of its parent discipline. These included questions relating to organizational structure, the use and careful application of a variety of methodologies, and the clear definition of a *unique* role or subject matter. All these problems were not made easier by a lack of willingness to reexamine the *roots* of intercultural communication studies by those now engaged in various activities as they tried to establish themselves in the field. As is true for the rest of the academic world, intercultural communication scholars must carve out their own professionally significant niches, which they hope will result in meaningful contributions, or simply recognition, advancement, and acceptance as equals by other social scientists within the academy. Of course, unwillingness to regularly reexamine roots as a *basis* for future development is not unique to this area-it is a weakness of every field of human study, including the natural sciences. While a growth or development orientation brings its own rewards, it also can lead to the repetition of prior mistakes by those who neither understand their bases nor are willing to learn from them. At the present time, as is true of communication studies in general, intercultural communication is more involved in describing and defining specific instances than in the development of any general theory. Of course, those methodologies that had been borrowed from prior communication studies, the social sciences, and, in turn, from the physical sciences have not resulted in the discovery of anything comparable to lawlike responses in human actions.

Many early contributors were concerned with the challenges faced in the United States by individuals who had to deal with confrontations between ethnic and racial segments of our population (Blubaugh & Pennington, 1976; Daniel, 1970; Rich, 1973; Smith, 1973). There was, furthermore, an emerging realization that the United States, following World War II, was suddenly and unexpectedly thrust into a world leadership role that resulted in almost daily interactions by individuals representing political, economic, cultural, and trade organizations. These situations required intercultural and language skills that had previously not been part of the training or education offered in the United States. In addition, these arenas of conflict were often far removed from an academic environment in which objectivity and scientific processes, not necessarily related to common, daily human experiences, were seen as ideals.

Much of the past work in intercultural communication has been anecdotal, and it has relied heavily upon situational descriptions. That approach was in no small measure encouraged by the seminal work of individuals like Edward T. Hall (1959, 1966). Hall's earliest approaches to the study of human behavior and interactions across cultural lines of demarcation were attempts to provide *specific* categories and measurements. The result was an impression that we might be able to identify and label "pigeonholes" into which we could easily sort cultural differences. His major contributions to our understanding that human beings use space differently in different settings because of different cultural demands were, nevertheless, flawed by the illusion of specificity or definiteness through the assignment of numerical values and measures. This illusion of precision, and the assumption of generalizability, provided the basis for a great deal of early enthusiastic growth in the available literature, only some of it of lasting value (Doob, 1961; Jules, 1963; Oliver, 1962; Smith, 1966). Once it became clear, however that mere categories or classifications had little necessary relationship to the complex realities faced by individuals concerned with human interactions across cultural lines of separation; the foundations were laid for an evolutionary process that still continues.

An attempt was made by Kohls (1983) to identify some significant milestones in the evaluation of intercultural communication study. He lists some publications, institutions, and events from the 1930s to the 1960s. Among these are: the establishment of the Experiment in International Living in Vermont (1932); The American Institute of Foreign Trade (1946), renamed The American Graduate School of International Management (1973); the Interagency Roundtable for Intercultural and Area Studies by the Government (1955); and the Area Studies Centers at major universities.

Other events, mostly of post-World War 11 vintage, that focused on international affairs and cross-cultural understanding also influenced the development of intercultural communication study, including the establishment of the United Nations and its subsidiary agencies and assistance programs; the United States Information Agency, renamed the International Communication Agency; the Fulbright Exchange Programs for academicians, students, and its foreign leader seminars; the Agency for International Development (a Marshall Plan for developing countries); and the Center for Technical and Cultural Interchange between East and West. These activities created a need to understand the interface of communication and culture.

Movements and events in the United States that marked an awareness of cultural differences and human rights concerns include: the "hippie revolution" of the 1960s, the demonstrations for and against the Civil Rights Act of 1964, the Immigration Act of 1965 dealing with immigrant quotas imposed on several countries, the influx of refugees from various parts of the world that continues to the present time, and the technological innovations that opened up more possibilities for cultural interactions in all parts of the world. From these historical happenings, studies about intercultural interactions began to accrue.

Within the fields of communication and speech communication, a number of individuals began to develop international contacts with those who had similar interests, during the period following World War 11. At this point, it is instructive to note that out of these early contacts and interests came the conviction held by William S. Howell, among others, to not contribute to the development of a new academic discipline. He argued that it would simply be another level added to the already existing professional structures or another attempt to justify its existence merely by *assuming* significant differences or unique contributions (Howell, 1975). It was argued that the very nature of the intercultural interactions that were being studied suggested that scholars concerned with such efforts should attempt to build new models of *cooperation* between and within already existing disciplines, such as communication, business management, and anthropology. That approach would have enabled scholars in various academic areas to make their contributions more readily available to individuals across academic "cultural" lines of division. To Howell and others, the question of whether or not intercultural communication should be a discipline, a field, or an area of study seemed unimportant. They preferred to deal with it as an emphasis that could be applied to and used in a variety of fields that were already well established and that had to be made more useful I a world of expanding human contacts. At the same time, certain amount of faddism could be noted. In some cases, unprofessional practitioners in the field of intercultural communication took advantage of existing needs, and attempted to fill the relative vacuum created by the absence of extensive scientific research and recognized publications by providing less than adequate information or questionable techniques.

Following the example of the social sciences, intercultural communication scholars attempted to overcome the negative effects of such faddism and self-serving approaches by employing methodological rigor. As had been tried earlier in the field of communication and in the social sciences, attempts began to abound in the 1970s and early 1980s to give meaning to that which was vague and inadequately understood by careful application of mathematical and statistical models (Gudykunst, 1983a). At the same time, calls for theory development abounded that were similar to those in other areas of communication study (Gudykunst, 1983b). Critics from outside the field noted that nothing significantly new happened if one merely added the word *culture* to communication without demonstrating that such interactions differed significantly from interpersonal, group, or media communication within one culture.

It did not help that in some cases vaguely anthropological settings or anecdotes were used to demand an even vaguer "cultural" *awareness*. To many who were attempting to apply models of physics to human behavior, this seemed more akin to voodoo than to science. Finally, in the

1970s, a variety of books and journals containing research findings were published that began to provide a meaningful corpus of knowledge. This corpus included an early effort by Bystrom, Casmir, Stewart, and Tyler (1971) to understand the explosively developing field, which resulted mainly in the realization of how complex and diverse the already existing information was. Other publications attempted to provide structure by developing encyclopedic formats intended to provide information concerning existing organizations, significant component parts, and divergent communication strategies (Hoopes & Ventura, 1979; Seelye & Tyler, 1977).

In much of this work, the influence of atomistic, reductionist assumptions as to how understanding is produced played a significant role. The ease with which physicists could predict that water could boil under specified circumstances in any environment could, however, never be replicated in intercultural communication studies, or for any other human interactional processes. Interrelationships were found to be complex, and they constantly reminded us of the earlier work by symbolic interactionists who had insisted that the process of socialization and acculturation could not easily be fitted into existing scientific models (Mead, 1934). Understanding universal principles thus proved to be a significant challenge, and the extensive listing of component parts did not produce closure.

Intercultural communication provided opportunities to identify and deal with important human needs, and the framework and controls developed in well established disciplines appeared to provide good bases to overcome disciplinary inadequacies as scholars attempted to apply already accepted standards or formats. This effort is reflected in the early textbooks on intercultural communication that came out in the 1970s. They were published in response to a need for textbooks in courses on intercultural communication, which at the time were proliferating at institutions of higher learning. Among those contributions were books by Harms, 1973; Condon, 1975; Ruhly, 1976; Sitaram, 1976; Dodd, 1977; Prosser, 1978b; and Sarbaugh, 1979.

Significantly, most of these publications were not truly "intercultural." They provided neither interactional opportunities for work with students and scholars in a variety of areas or opportunities for "practitioners" to readily learn or benefit from the work of researchers, theoreticians, and educators. Some of these books became cultural *artifacts, representing* the concerns of specialists in one academic field rather than intercultural *resources* directed to a variety of individuals, institutions, or interests. Publications during the early 1980s often still indicated the lack of a truly *intercultural* emphasis in communication studies. There also could be noted the absence of a unified effort by practitioners and scholars to reach conclusions based on all, or a significant portion of, the efforts and insights of the past 20 to 25 years. Thus while intercultural communication has become established at American universities and colleges as an identifiable subject matter that can be taken as a major at both the undergraduate and graduate levels, there is still a need for a unifying concept, construct, or theoretical base that would affirm and demonstrate its uniqueness vis-^-vis other areas of communication study.

SUMMARY

As technology advances our ability to communicate with others, our world becomes increasingly smaller and more interconnected. Diversity is increasing in every country and everywhere around the globe. There are many reasons why you should study intercultural communication: personal, political, educational, and occupational, to name a few. Whatever the reason you may have for studying intercultural communication, you have begun your lifelong journey toward becoming an interculturally competent communicator. It is a journey that does not end once you have finished reading this book or have completed this class. Rather, it is a journey that continues with every interaction and experience you have and share with other individuals.

In this chapter, our readings explored three areas of intercultural communication. First, we examined what intercultural communication looks like how it is defined. As you begin your journey toward becoming a culturally competent communicator, you likely will create your own definition of intercultural communication. The definition in this chapter provides a starting point for you in the process of creating your own definition. Second, we explored why we should study intercultural communication, based upon readings describing the increasing diversity of the United States and the interconnectedness of the world, or *globalization*. These two imperatives are important reasons to study intercultural communication as our world becomes smaller nationally and connected internationally. The readings in our third section revealed the history and development of intercultural communication. Here, we learned about some key moments in the timeline of the development of intercultural communication as a field, as well as the development of influential intercultural research.

DISCUSSION QUESTIONS

1. When you think about culture, what comes to mind?
2. In what ways has your cultural background influenced the way you communicate? How much do you know about the cultural history of your own country?
3. Is it possible for someone to view life through the eyes of another person? Why would such an ability be necessary in the world of global business and technology, education, or the health professions?

IMMIGRATION

CHAPTER 2

STUDY OBJECTIVES

After completing this chapter, you will be able to:
- Identify key events involving the United States and the history of immigration.
- Identify and describe the positive and negative effects of immigration in the United States.
- Understand the issues that surround the immigration reform debate.

INTRODUCTION

In recent years, immigration has become a topic that reporters and commentators in the news media frequently discuss. It is a topic that covers both legal and illegal immigration, and it can often be overwhelming to talk about, much less understand. At the time when the editors were putting together this book, there had been thirteen bills introduced into the first session of the 113th Congress regarding immigration, but none of these bills concerned major reform (American Immigration Council 2014). If you feel overwhelmed by this fact, there is no need to worry; the topic of immigration is a complex, multidimensional topic. Understanding immigration is even more complex without being knowledgeable of the history of immigration in the United States, the changing cultural landscape, or the reasons why people immigrate in the first place.

The cultural landscape of the United States is changing. Culturally, the United States looks a lot different than it did when your parents were your age, or even a decade ago. As a result of this change, immigration has been a popular topic for debate among policy makers in recent years. Certainly, the topic of immigration is dynamic, and as with any issue or topic, there are multiple perspectives to be considered.

The topic of immigration is not a clear-cut, definitive, "black and white" issue. Rather, immigration is more of a grey-area issue. To help provide some clarity for your thinking, this chapter provides some background information regarding immigration. Hopefully, by the end of this chapter, you will feel more confident about your knowledge of the arguments for and against immigration policies, particularly in the United States. Also, you may begin to think about the journey upon which New Americans in making the United States their home.

In this chapter, our first reading examines why studying and understanding immigration matters. Providing some background on immigration, our second reading explores the effects of immigration on the United States and the current immigration debate. Our third reading comes from the Immigration Policy Center and examines immigration reform and the history and principles that drive support for overhauling immigration law. The end of the chapter provides an opportunity for you to consider these readings more deeply with a number of discussion questions.

Moving Forward

Although our first reading is quite brief, it provides a rationale for why the study of immigration matters. As you read this short selection, consider how much the United States has changed culturally since the time you were born, since the time your parents were born, and since the time your grandparents were born. In terms of culture and diversity, you, your parents, and your grandparents experienced a very different United States. What might you expect the United States to reflect in ten or twenty years?

RATIONALE FOR STUDYING IMMIGRATION

The study of intercultural communication is important in any society or culture. This is especially true in the United States, which has made intercultural openness a central feature of its cultural persona. The United States is currently experiencing the greatest period of immigration in its history. Although the late 19th and early 20th centuries witnessed a greater proportional population increase due to immigration, the actual number of legal immigrants entering the United States since 1980 was greater per decade than in any previous time in history. When illegal immigration is factored in, the current period of immigration is unsurpassed in American history, yielding a nation whose cultural heritage is changing, and, as a corollary, its communication is changing as well.

Moving Forward

Our next reading gives a brief historical overview of immigration in the United States up until recent years. This reading explains the demographic, economic, social, and cultural effects that immigration has had on the United States. As you read about the effects of immigration, for each area, try to come up with an additional positive and negative effect that the authors did not mention. How would these effects have an impact locally or nationally?

Once you feel comfortable exploring these effects, move on to the next reading, The Great Debate. This section of the reading introduces the arguments that surround immigration, revealing that although there may be increased attention to the topic of immigration, the immigration debate is not new. As a country, we have been discussing immigration in some form since the 18th century. This reading will provide an insight into why immigration is a difficult topic to discuss. As you read, think of some arguments that voices on either side of the debate may have. If you have a stance on this issue, think of the arguments that represent the opposite side of your stance, and try to understand the reasoning for those opposing arguments.

ECONOMIC EFFECTS OF IMMIGRATION

"In 1790, there were 4 million Americans in our first census. Today, there are 301 million in the country, a 75-fold increase. Now, what happened to that nation, which suffered from the most terrible population explosion? It became the most prosperous and influential nation in human history—so what's the problem?"[1]

—Ben Wattenberg, Senior Fellow at the American Enterprise Institute (AEI)[2], in response to opposition to immigration, in August, 2007

"Standard economic theory predicts that the shifts in the supply of labor caused by immigration should produce some economic gains for natives. But every attempt to measure the size of those gains based on actual data shows that it is extremely small ... Moreover, those gains are generated by the wage losses suffered by natives in competition with immigrants, who in the case of illegals tend to be the poorest and least-educated Americans. Lowering their wages so that the rest of society can be made imperceptibly richer is hardly sound public policy."[3]

—Steven Camarota, Director of Research, Center for Immigration Studies, June 2006

---

1 Randy Hall, "Report: Immigration Could Add 100 Million to US by 2060," www.cnsnews.com, August 31, 2007.

2 The American Enterprise Institute was founded in 1943. It is a private, nonpartisan, not-for-profit institution dedicated to research and education on issues of government, politics, economics, and social welfare. (Source: www.aei.org)

3 Steven Camarota and Tamar Jacoby, "What to do on Immigration," www.cfr.org, June 23, 2006.

Introduction

On August 10, 2007, George W. Bush (Bush), President of the United States (US), announced new measures to address some of the challenges thrown up by the high levels of immigration into the US. The announcement followed the rejection of the Comprehensive Immigration Reform bill—a bill that dealt with immigration issues including those relating to homeland security—in both legislative bodies. Bush said that the new measures represented steps that his administration could take "within the boundaries of existing law to better secure [US] borders, improve worksite enforcement, streamline existing temporary worker programs, and help new immigrants assimilate into American society."[4]

Economists have always been interested in understanding the role of immigrants (foreign-born persons) and the part they play in the economy of the host country. For them, the US with its history of immigration, offered the ideal opportunity to study the economic implications of a continuous flow of immigrants. Large-scale immigration into North America started in the 16th century, with people coming in from Europe. Hordes of immigrants populated the towns, cities, and villages of the country and took up jobs as laborers, farmers, physicians, etc.

Until 1882, the US authorities did not restrict the entry of immigrants. However, with the rapid increase in population, the US government decided to regulate immigration and a new immigration policy was implemented. Over the years, the US government introduced different acts in its efforts to control immigration. Nonetheless, as of 2000, immigrants constituted 11% of the total population of the US.

The terrorist attacks of September 11, 2001 (9/11) polarized public opinion on immigration. Debates on the topic on the floors of legislative bodies as well as in the print media grew more heated. In response to the attacks, the US government tightened immigration regulations. Some analysts supported the new regulations and even demanded further restrictions on immigration on the grounds that high levels of immigration caused population increase, stagnation or reduction in the wages of blue-collar workers, and job losses for US citizens, besides having far-reaching social and cultural consequences. However, a majority of analysts were not in favor of further restricting immigration. They argued that immigrants had made a positive contribution to the US economy. With the decline in fertility rates among US-born citizens, immigration would play a key role in future population and economic growth of the US, they added.

The US government drafted the Comprehensive Immigration Reform Act to address the problems associated with immigration. However, the bill, introduced in the US Senate on May 9, 2007, failed to muster sufficient votes.

---

4 Michael Sung, "Bush Administration Unveils New Immigration Reforms," www.jurist.law.pitt.edu, August 10, 2007.

Background Note

According to one section of anthropologists, the first humans entered the Americas through the Bering Strait[5] around 11,000 years ago from Eurasia[6]. These people were believed to be the ancestors of the present-day Native Americans. However, it was Christopher Columbus' voyage to the continent of America in 1492 that triggered what later became a large-scale migration of the people of Europe into the "New World".

The migration of Europeans to what was later to become the US started as a trickle. Initially, Spanish explorers came in small numbers. However, in the 16th century, after Spain conquered Florida, California, and the south-west region of America, some 200,000 Spaniards came and settled in these regions[7]. The English government also started sending explorers during this period. In 1607, James I[8] granted permission to English merchants to establish a permanent settlement in Virginia. The English wanted to establish colonies in America so as to shift some of their surplus population and also create new markets for their products. The Dutch first arrived in America in 1609 and by 1614 Dutch merchants had established a trading post at Fort Orange. The Dutch West India Company offered free land along the Hudson River to Dutch immigrants so as to encourage settlement. The arrival of people from England grew steadily and by 1650 the population of Virginia had reached 15,000.

The American continent was sparsely populated then and the new settlers needed more people to start industries and populate the newly established towns and cities. In this period, almost anyone who managed to make the long journey from the old world was allowed to enter the country.

On July 4, 1776, the United States of America was born. In 1790, the US government declared that "free white persons" who had resided in the US for at least two years and were loyal to the US Constitution were eligible to become citizens of the US.[9]

The subsequent waves of immigrants into the United States came from all regions of Europe. There were people from Sweden, the Netherlands, Spain, Italy, and Eastern Europe. In the mid-800s, the potato famine in Ireland and political disorder in Germany impelled thousands of immigrants from these countries to come to the US. In the late 19th century, a large number of Russian Jews immigrated to the US (Refer Exhibit I for more information on immigration to the US from Europe).

In the mid-19th century, a large number of Chinese started immigrating to the US. They took up low-paying jobs in the mining and construction industries. In the 1860s and 1870s, the Chinese formed approximately 10–15% of the population of many western states. While industrialists were in favor of Chinese immigration to the US as they stood to gain from the cheap labor, political parties, labor unions, and popular opinion were against it. The anti-Chinese agitation forced the US Congress to pass the Chinese Exclusion Act in 1882,

---

5   The Bering Strait, named after Vitus Bering, a Russian explorer, is a sea strait between Russia and Alaska. Some scientists believe that in the last Ice Age, the strait had frozen over, allowing the passage of animals and humans into the American continent.

6   www.ngc.org

7   St.Augustine in Florida is considered the first European settlement in America. It was one of the 200 settlements that the first Spaniards established in the region.

8   James I was the ruler of England, Scotland, and Ireland from 1603 to 1625. Prior to 1603, he was the ruler of Scotland.

9   The "free white persons" requirement remained on the federal books until 1952.

restricting Chinese immigration to the US for ten years. The US government later framed several acts to bar Asians from entering the US. The Gentlemen's Agreement of 1907 restricted the Japanese, the Barred Zone Act of 1917 banned Asian Indians, and the Tydings-McDuffie Act of 1934 excluded Filipinos. The restrictions on Chinese and other Asian immigration continued till 1943.

In the 19th and 20th centuries, the US government introduced several more acts to control immigration (Refer Exhibit II for immigration laws in the US over the years). The foreign-born population of the US declined from 14.2 million in 1930 to 10.3 million in 1950. In the 1970s, immigration from European countries to the US decreased significantly as Europe experienced high levels of economic growth and was itself facing labor shortages. The Europeans were replaced by people from Latin America and Asia as the largest group of immigrants into the US. Between 1970 and 1990, the foreign-born population of the US increased drastically from 9.6 million to 19.8 million.

In the early 1990s, the US government decided to relax its immigration policy. The Immigration Act of 1990 raised the annual cap of legal immigrants from 500,000 to 700,000. The lenient immigration policy continued till the early 2000s. According to the National Immigration Law Center,[10] immigrants constituted about 11 percent of the US population in 2000[11] (Refer Exhibit III for immigration on the basis of country of origin in 1890 and 2000). In July 2001, Bush said, "Immigration is not a problem to be solved; it is a sign of a confident and successful nation. Their arrival should be greeted not with suspicion and resentment, but with openness and courtesy."[12]

However, after the 9/11 terrorist attacks by 19 foreign nationals, the US federal government tightened immigration regulations. According to the Department of Justice, one of the 19 hijackers had entered the US on a student visa. In view of this fact, Bush announced on October 2001 that the immigration department would tighten control on foreign student visas.[13] He said, "We're going to tighten up the visa policy. That's not to say we're not going to let people come into our country. Of course we are. [But] never did we realize people would take advantage of our generosity to the extent they have."[14]

In October 2001, the US Congress passed the "USA Patriot Act," which gave powers to the domestic law enforcement and international intelligence agencies to identify and take persons who were suspected to have links to terrorism into custody and deport them, if need be. Bush said, "We welcome legal immigrants and we welcome people coming to America. We welcome the process that encourages people to come to our country to visit, to study, and to work. What we don't welcome are people who come to hurt the American people. And, so, therefore, we're going to be very diligent with our visas and observant with the behavior of people who come to this country."[15]

---

10 Established in 1970, the National Immigration Law Center protects and promotes the rights of immigrants with low incomes and their family members. It aims to provide these immigrants with unrestricted access to social welfare programs funded by the government

11 "Facts about Immigrant Workers," www.nilc.org, April 2005.

12 "Bush Calls for Relaxed Immigration Rules," www.cnn.com, July 10, 2001.

13 About 600,000 foreign students are admitted each year to US Colleges and Universities.

14 "Bush to Tighten Visa Restrictions," www.opendoors.iienetwork.org, October 29, 2001.

15 "U.S. to Tighten Up its Visa Policy," www.usinfo.state.gov, October 29, 2001.

In March 2003, the functions of the Immigration and Naturalization Service (INS)[16] were transferred to three agencies: the United States Citizenship and Immigration Services (USCIS), the United States Immigration and Customs Enforcement (ICE), and the United States Customs and Borders Protection (CBP), within the Department of Homeland Security.

In 2006, the US immigration authorities granted legal residence to around 1.2 million immigrants. Official records indicated that on the whole, in the 231 years since the US became independent on July 4, 1776, 70 million immigrants had settled in the US[17] (Refer Exhibit IV for the flow of immigrants to the US between 1900 and 2006).

Why Does the US Attract Immigrants?

Ever since the Americas were discovered by explorers, they attracted millions of immigrants. The US, in particular, became a magnet of sorts for prospective immigrants. Although there were several reasons for this, the main reason was better economic prospects. Immigrants usually came from countries where there were few opportunities. The US, sometimes referred to as the 'Land of Opportunities', was where these immigrants hoped to achieve a higher standard of living—something that they felt their own country would be unable to provide.

The US was home to some of the best universities in the world and had been attracting students from all corners of the globe. A good proportion of these students decided to stay back in the country after completing their studies (Refer Exhibit V for the names of some of the world's best educational institutions). The country also offered well-paying career options for professionals as well as blue-collar workers. Thousands of doctors, nurses, teachers, and numerous engineers, scientists, IT professionals, farm laborers, meat packers, and factory workers moved to the US every year for better opportunities (Refer Exhibit VI for a list of the largest companies in the world by revenues in 2006–07).

The US economy was the largest and one of the most vibrant economies in the world. The US was ranked third in 'starting a business' and first in 'employing workers' (Refer Exhibit VII for the best countries in terms of doing business according to The Doing Business Project[18]). A robust economy and the favorable regulatory environment attracted workers and entrepreneurs from around the world to the US.

A lenient asylum policy was another reason for immigrants choosing the US over other countries. The US government offered asylum to people regardless of their country of origin, if they 'were not capable or unenthusiastic to return to their own country because of harassment or a justifiable fear of harassment'. If the authorities found the applicant eligible for asylum, (s)he was allowed to remain in the US and apply to become a lawful permanent resident after one year. In 2006, 51,000 people applied for asylum in the US, which was approximately 17% of all applications received by industrialized countries.[19]

---

16   The Immigration and Naturalization Service (INS), initially a part of the US Department of Justice (DoJ), handles legal and illegal immigration and naturalization services.

17   "Cultural Diversity and Immigration: A U.S. Perspective—Remarks at the Taste of Diversity," www.amsterdam.usconsulate.gov, June 28, 2007.

18   The Doing Business Project compared 170 countries on 10 parameters such as starting a business, dealing with licenses, registering property, getting credit, employing workers, protecting investors, trading across borders, enforcing contracts, closing a business, infrastructure, and transparency.

19   "Asylum Levels and Trends in Industrialized Countries, 2006," www.unhcr.org, March 23, 2007.

According to the United Nations Human Development Report 2006, the US ranked eighth among 177 countries on the Human Development Index (HDI)[20]. Though there were seven countries ranked higher than the US on the HDI, the US attracted the most number of immigrants partly because of its size and partly because of the vibrancy of its economy (Refer Exhibit VIII for the top 5 destination countries in terms of number of immigrants).

Effects of Immigration

Immigration has had a significant demographic, economic, and social impact on the US economy.

Demographic Effects

With a steady flow of immigrants, the demography of the US had been changing over the years. Immigration had contributed significantly to the increase in US population, though there were other factors like a declining infant mortality rate (from 100 per 1,000 births in 1900 to less than 10 per 1,000 births in 2000), and an increasing average life expectancy (from 47 years in 1900 to 77 years in 2000). According to the Census Report published in 2002, the country's population grew from 76 million in 1900 to 300 million in 2006. Of these 300 million, there were approximately 37.5 million immigrants and several million more born to immigrants.[21]

The high levels of immigration meant that the US had a relatively high fertility rate (2.09 as of 2007) that mitigated the problem of an aging population, which was turning out to be a major issue in many developed countries.

Immigration had resulted in drastic changes in the racial mix over the years. In 2000, about one out of four Americans was of a race other than white, compared to about one out of eight in 1900 (Refer Exhibit IX for the distribution of the total US population by race in 1900 and 2000). According to the Census, the population of Hispanic origin had more than doubled between 1980 and 2000. A major contributory factor to this was the large number of illegal immigrants who crossed the US border with Mexico. It was observed that the South and the West regions attracted a larger number of people of Hispanic-origin than the Midwest or the Northeast regions (Refer Exhibit X for the distribution of the Hispanic population by region between 1980 and 2000, and Exhibit XI for the immigration patterns in the 1990s).

The fact that new immigrants preferred some regions to others had significant political repercussions. As illegal immigrants generally settled down in groups, they contributed to the increase in population of some districts/states. When these districts were reapportioned,[22] the political power of the residents of the districts increased. According to census data, between 1990 and 2000, the number of seats representing California had increased by nine due to immigration.

---

20 The Human Development Index (HDI) is a comparative measure of life expectancy, literacy, education, and standards of living for countries worldwide.

21 "Number of Immigrants in U.S. Hits 37.5 Million," www.english.peopledaily.com.cn, September 14, 2007.

22 Reapportionment means that if one state gains a House district, another state must lose one. This is because the total number seats in the US House of Representatives is fixed at 435.

Illegal immigration also created problems of a different kind. As congressional districts were supposed to be almost equal in population size, districts that had a high number of illegal immigrants increased the political power of legal residents[23]. For example in 1996, the number of votes required to elect a representative in some districts of California and Texas was about one-quarter of the number needed in the average Michigan district.[24]

Economic Effects

The US economy has been dependent on immigrants since the 16th century. In the early years of immigration, a large proportion of the English people who came to America were farmers and they continued to work on farms in their adopted country. The US also attracted people with technological skills. For example, Samuel Slater, an expert in making textile machinery, arrived in the US in 1789 and four years later established America's first cotton factory at Pawtucket, Rhode Island.

Immigrant workers usually took up jobs that US citizens avoided. According to official records, a high percentage of immigrant workers were construction workers, poultry plant workers, meat packers, gardeners, hotel maids, restaurant workers, building demolition workers, and fruit and vegetable pickers. Jobs in poultry plants across southern US were dominated by Mexican immigrants.

Immigrants acted as a positive economic force by establishing businesses. For example, in Los Angeles County during the period 1972 to 1992, while the Hispanic population grew by 200%, the number of licensed Hispanic-owned firms grew by 700%.[25] The growing number of immigrants also stimulated demand and contributed to the rapid expansion of the consumer market. According to a study by the Alexis de Tocqueville Institution[26], cities which had high immigration rates created jobs at twice the rate that cities with low immigration rates did. The study also found that residents of high-immigration cities were 15% more affluent than those in low-immigration cities and the tax burden was 9% lower in cities with a high number of immigrants.[27]

Social and Cultural Effects

Immigration also had a social and cultural impact on US society. Owing to the large number of immigrants, the US had become a multicultural society. There was diversity in food, language, art, and culture.

However, the increasing number of immigrants into the US also led to xenophobia among some of its citizens as they feared that high levels of immigration could cause the US to

---

23 If illegal alien non-citizens are counted in the decennial Census upon which districts are apportioned, then states with larger illegal alien populations are likely to end up with more districts and therefore more representation in the House. This effectively dilutes the votes of citizens in states having relatively low population of illegal aliens. Similarly, congressional districts in those states with proportionately higher numbers of illegal aliens end up representing a large illegal alien, non-citizen, non-enfranchised population. (Source: www.14thamendment.us)

24 "Immigration Fuelling Population Boom," www.ncpa.org.

25 "Alexis de Tocqueville Institution: Immigration Creates Economic Growth." www.ncpa.org.

26 The Alexis de Tocqueville Institution is a Washington, D.C.-based right-wing think-tank that conducts policy research and produces reports on immigration.

27 "Alexis de Tocqueville Institution: Immigration Creates Economic Growth." www.ncpa.org.

lose its Anglo-Protestant culture. In the 1860s, groups that advocated white supremacy used violent methods to oppose Blacks, Jews, Catholics, etc. The Irish were targeted in this period for their loyalty to the Pope and their refusal to adapt to the new American culture. According to records, small-scale riots between Catholics and nativists broke out in several American cities in the 1860s.

In the late 18th century, anti-immigration views started to gain ground as there were large inflows of immigrants from cultures that were quite different from the existing American culture. The Chinese were targeted in the early 1900s. In the 1960s, some were wary of involving immigrants, especially those of Chinese origin, in defense services and space research, as they feared that it could be a threat to US national interests. Post-9/11, xenophobia seemed to have touched new heights.

Some analysts believed that xenophobia was the result of some immigrants preserving their culture as a symbol of their national identity and preferring to stay separate from the mainstream culture. According to them, this tendency made the Americans feel that immigrants were not loyal to the US and this led to animosity toward them.

The Great Debate

The issue of immigration had been a topic of debate since the late 18th century. Critics had been arguing that immigrants depressed wages, especially of low wage earners, disregarded the principles of freedom and democracy, refused to learn English, and weakened public service. The arguments remained the same over the years; however, with the substantial increase in immigration levels, the issue began attracting far more attention. Between the late 1990s and 2006, around 10 million legal immigrants and approximately 12 million undocumented immigrants joined the US population.

With the rapid growth in the number of Hispanics, the number of non-English speaking people in the US was growing. Some critics cited studies that showed that the lack of English proficiency among immigrants had resulted in businesses (employing immigrants) losing more than US$ 175 billion a year due to loss of productivity, work-related miscommunication, etc.[28] Others feared that the US would become a bicultural nation.

Some were of the view that guest worker visa holders (H1-B visa) took jobs away from US-born workers (Refer Exhibit XII for the different visa categories in the US). For example, they believed that the salaries of American IT professionals had decreased or stagnated and the overall number of US-born citizens in computer-related occupations had dropped because of the H1-B visa program. Although H1-B visa holders themselves were not immigrants, a significant number of them stayed back (by applying for the Green Card when a company sponsored their application) and thus became immigrants.[29] Analysts were of the opinion that in order to restrict immigration, government should cut the number of H1-B visas further[30].

---

28   Gary Strauss, "Consumers Frustrated by Verbal Gridlock," www.moritzlaw.osu.edu, February 28, 1997.
29   The H1-B visa is issued for up to three years but may be extended. This provides a maximum stay of six years.
30   In the late 1990s, as the US needed thousands of technology experts to tackle the millennium bug, the H1-B visa cap was raised from 65,000 to 115,000. In 2001, the government raised the cap again to 195,000. However, in 2005, the government slashed the H1-B cap back to 65,000.

The high level of immigration was also believed to be the reason for wages remaining low in low-skill jobs. For example in the agricultural sector, the wages of farm workers had stagnated or declined in several regions.

Some critics were suspicious of high-skilled immigrants, arguing that they would use the experience and training that US-based companies provided them to start enterprises in their country of birth, which would eventually become competitors to these firms.

The anti-immigration lobby also pointed out that immigrants sent back huge amounts of money to their countries of birth. These remittances, according to them, were a drain on the US economy. For example, the Inter-American Development Bank estimates indicated that immigrants in the US sent more money to their families in Latin American and Caribbean countries than all the official foreign aid sent to that region.[31] Critics suggested that limiting immigration would reduce the dollar outflow.

According to one study done by Harvard political scientist Robert Putnam, based on detailed interviews of nearly 30,000 people across America, the greater the diversity in a community, the fewer the people who voted and volunteered, the lesser the amounts given to charity, and the lesser the time spent on work on community projects. The study went on to conclude that in the most diverse communities, neighbors trusted one another only about half as much as they did in the most homogenous settings. The study found that virtually all measures of civic health were lower in more diverse settings. "The extent of the effect is shocking," said Scott Page, a University of Michigan political scientist.[32] This study provided ammunition to the opponents of immigration.

With increasing incidents of terrorism, some analysts also said that allowing more immigrants in would help spread terrorism further. They were of the view that reforming the immigration policy could help the US fight terrorism.

Some analysts were concerned about the high levels of illegal immigration. Critics of immigration were of the opinion that as many illegal immigrants were relatively unskilled and poor, they increased poverty levels in the US. They claimed that illegal immigrants put pressure on the public health care system without contributing to public finance (through direct taxes).

High levels of illegal immigration, according to some analysts, resulted in higher taxes for legal residents. As illegal immigrants generally competed for jobs with the least educated among the US-born citizens, they affected the income of the working class. According to a study by Harvard professors George Borjas and Lawrence Katz, the wages of high school dropouts in California, a major destination for illegal immigrants, declined by 17% between 1980 and 2004. Analysts said that this data indicated that illegal immigrants had brought down the wages of blue-collar workers. This study attracted the attention of politicians, the media, and the general public. Critics of immigration used it to argue that immigration affected the earnings of US-born citizens. However, similar studies in Ohio, a state with a low proportion of illegal immigrants, revealed that the wages of Ohio's high school dropouts had fallen 31 percent between 1980 and 2004. The Harvard economists too acknowledged that their study did not consider all the economic effects of illegal immigration, such as the fact that certain businesses would not exist in the US without cheap immigrant labor.

Supporters of immigration were of the view that the benefits of immigration far outweighed its disadvantages. Each year, thousands of physicists, engineers, computer specialists,

---

31   "Remittances Boost Latin Economies," www.ncpa.org, October 22, 2002.
32   Michael Jonas, "The Downside of Diversity," www.boston.com, August 05, 2007.

and other professionals immigrated to the US. According to them, these immigrants generated a 'brain gain' for the US. According to them, the greatest strength of the US was its capacity to attract knowledge workers from around the world.

According to some sociologists, the constant flow of immigrants had made the US the center of innovation. Explaining this, they said that in a heterogeneous society, culture clashes were more common, and so old beliefs were constantly questioned. This generated innovative solutions that a group of people with more homogenous backgrounds and approaches might not have arrived at.

Most analysts felt that though immigrants could cause some problems for US-born people, their overall contribution to the US economy was positive. According to one American columnist, opponents of immigration had their "reasons as well as prejudices."[33] According to James P. Smith, senior economist at Rand Corp, "Immigrants may be adding as much as $ 10 billion to the economy each year. It's true that some Americans are now paying more taxes because of immigration, and native-born Americans without high school educations have seen their wages fall slightly because of the competition sparked by lower-skilled, newly arrived immigrants. But the vast majority of Americans are enjoying a healthier economy as the result of the increased supply of labor and lower prices that result from immigration."[34]

The popular opinion among economists was that efforts to restrict immigration would hurt US companies, especially those in the high-tech industry. According to reports, there were a growing number of US-born students who were less inclined to take up courses in mathematics, computers, or technology. As a result, the US high-tech industry was apparently facing a shortage of people with advanced technical skills, forcing it to look overseas for such people. However, as US immigration laws restricted the number of guest workers into the US, the shortage was expected to worsen in the near future.

Critics of immigration blamed the government's immigration policy for the phenomenon. They said that without an appropriate immigration policy, the problems created because of immigration could not be solved. With the increasing number of illegal immigrants in the country, pressure from employers to increase the H1-B visa cap, growing incidents of terrorism, and other problems associated with immigration, the government also felt the necessity of regularizing the immigration policy.

---

33 "Cultural Diversity and Immigration: A U.S. Perspective—Remarks at the Taste of Diversity," www.amsterdam.usconsulate.gov, June 28, 2007.

34 "Overall U.S. Economy Gains from Immigration, but its Costly to Some States and Localities," www.8.nationalacademics.org, May 17, 1997.

Moving Forward

Our final reading in this chapter comes from the Immigration Policy Center (IPC). The following is the official statement describing the IPC:

> The Immigration Policy Center (IPC) is the research and policy arm of the American Immigration Council. IPC's mission is to shape a rational conversation on immigration and immigrant integration. Through its research and analysis, IPC provides policymakers, the media, and the general public with accurate information about the role of immigrants and immigration policy on U.S. society. IPC reports and materials are widely disseminated and relied upon by press and policy makers. IPC staff regularly serves as experts to leaders on Capitol Hill, opinion-makers and the media. IPC, formed in 2003 is a non-partisan organization that neither supports nor opposes any political party or candidate for office.

In this reading, the IPC provides an overview of the legal system, the basic principles of immigration reform, and the reasoning that drives reform. As you move throughout this reading, think about what obstacles the IPC faces in carrying out its mission statement. If you worked for the IPC, how might you suggest overcoming some of the obstacles you identified? Does intercultural communication play a role?

THE EVOLUTION OF U.S. IMMIGRATION POLICY

For more than a decade, efforts to systematically overhaul the United States immigration system have been overshadowed by other events—from foreign wars and national security concerns to the financial crisis that threatened to bring down the world economy. In addition to this ever-changing list of national crises, years of partisan political fighting and the resurgence of a volatile restrictionist movement that thrives on angry rhetoric have made opportunities for advancing genuine reform few and far between. As a result, many in both parties opted for a political strategy that emphasized immigration enforcement over immigration reform, holding to the argument that efficiently deporting non-citizens would reduce illegal immigration and pave the way for more sensible outcomes in the future. Instead, the unprecedented spending on immigration enforcement, the extraordinary rise in deportations, the passage of state anti-immigrant laws, and the almost daily anecdotes of separated families and discrimination finally took their toll. Voters signaled in the 2012 federal elections that they were tired of enforcement-only immigration policies and the senseless pain they caused. Now more than ever, the opportunity to craft immigration laws that reflect American values and needs is a distinct possibility. The White House, Members of Congress, and countless organizations have issued new ideas and principles for making the system work. These proposals vary and will likely change even more as proposals translate into legislation, but there are a number of common themes that exist. This paper lays out an overview of the underlying legal system, the most basic principles of reform, the reasons behind them, and how they are likely to be reflected in coming legislation.

The Immigration and Nationality Act in a Nutshell

Although Americans routinely acknowledge that the United States is a nation of immigrants, the system of laws that govern who can immigrate, who can visit, who can stay, and under what conditions is largely unknown to most people. The Immigration and Nationality Act (INA) of 1952 is a complex and often confusing collection of laws that does everything from setting forth qualifications for naturalization to regulating foreign students to managing temporary workers to authorizing humanitarian protections such as asylum and refugee admissions. The INA also contains quotas or limits on the number of legal immigrants who may come to the country each year, numbers which were last adjusted in 1990. In addition, the INA has authorized "relief" from deportation over the years. Providing relief through various laws allowed an individual to make the case that he or she should be permitted to enter or remain in the United States, despite being in violation of immigration laws, based on family unity, contributions to the community, or other humanitarian concerns. Similarly, the INA has been amended numerous times both to expand access to the United States (based on characteristics of immigrants such as country of origin, occupation, and humanitarian factors) and to restrict access (based on criminal convictions, occupations, or political affiliations). Critics of these amendments routinely argue that we are either too generous or too restrictive in whom we allow to enter and remain in the United States, setting the stage for political arguments that have little to do with immigration itself and far more to do with issues of race, economics, culture, and identity.

What Kinds of Events Prompt Changes in Immigration Law?

Immigration reform is often fueled by other aspects of social change when the American public realizes that immigration law lags behind other social reforms. For instance, against the backdrop of the civil rights movement, the 1965 amendments to the INA eliminated biases in the law that favored European immigrants over all others. Following the refugee crises brought on by the Vietnam War, Congress enacted refugee and asylum provisions in 1980 that brought the United States into compliance with international standards of refugee protection. In 1986, driven by increased unauthorized immigration and few means to control it, Congress created a trade-off—legalization of approximately three million unauthorized immigrants in exchange for requiring all workers to establish their eligibility for employment in the United States.

By 1996, when unauthorized immigration was still not in check, many in Congress blamed the more generous provisions of the INA for the problem. As a result, lawmakers, led by then-House Judiciary Immigration Subcommittee Chairman Lamar Smith (R-TX), enacted a harsh new immigration removal scheme that eliminated or restricted many forms of relief, required mandatory detention and removal for many immigration violations, and authorized extensive or permanent bars on admission following a deportation. In subsequent years, the severity of these measures and the hardships experienced by many unauthorized immigrants who had fled civil wars and violence in Central America, Haiti, and the former Soviet Union led Congress to pass some small legalization programs, but nothing on the scale of the 1986 law.

On September 10, 2001, President George W. Bush and Mexican President Vicente Fox were making plans for a new temporary worker program and other immigration reforms, brought about by a booming economy, efforts to build a stronger partnership with Mexico, and a rise in unauthorized immigration. Of course, that initiative and many others fell by the wayside on September 11, to be replaced with enhanced national security and anti-terrorism laws, many of which attempted to regulate possible threats to the country through restrictions on immigration.

Nonetheless, bipartisan efforts to achieve a comprehensive immigration reform package began again in earnest by 2004, led by Senators Edward M. Kennedy (D-MA) and John McCain (R-AZ) and Cong. Luis Gutierrez (D-IL) and Jeff Flake (R-AZ). At the same time, continued immigration restriction sentiments in Congress, particularly in the House, led to passage of a House bill in 2006 that would have made simply being in the country unlawfully a crime. The Senate responded by passing a bipartisan comprehensive immigration reform bill, but the two immigration bills were never taken up by the other chamber. In 2007, a second bipartisan effort came to the Senate floor twice, but could not obtain enough votes to overcome procedural hurdles.

Why is Comprehensive Immigration Reform Back in The News?

There is little doubt that the results of the November election, particularly the impact of Latino, Asian, and New American voters, jump-started the conversation on immigration reform, but the political momentum has increased each year since 2007. In fact, some might argue that the legislative push in 2013 can be traced back to the extremely punitive 1996 law. After almost 20 years, the supposed reforms of 1996 have led to years of troubled enforcement policies, further undermined a system that could not respond quickly to changes in the economy, and often ignored the important contributions made by immigrants to this country.

The persistent legacy of the 1996 law, which enhanced immigration penalties but eliminated many forms of relief, has been a series of ever-expanding efforts to deter illegal immigration through higher penalties and fewer options. The law also expanded mandatory detention and expanded immigration enforcement—including mass worksite raids and greater federal/state/local law-enforcement cooperation through programs like Secure Communities—which has ratcheted up the numbers of non-violent, non-criminal immigrants arrested for immigration violations. Despite the fact that many of the unauthorized have lived in the country for a decade or more and have U.S.-citizen and lawful permanent resident (LPR) family members, deportation has been almost inevitable because there is little relief available under the INA. The damage that millions of deportations have inflicted on U.S. families and communities is well-documented.

The long-standing inadequacy of existing channels for legal immigration has also served as a motivation for change. That inadequacy, coupled with more than a decade of strong economic growth prior to the 2008 recession, created a jobs magnet in the United States, while also decreasing the likelihood that unauthorized immigrants would return to their home countries. Since the recession, unauthorized immigration has slowed to a trickle given the contraction of the U.S. labor market and improving economic conditions in Mexico. Yet 11 million unauthorized immigrants still call the United States home.

Emerging from the recession, however, was also a growing consensus that the contributions of immigrants in speeding an economic recovery were critical. This was reflected in the growing number of arguments in favor of expanding both temporary and permanent access to high-skilled labor, as well as major reports on the role of immigrants as entrepreneurs and innovators. Many business leaders became more sensitive to the issue following state-led efforts to restrict immigration, and numerous reports assessing the value of immigrant contributions to the economy have poured out over the last few years.

This mindset helped to foster greater openness to the idea that immigrant contributions far exceed the perceived problems of immigration. Demographic changes have further helped to solidify that point of view. Similarly, the activism of young unauthorized immigrants around the DREAM Act further expanded a general understanding of the shortcomings of the current immigration system, while at the same time lifting up the enormous contributions that these young people hoped to make to their country.

Further, notwithstanding the decline in unauthorized immigration in recent years, the economic, demographic, and political strength of immigrants and their children is growing. Meanwhile, evidence mounts that anti-immigrant measures such as Arizona's SB 1070 result in discrimination, racial profiling, and hate crimes against people of color. All of these factors have contributed to the growing awareness that an immigration crisis exists in the United States. Political polling following the 2012 elections further clarified that many voters, particularly those of Latino and Asian descent, think that a politician's negative views on immigration reflected a bias against them, regardless of their place of birth. Thus, the current efforts to reform immigration laws are the culmination of years of effort, but also of the political realities of America in 2013.

Is it Necessary to Try to Fix All The Immigration Laws at Once?

For years there has been debate over whether immigration reform should be "comprehensive," "piecemeal," or "incremental." As a practical matter, immigration law should be something that is updated and revised constantly to reflect current economic and political conditions, to reflect changes in social issues, and to respond to foreign policy and humanitarian concerns. Congressional gridlock, and the particular paralysis that has stalled immigration reform, has meant that issues which should have been addressed periodically, such as adjustments to overall legal immigration admission numbers, don't happen in a timely way. That makes it even more difficult to address more dramatic challenges, such as the plight of 11 million unauthorized immigrants. Even as the President and Congress contemplate systematic overhaul of the immigration system, Members of Congress are introducing individual, more targeted bills. Both are necessary and can play a role in improving the system. The key, however, is coordinating the various proposals so that the overall effect is a more cohesive set of laws that acknowledge the biggest issues of immigration reform today: the need for an improved legal immigration system that is generous enough to discourage unauthorized immigration and provide a solution for the 11 million unauthorized immigrants, allowing them to transition from an underground existence to lawful permanent residence and, ultimately, U.S. citizenship. For a variety of reasons, these two components are critical and should be considered simultaneously, regardless of how many individual bills are initially introduced to put the issues on the table.

What Other Reforms are Likely to be Under Consideration?

There is a humanitarian and political imperative to resolve the legal status of the roughly 11 million unauthorized immigrants in the United States, and this has been a central component of virtually every immigration overhaul proposal offered since 2004. Other critical components to a systemic approach include creating a fair, but realistic system to regulate future immigration needs, securing our borders through efficient application of smart enforcement strategies and technologies, ensuring that our immigration system welcomes new immigrants, and ensuring that all immigration laws respect the principles of due process on which this country is based.

What are the Basics of Reform?

1. Creating a pathway to citizenship for unauthorized immigrants that is fair but feasible.

Today, the vast majority of Americans support some form of legalization for unauthorized immigrants. While the details of that process may vary, polls show that the public wants a system put in place that permits legal status and ultimately citizenship, if the immigrant establishes commitment to the United States. Routinely, that commitment is demonstrated through some form of initial registration, a willingness to learn English, and full payment of any outstanding taxes. Many of the fiercest debates—behind the scenes, in committee, and on the House and Senate floor—will likely turn on other requirements or conditions placed on individuals. For instance, the amount of fees and fines may determine who can actually apply for the program and who will be unable to afford it.

The scope of the program—whether you can apply for legalization based on presence on the date of enactment, at the time the bill was initially introduced, or sometime further back—will expand or narrow the number of people who can participate. While persons with major criminal convictions will clearly be excluded from the process, Congress will have to decide whether all criminal convictions—including misdemeanors or crimes committed long ago—will also bar someone from eligibility. For example, will convictions for immigration violations, such as entry after deportation, be held against an applicant?

Congress will also have to decide how many years an applicant must wait to transition from some form of provisional legal status to becoming an LPR. The amount of time could depend on whether or not LPR status is contingent on first clearing out the backlog of applicants in legal immigration visa categories, whether someone qualifies under special categories like

DREAM Act or AgJobs, or whether someone is applying independently or as the derivative of a spouse's or parent's application. Each of these questions has implications for thousands, if not millions, of people, and that will make the final legalization package a series of compromises with clear winners and losers.

2. Ensuring that immigration policy supports families and American values.

While the economics of unauthorized immigration is frequently the focus of the immigration debate, the breakdown of the family immigration system is equally destabilizing and also spurs a significant amount of unauthorized immigration. Current backlogs in family-based immigration lead to delays of up to 20 years for the legal migration of family members. Moreover, recent attempts to undermine family-based immigration have ignored the significant role family support plays in the success of immigrants, and thus of the American dream. The long delays and outdated procedures have generated several policy proposals that could form the basis for reforming family-based immigration. Among the issues likely to be debated include increasing the overall number of visas available in order to reduce current backlogs, whether those increases will be temporary or permanent, and whether increases in family-based immigration can be made while simultaneously increasing employment-based immigration.

Critics of the current family-based visa categories may argue that only nuclear-family members should have access to family-based immigration. They say siblings of U.S. citizens should compete for visas under a merit or employment-based system. Such arguments are often justified by claiming that family immigration leads to "chain migration" or a constant flow of more and more immigrants as each new immigrant brings in additional family members, but the actual number of people who immigrate based on any relationship to a U.S. citizen is quite low. There have also been proposals that would tie elimination of family backlogs to the ability of unauthorized immigrants to become LPRs, on the theory that it is unfair to make family-based immigrants wait longer for their visas than unauthorized immigrants would. Proposals like these, however, often fail to explain that the family-based backlogs are of Congress's own making and can be fixed by raising current limits.

Other issues likely to arise, in either an initial package or as a bill moves through Congress, include expanding the eligibility of same-sex partners to petition for spouses and children, allowing the spouses and children of LPRs to be treated as immediate relatives (eliminating waits of several years for LPR families to reunite), and providing broader discretion to grant waivers for persons with an immigration violation to remain in the country based on family or other humanitarian needs.

Another proposal that may be brought into the discussion is the introduction of a point-based immigration system. In a point system, immigrants are admitted based upon a list of characteristics that a country finds valuable, such as education, occupation, work experience, language ability, or age. While the 2007 Senate immigration bill contained a point system, it was a hurriedly produced experiment that was driven by political compromise rather than evidence that a point system would work. In order to be consistent with both American tradition and the country's varied economic needs, any effort to experiment with a point system would have to be a supplement to—and not a substitute for—the existing systems of family-based, work-based, and humanitarian immigration.

3. Ensuring that immigration enforcement enhances national security and community safety without undermining due-process protections.

Most experts and analysts, including those in law enforcement, think legalization is one of the key elements to ensuring our country's safety because it would allow the federal government to focus on genuine threats posed by those seeking to do the country harm, rather than individuals who lack status but have committed no other crimes. Recent reports have also emphasized that many of the markers and targets proposed for enforcement, especially border enforcement, have been met in recent years. Other studies have suggested that a decade of increased spending for immigration enforcement has produced diminishing returns with respect to ending unauthorized immigration, and that the economy, rather than enforcement measures, is a better predictor of unauthorized immigration. Despite these developments, enforcement measures will continue to appear in overhaul bills. These could include additional proposals to strengthen the border and ports of entry, as well as some increased penalties for existing immigration violations. Immigration reform advocates may also push for limits on immigration detention and reduced use of state and local law-enforcement officers to enforce immigration laws.

Shifts in public support away from immigration enforcement may limit additional immigration control measures. However, one area that appears likely to be expanded is the mandatory electronic employment-verification system, E-Verify. While E-Verify continues to have many critics, the debate over its further implementation is likely to turn far more on the level of employer and employee protections embedded in the system, the amount of time it will take to fully implement a mandatory program, what type of exemptions may exist for individual employers, and how businesses protect themselves from liability for hiring unauthorized workers.

4. Ensuring that the legal immigration system is sufficiently robust to meet the needs of the American economy, does not put native-born workers at a disadvantage, and does not encourage new waves of illegal immigration when job demand is high.

One of the major criticisms of the Immigration Reform and Control Act (IRCA), which legalized nearly three million unauthorized immigrants in the late 1980s, was the failure to include provisions for dealing with future workforce needs. The authors assumed employer sanctions would deter future unauthorized immigration, but they did not account for an increased need for immigrant workers. Because overall immigration numbers were not adjusted to meet demand (and have remained essentially stagnant since 1990), the growing economy, widely available jobs, and inefficient enforcement fueled continued unauthorized immigration. Consequently, regulating the flow of immigration so that it reflects constantly shifting employment needs is critical to a systematic overhaul of the immigration system. It may also be one of the most difficult pieces of the puzzle to negotiate. Some issues, such as increasing the number of visas available in science, technology, engineering, and mathematics (STEM) fields, or encouraging foreign entrepreneurs to invest in the United States, have widespread support among Republicans and Democrats.

Other components of "future immigration flow," particularly regulating the temporary workforce, are more controversial because they raise difficult questions about the dynamic between the native-born workforce and immigrants. The concerns range from unfair competitive advantages to defining labor shortages to ensuring adequate worker protections. Some argue for the necessity of a short-term and dependable supply of foreign labor, while others argue that businesses should be able to find and recruit needed workers wherever they may be. And other critics maintain that relying primarily on temporary workers, whether professional or day laborers, to meet job demand depresses wages and discourages American workers from obtaining the skills and training they need to succeed. Congress likely will piece together a series of bills that address different aspects of these issues, and may attempt to solve the problem of anticipating future need through various market-driven schemes. That could be through some form of an independent commission tasked with regulating immigration numbers, through lifting some caps on employment categories, by creating new visa categories, or some combination of these ideas. Congress may also choose to put some temporary increases in places with enhanced labor protections and defer the larger fight to another day. Regardless of whatever compromise is reached on this topic, the future-flow issue promises to be one of the most carefully watched and controversial aspects of reform.

5. Long-term commitment to citizenship

Although it frequently receives less attention, continued support of integration and naturalization for immigrants remains a goal of systematic immigration reform. A truly successful legalization program, for instance, should include support for teaching English as a second language and civics education in order to ensure that new immigrants are fully prepared to participate in American life. The high cost of becoming a citizen is a frequent critique of the U.S. immigration system, yet Congress has routinely cut support for the Office of Citizenship in the last few years. Viewing citizenship as an investment in the future should be a given in any major reform package, but it remains to be seen whether Congress will be willing to invest funds in citizenship education during a period of fiscal austerity.

Conclusion—But There's More

This is only a brief analysis of what we are likely to see in the coming months. A host of issues will likely be raised at some point in the debate: the restoration of many due-process protections for immigrants in court, reform of the immigration court system itself, access to counsel for minors and persons with disabilities, expansion of the protections for battered spouses and children under the Violence Against Women Act (VAWA), eliminating barriers to asylum such as the one-year filing deadline. Some of these issues may proceed under other pieces of legislation, such as VAWA reauthorization. Some of them may be debated but left for another day. The breadth and scope of these issues—both those that we know must be considered and those that we know should be considered—underscore why the time for a genuine debate over immigration reform is not only much anticipated, but long overdue.

Mary Giovagnoli, "Overhauling Immigration Law: A Brief History and Basic Principles of Reform," http://www.immigrationpolicy.org/perspectives/overhauling-immigration-law-brief-history-and-basic-principles-reform. Copyright © 2013 by American Immigration Council. Reprinted with permission.

SUMMARY

The United States is experiencing a shift it its cultural landscape. As this shift continues the topic of immigration and immigration reform will continue to be highlighted by policy makers, major news media, and news sources. It is a topic that highlights the need for competent intercultural communicators. Having read this chapter, learning more about the history of immigration in the United States and the discussion surrounding immigration reform, you should now be aware that discussing the topic of immigration is multidimensional and difficult.

In this chapter, the readings first focused on the rationale for studying and understanding the conversation surrounding immigration. We examined why understanding immigration is important, not only as a student but as a citizen, as well. Then, we explored the historical background of immigration in the United States, evaluated the effects of immigration, and delved into understanding the debate that encircles immigration. Finally, we read about immigration reform, learning its background history in the United States, the principles driving supporters of immigration reform, and the next steps in reform. As you become more knowledgeable regarding immigration and immigration reform, make sure to contribute to the conversation—whatever your position—especially as you become more competent as an intercultural communicator. Check out the discussion questions below that should put your immigration knowledge to the test.

DISCUSSION QUESTIONS

1. What is your closest connection to the topic of immigration? When you communicate about immigration, to what extent is your opinion informed by experience versus what you have read about or heard from others?
2. How has communication involving immigrants changed over the course of history in the United States? Why has this change occurred?
3. How has our fear or distrust of people considered as foreign affected our communication with them? What communication strategies might help to reduce this fear or distrust?
4. How does the status of "new" versus "old" Americans, and the way we communicate with them and others change as they remain in the United States?

NONVERBAL ISSUES IN INTERCULTURAL COMMUNICATION

CHAPTER 3

STUDY OBJECTIVES

After completing this chapter, you will be able to:
- Identify and explain the different types of nonverbal codes.
- Describe nonverbal communication's role in intercultural communication competence.
- Evaluate how culture plays a role in nonverbal communication.

INTRODUCTION

As the King and his suite neared Akasaka, the palace of the Emperor, a bugle announced their arrival. The Emperor Meiji of Japan stood alone in a room adjacent to the entrance of the palace. He was dressed in European military uniform and the crest of his coat was decorated with orders. As [King] Kalakaua left the carriage and entered the palace, he stepped up to the Emperor alone and extended his arm to shake hands. For the first time in Japanese history an Emperor exchanged handshakes with a foreign sovereign. (Ogawa, 1973, p. 91)

Instead of the traditional bow, this momentous meeting between two monarchs in 1881 began with a simple handshake, which served as a precursor to friendly international relations between Japan and Hawaii. More recently, the offering or withholding of a handshake between Middle Eastern leaders, reflected in this seemingly inconsequential greeting ritual, the status of peace negotiations.

So, too, are the warp and weave of daily interactions fashioned from a thousand and often presumably insignificant nonverbal gestures. A gaze broken too soon, a forced smile, a flat voice, an unreturned phone call, a conversation conducted across the barrier of an executive desk—together, such nonverbal strands form the fabric of our communicative world, defining our interpersonal relationships, declaring our personal identities, revealing our emotions, governing the flow of our social encounters, and reinforcing our attempts to influence others. Understanding human communication requires understanding the multiple nonverbal codes by which it is transacted and the communicative functions those codes accomplish.

Amy S. Ebesu Hubbard and Judee K. Burgoon, Excerpt from: "Nonverbal Communication," *An Integrated Approach to Communication Theory and Research, ed. Don W. Stacks and Michael B. Salwen*, pp. 336. Copyright © 2009 by Taylor & Francis Group. Reprinted with permission.

Some scholars believe that studying nonverbal communication is more important than studying verbal communication, as our nonverbal communication provides more detail than our words. For example, our verbal and nonverbal messages do not always match each other. Have you ever observed someone who appeared upset; yet when you asked them why they were upset, they answered that they were fine? In this chapter we explore the paradox of nonverbal communication and discover that it is not just how you express yourself physically; rather, culture plays a large role in an individual's use and interpretation of nonverbal communication.

In order to understand how culture affects nonverbal communication, we need a definition of nonverbal communication. Our first two readings introduce, define, and explain different nonverbal codes and the role that nonverbal skills play in communication competence. Then, we explore how not all nonverbal communication carries the same weight and how culture influences nonverbal communication. In this section, our readings focus on how the different aspects of nonverbal communication that we explored in our first two readings are affected by culture. The third reading examines the effect of culture on paralanguage, and our last reading explores the role culture plays in nonverbal communication and culture-specific nonverbal communication. After you have read these selections, you can apply your knowledge about culture and nonverbal communication via the discussion questions included at the end of the chapter.

Moving Forward

Nonverbal communication consists of more than just body language. The following reading delves into the realm of nonverbal communication, defining and exploring each of the different nonverbal codes. Before we take a look at how culture plays an important role in nonverbal communication, we first need to understand what elements make up nonverbal communication. As you think about this reading, make sure to note each nonverbal code and think about how each code contributes to communication. How do kinesics, haptics, proxemics, physical appearance, vocalics, chronemics, and artifacts play a role in your daily life? Can you identify a recent time where you used one or more of these codes or observed somebody else using these codes?

NONVERBAL COMMUNICATION CODES

Sayings that attest to the importance of nonverbal communication in our lives vary from "A picture is a worth 1,000 word" to "Appearances are deceiving." But what are we talking about when discussing nonverbal elements of communication? Many people think of "body language" when discussing nonverbal messages. However, thinking of nonverbal only as body language ignores several important elements. For our purposes, nonverbal communication will be defined as "those behaviors other than words themselves that form a socially shared coding system" (Burgoon, 1994, p. 231). Two primary aspects of this definition are worth noting: First, it includes a wide variety of behaviors besides "body language." Second, it assumes people recognize the meaning of these behaviors within their social or cultural setting. These two aspects of nonverbal will become very clear by the end of this selection.

Scholars often claim that nonverbal messages are more important than verbal ones (see Burgoon, Buller, & Woodall, 1996). Their claim is based on several arguments. First, studies suggest that nonverbal messages make up a majority of the meaning of a message (see Andersen, 1999). Think of the times you've watched people from a distance, not being able to hear what they're saying but being able to see them. Based only on their nonverbal messages, you are able to understand a lot about their relationship and their interaction. You may be able to determine whether they are friends or dating partners, whether they are having a pleasant or unpleasant interaction, and whether they are in a hurry or not; all these interpretations occur without hearing a word. Although the importance of nonverbal messages for the meaning of an interaction varies, they play at least some role in every interaction. Second, nonverbal communication is omnipresent. In other words, every communication act includes a nonverbal component; nonverbal behavior is part of every communicative message. From how we say something to what we do and how we look when saying it, nonverbal messages are constant influences on our interpretation of what others are communicating to us. Third, there are nonverbal signals that are understood cross-culturally. Unlike verbal messages, which carry meaning strictly within the relevant language culture, nonverbal messages can be used as a communication tool among individuals from vastly different language cultures. For example, individuals from a wide variety of cultures recognize smiles to indicate happiness or recognize hunger from the act of putting fingers to your mouth. Finally, nonverbal messages are trusted over verbal, messages when those two channels of information conflict. Because we (somewhat erroneously) believe that nonverbal actions are more subconscious than verbal messages, we tend to believe the nonverbal over the verbal. All these arguments for the importance of nonverbal messages will be defended by the end of this selection.

The selection is divided into roughly two sections. The first section overviews the various types of nonverbal messages (i.e., codes), starting with body movements (i.e., kinesics) and ending with physical aspects of the environment that affect behavior (i.e., artifacts). You should have a good sense for the breadth and importance of nonverbal communication by the end of that section. The next part of the selection overviews the ways we use nonverbal messages (i.e., functions). Nonverbal messages can be used to accomplish a wide variety of outcomes, from allowing the smooth flow of an interaction to deceiving others. Theories will be applied throughout the selection but will be concentrated in the discussion of functions.

Nonverbal Codes

As noted earlier, nonverbal behaviors include a lot more than "body language." Although scholars disagree on the exact number, there are seven codes (or categories) of nonverbal behavior that will be reviewed in this selection: kinesics, haptics, proxemics, physical appearance, vocalics, chronemics, and artifacts. I will define each code in turn and discuss some of the associated behaviors.

Kinesics

What do you think of when you ponder nonverbal behavior? If you're like many people who have not studied nonverbal communication, you think of gestures, body movements, eye contact and the like. In other words, you think of only one of the seven codes that exist to describe nonverbal behavior. The kinesic code includes almost all behaviors that most people believe make up nonverbal ways of expression, including gestures, eye contact, and body position. Burgoon et al. (1996) defined kinesics as referring to "all forms of body movement, excluding physical contact with another" (p. 41). As you can imagine, these movements number in the hundreds of thousands, but there are classifications of kinesic activity that help us better place the movements into discrete categories. Perhaps the most, widely used is Ekman and Friesen's (1969) distinction among emblems, illustrators, regulators, affect displays, and adaptors. This typology describes kinesic behaviors according to their intended purpose.

Emblems are body movements that carry meaning in and of themselves. Emblems stand alone, without verbal accompaniment, and still convey a clear message to the recipients. Common examples of emblems include a thumbs-up gesture, "flipping someone the bird," using the thumb and index finger to signal "OK," and moving two fingers across your throat to signal someone to stop. In fact, sports are often an arena where celebratory emblems are displayed or become a part of our cultural fabric. An example is the "raise the roof" signal, an emblem signaling celebration that quickly caught on among sports players and is now understood relatively widely in this culture. The historical development of emblem form and meaning is fascinating and varies dramatically from culture to culture. Certain cultures (e.g., Italy, France, Egypt) rely on emblems for the delivery of meaning much more so than other cultures, but all cultures include emblems as part of their communication channel.

Unlike emblems, *illustrators* do not carry meaning without verbal accompaniment. Instead, illustrators are body movements that help receivers interpret and better attend to what is being said verbally. The sort of "nonsense" hand gestures that often accompany a person's speech, especially when speaking publicly, are one form of illustrators. Yet these "nonsense" gestures actually serve important functions: They help focus the receiver's attention on what is being said, they help the sender emphasize a part of his or her speech, they help the sender clarify what is being said, and so on. A father who scolds his child may accentuate the seriousness of the message by waving a finger in the youngster's face, or a traveler may clarify a description of her lost luggage by drawing a "picture" of its shape in the air as she describes it; these are simply two examples of how we use illustrators to assist the verbal component.

Regulators are body movements that are employed to help guide conversations. They may be used to help signal a desire to speak, or a desire not to be called on, or to communicate to the speaker that you are or are not listening. Perhaps the most common example of a regulator is the head nod. We consistently use head nods during conversation to signal to speakers that we are listening, a sign that encourages them to continue. Other behaviors that function as regulators of our conversation include maintaining eye contact, turning our bodies toward or away from the speaker, and looking at our watch.

Adaptors are body movements that "satisfy physical or psychological needs" (Burgoon et al., 1996, p. 42). These movements are rarely intended to communicate anything, but they are good signals of the sender's physiological and psychological state. There are three categories of adaptors: self-adaptors, alter-directed adaptors, and object adaptors. *Self*-adaptors are movements that people direct toward themselves or their bodies; examples include biting fingernails, sucking on a thumb, repeatedly tapping a foot, adjusting a collar, and vigorously rubbing an arm to increase warmth. *Alter-directed* adaptors include the same sorts of behaviors found among self-adaptors except that they are movements people direct to the bodies of others; examples include scratching a friend's back itch, caressing a partner's hair, adjusting a partner's collar, or dusting off a friend's rarely worn jacket. Alter-directed adaptors often signal to the target person or to the audience the level of attachment between the individuals in the exchange. *Object* adaptors are movements that involve attention to an object; common examples include biting on a pen, holding a (sometimes unlit) cigar, or circling the edge of a cup with a finger.

Finally, *affect* displays are body movements that express emotion without the use of touch. Like emblems, affect displays often do not require verbal accompaniment for understanding. In fact, several studies have shown that people across cultures understand certain nonverbal facial expressions as reflective of particular emotions (see Ekman & Oster, 1979; Izard, 1977). By manipulating three facial regions (the eyes and eyelids, the eyebrows and forehead, and the mouth and cheeks), people can create affect displays that are recognizable world wide. For example, sadness is expressed by somewhat constricting the eyes and forehead region, while flattening the cheeks and displaying a slight downward curvature of the mouth.

Although Ekman and Friesen's category system captures most gestural movements, it doesn't describe all kinesic behaviors. Perhaps most importantly, it gives short shrift to the types and functions of eye contact. A popular saying exults that "the eyes are the window to the soul" Research on eye behavior supports these beliefs. Eye contact has been shown to vary dramatically in form and to differ significantly in function (for review, see Gramet, 1983). It clearly occupies a central place as a channel for message transmission and will emerge in studies reviewed throughout the selection.

Haptics

A second general category of nonverbal behavior is labeled haptics and refers to all aspects of touch. Perhaps no other code has stronger communicative potential than does touch. Research has shown that individuals place considerable weight on the meaning of touch and that touch has important developmental benefits (see Jones & Yarbrough, 1985). In fact, several studies have found that the absence of touch from parents has serious consequences for children's growth (for review, see Montagu, 1978). Close, physical contact with the caregiver seems to give children the critical sense of protection and security that cannot be attained in other ways. As such, it is not surprising that holding babies is often the behavior that can best calm them and that physicians spend some time explaining baby-holding techniques to new parents.

Touch does not only play an important role during early childhood, it is a critical part of our life as we age as well (see Barnard & Brazelton, 1990). Indeed, the elderly may be most affected by the harmful consequences of touch deprivation (see Montagu, 1978). When lifelong partners pass away, the elderly often lose the one source of affectionate touch on which they have relied for much of their lives. Although certain associations (e.g., long-time neighbors, family members) may help alleviate some potential for loneliness, it is unlikely that their needs for touch will be fully satisfied by these connections.

As with kinesics, haptic behaviors may be classified in multiple ways, some focused on type and others focused on function. Among the type of haptics discussed, scholars have distinguished between the form of touch and its qualities. On the one hand, the form of the touch sends an important communicative message. For example, we could easily separate nuzzles from kisses, rubs from hugs, pokes from hits, pushes from punches, and so on.

Proxemics

The proxemic category of nonverbal behavior captures the way we use space. From analyses of overpopulation in certain nations, to the impact of small dorm room space, to overcrowding in prisons, studies consistently show harmful, effects of limited space. Although cultures differ dramatically in the amount of space that is typically given, we are all born with at least minimum needs for space. Threatening those space needs, especially for prolonged periods, produces high stress that, in turn, affects our psyche and behavior dramatically (see Edwards, Fuller, Vorakitphokatorn, & Sermsri, 1994). It is not surprising then, that confinement in a very small and dark room is commonly used as a method of torture (www.amnesty.org) and that such torture has devastating psychological impact. Indeed, Lester (1990) found an increase in suicide rates associated with overcrowding in prisons. Donoghue (1992) reported overcrowding as a factor contributing to stress among teenagers in the Virgin Islands. Curiously, he noted that sexual activity (sometimes leading to pregnancy) was one of consequences. Also, Gress and Heft (1998) showed that, the number of roommates in college dorms negatively affected the residents both emotionally and behaviorally. One way in which this need for space is expressed is through our behavior around territories.

Territories are physically fixed areas that one or more individuals defend as their own (Altman, 1975). To maintain the spatial needs provided by these territories, we set up markers so that others know the territory's boundaries (Buslig, 1999). For example, students may put books on the seat next to them to ensure that the seat is not taken, or spread their belongings across a wide area of a table to indicate the area as their own. Fences around property, "Keep Away" and "Do Not Disturb" signs, and markers around beach blankets are other common examples of signaling territory. Interestingly, locations where space is limited are particularly prone to markers of territory. Roommates often send very clear signals about the boundaries of their territory by hanging unique posters or signs that mark the area as their own. The importance of these territories to our well being is evident in the way individuals react to their violation. Intrusions into territory have been shown to produce elevated stress, and behavioral responses varying from withdrawal to confrontation (for review, see Lyman & Scott, 1967).

Unlike territories, which are fixed physical entities, *personal space* is a proxemicbased need that moves along with the individual. It is an "invisible bubble" that expands and shrinks according to context, but follows each individual, protecting him or her from physical threats (Hall, 1966). Violation of that personal space bubble produces responses similar to those found for the violation of territory. In North America, typical personal space has a circumference of approximately 3 ft, but the size of that space varies dramatically and is influenced by a variety of factors, from the target of your conversation to its location (see Burgoon et al., 1996). For example, you would likely feel much more uncomfortable standing 2 ft away from someone in a relatively empty elevator than in a crowded elevator. We recognize that certain contexts necessitate the temporary violation of our personal space, but we also keenly anticipate extracting ourselves from that context and restoring the security that comes with maintaining those personal space needs. A behavior that is commonly used both to violate personal space and restore it is eye contact. Have you ever felt that your personal space has been violated by someone simply staring at you, even from a distance? Many people report such a sensation. Have you ever looked away from someone who got too close physically? That sort of behavior is a common response to the violation of personal space in elevators, for example (see Rivano-Fischer, 1988).

Physical Appearance

The physical appearance category of nonverbal behavior includes all aspects related to the way we look, from our body type, to body adornments (e.g., tattoos, rings), to what we wear. Perhaps no other category of nonverbal behavior has a stronger effect on initial impressions than our physical appearance. The two general types of physical appearance that will be addressed in this selection are body type and attire.

Researchers have identified three general body types: ectomorphs, mesomorphs, and endomorphs (see Burgoon et al., 1996). *Ectomorphic* bodies are characterized by thin bone structures and lean bodies, *mesomorphic* bodies have strong bone structures, are typically muscular and athletic, and *endomorphic* bodies have large bone structures, and are typically heavy-set and somewhat rounded. An individual's body type is partly based on genetic elements such as bone structures and partly based on other elements such as diet and levels of activity. Regardless of the source of one's body structure or the degree to which it has any actual effect on behavior, research has clearly shown that people have strong impressions of others based on their body type. Specifically, ectomorphs are perceived to be timid, clumsy, and anxious, but also intelligent; mesomorphs are seen as outgoing, social, and strong; and endomorphs are considered lazy, jolly, and relatively unintelligent (Burgoon et al., 1996). Some factors may affect these perceptions. For example, women ectomorphs and male mesomorphs may be perceived more favorably than their other-sex counterparts. Unfortunately, research has not sufficiently addressed these possibilities. However, one pattern that has been well documented is that, regardless of actual body size, women are more likely than men to perceive their bodies negatively (for review, see Cash & Pruzinsky, 1990). Such "body image disturbances" have devastating consequences, affecting self-esteem, leading to eating disorders, and even increasing suicide rates (e.g., Phillips, 1999; Stice, Hayward, Cameron, Killen, & Taylor, 2000). Why do many women have such dislike for their bodies? Although the answer to this question is not at all simple, it is undoubtedly based, at least in part, on a cultural obsession with images of overly thin women (see Botta, 1999).

However, body shape is not the only aspect of physical appearance that has been shown to affect people's perceptions of us. Another strong influence on perceptions is height. Taller men and women are more likely to be seen as competent, dominant, and intelligent (see Boyson, Pryor, & Butler, 1999). Interestingly, however, the advantage of height does not extend to perceptions of women's attractiveness. Instead, shorter women are perceived as more attractive and date more frequently than taller women (Sheppard & Strathman, 1989). Men and women who fall well above or below this preferred standard encounter lifelong difficulties, including a diminished likelihood of relational success and struggles with perceptions of credibility across a wide range of evaluative contexts (see Martel & Biller, 1987). To combat these perceptions, .short people sometimes change their environment to hide their height. For example, Robert Reich, who served on three presidential administrations and is under 5 ft tall, would speak behind a podium and use a step stool, making media viewers unaware of his short stature.

One explanation for the strong perceptions associated with body type and height comes from Evolutionary Theory. Evolutionary theorists (otherwise called sociobiologists) argue that our attraction to others is based in large part on our perceptions of their genetic makeup (see Buss, 1994). They suggest that, much like other mammals, the strongest members of our species receive the greatest attention and are considered the most attractive. For us, signs of health, wealth, and intelligence are the primary determinants of "strength." As such, it is not surprising to these scholars that people's body type (which may be associated with health) and height (which often translates to physical superiority) affect their life success.

Finally, the clothes we wear are a part of our physical appearance that also affects people's perceptions of us. The clothes we wear strongly influence perceptions of credibility, status, attractiveness, competence, and likability (e.g., Kaiser, 1997). This should come as no surprise to anyone who has seen students proudly display their *Abercrombie & Fitch* shirts, observed the respect often afforded to those wearing their military uniforms, or shook their head in frustration at someone who leaves for an interview in completely disheveled clothes. Indeed, individuals wearing formal clothes are seen as more credible and more persuasive than those wearing informal clothes, affecting their success across a range of interaction contexts, from job interviews to dates. Other aspects of physical appearance that relate to people's judgments include tattoos, rings, and hair styles, in sum, studies unequivocally demonstrate that physical appearance, both things under individuals' control (e.g., attire) and those not (e.g., height), strongly influence perceptions.

Vocalics

Vocalics, a category that people sometimes have difficulty recognizing as a nonverbal component, reflect all aspects of the voice, including loudness, pitch, accent, rate of speech, length of pauses between speech, and tone, among many others. Vocalic elements carry much of the meaning of a message and communicate a lot about the sender. Its importance can be reflected by a simple exercise. Try saying the same words (e.g., "Come over here") with slightly different vocalic qualities. Depending on how we say these words, we could communicate anger, passion, sadness, love, or a variety of other emotions. Indeed, studies have shown that we make relatively accurate judgments about a person's sex, age, height, and cultural background based on vocal cues alone (see Argyle, 1988). Like many of the codes discussed so far, vocalic elements also affect perceptions of attractiveness and competence (Semic, 1999). Deeper voices among men, like that of Barry White for example, are considered sexual and romantic, whereas high-pitched voices among men are considered feminine and weak. Other vocal qualities such as accent and speech rate are also associated with intelligence. For example, certain accents (e.g., British accents) may be considered sophisticated whereas others may not (e.g., thick Boston accents). This difference in the attractiveness of accents is illustrated in the movie *My Fair Lady* which is based on the premise that individuals sometimes must change their accent to affect judgments of their credibility.

One theory that has been applied to understand vocalic shifts is Communication Accommodation Theory (CAA, see chap. 16, this volume). Central to CAA is the belief that we converge our speech toward the style of individuals with whom we want to be associated and diverge away from that of individuals with whom we do not want association (see Giles, Mulac. Bradac, & Johnson, 1987). Examples of this behavior can be found across a wide range of contexts, including interactions between individuals of different ages (e.g., adults and the elderly), individuals from different cultures, individuals with different levels of status, even individuals of different sexes (see Gallois, Giles, Jones, Cargile, & Ota, 1995). So, if you were from the eastern United States and were to spend considerable time in the South, you would likely develop somewhat of a Southern accent, at least when around your friends from the South. That accent accommodation is a way of signaling connectedness with the South. Not surprisingly, the degree to which you are willing to accommodate others in your language has also been shown to significantly affect their perceptions of you. Failure to accommodate your vocalic patterns to others implicitly signals to them that you are not interested in joining their cultural group. On the other hand, a willingness to accommodate communicates attraction.

Chronemics and Artifacts

Chronemics and artifacts are the last two categories of nonverbal behavior that we will discuss in this selection. Rarely considered when discussing nonverbal messages, these codes nevertheless play a strong role in our interactions. The chronemic code captures our use and perception of time, including (among other things) our perception of the "appropriate" duration of an event, the number of things we do at once, the importance of punctuality, our use of time in our language, and the desired sequencing of events (Andersen, 1999). The North American culture is preoccupied with the notion of time; life is fast-paced and individuals are seemingly always struggling against time constraints. Two hours seems to be the maximum time that one expects to allot for entertainment or food events; movies are typically 2 hr or less, plays may go 3 hr but will have a prolonged recess to affect the perception of time, and quests often start getting anxious when meals take longer than 2 hr. Other countries differ dramatically from this North American norm. Although we rarely think of these time norms, they become very evident when we visit other countries. For example, Mediterranean countries often take 3 to 4 hr for a meal, making it as much as a social event as it is time for nourishment. This selection will focus on three chronemic elements: duration, punctuality, and the distinction between polychronism and monochronism.

The expectations surrounding event duration are captured in part by the example provided previously. For every event or interaction, we have culturally and socially based expectations about its duration (Gonzalez & Zimbardo, 1999). Whether it be the amount of time a professor spends in an office meeting with a student, the amount of time set aside for a lunch date, or the amount of time before contact is made following a successful first date, these expectations strongly affect our perceptions of others' competence or attractiveness. Imagine if you had strong expectations that someone not call you back until 2 or 3 days after a first date but the person calls you within minutes after dropping you off. That violation of your chronemic expectations would undoubtedly affect your perceptions of him or her. In a similar vein, perceptions associated with punctuality vary according to the context and have important consequences. Punctuality is held with relatively high esteem in the North American culture, especially for more formal engagements. Arriving late to an interview, even if 5 min, is considered inexcusable, but 5 min late for a lunch date may be acceptable. However, even informal occasions have relatively strict punctuality expectations; arriving 30 min late for a lunch date is not appropriate, for example. In other cultures, however, there is a recognition that the time set for an appointment is rarely adhered to, and expectations are that the appointment may begin 30 to 45 min following the originally set appointment time.

Failing to meet these culturally and contextually driven expectations have important implications for assessments of individuals (see Burgoon & Hale, 1988).

A final concept related to chronemics that will be considered in this selection is the distinction between polychronism and monochronism (Hall & Hall 1999). Polychronism reflects the act of doing multiple activities at once, whereas monochronism characterizes a focus on one activity at a time. For example, interacting with someone while you are cleaning your apartment, or watching TV while talking to someone considered a reflection of (dis)interest in the conversation. Of course, certain careers (e.g., secretarial work, CEOs) require that individuals are adept at polychronistic activity, and some cultures consider polychronism a sign of importance, so monochronism is not universally preferred.

The final nonverbal code is *artifacts,* a category that includes "the physical objects and environmental attributes that communicate directly, define the communication context, or guide social behavior in some way" (Burgoon et al., 1996, p. 109). Hall (1966) classified artifacts into two main types: fixed-feature elements an semifixed feature elements. Fixed features include aspects of our surroundings that are not easily movable and are unlikely to change. Among these features is the structure of our surroundings, including the architectural style, the number and size of windows, and the amount of space available. Studies have shown that such architectural features directly impact the sort of communication that occurs (see Sundstrom, Bell, Busby, & Asmus, 1996). For instance, people who work in small cubicles are much less productive and less satisfied than people who work in their own office space, especially when the office space includes windows. Semifixed features are defined as aspects of our surroundings that are somewhat easily movable. Examples include rugs, paintings, wall color, the amount of lighting, and the temperature, among others. Considerable evidence suggests that these features also strongly affect both psychological health and communication outcome (for review; see Sundstrom et al., 1996). For example, research has shown that the semifixed aspects of a hospital affect the speed of patient recovery (Gross, Sasson, Zarhy, & Zohar, 1998).

In sum, nonverbal messages affect our interactions in hundreds of ways, from movement in our face, to our body posture, our gestures, the space between us, the ways we touch, the intonations in our voice, the way we use time, and the surroundings in which we find ourselves. Together, these nonverbal features inescapably guide the way we act and the outcome of our interactions. However, noting the population of nonverbal message types is only part of the equation. Each of these nonverbal behaviors can serve a variety of functions or purposes.

Moving Forward

Now that we have an understanding of nonverbal codes and the role they play in communication, we continue defining nonverbal communication by moving onward to the nature of nonverbal skills in communication competence. The next reading discusses the ability to send and receive nonverbal messages and emotional intelligence; and how both of these skills are related to nonverbal communication. As you move throughout this reading, break down an encounter that you recently may have had with a friend, roommate, or classmate; and identify the moments when you may have used the communication skills that the authors discuss.

THE NATURE OF NONVERBAL SKILLS

Nonverbal skill is an integral aspect of overall social competence or social skill. Social competence, according to Feldman, Philipott, and Custrini (1991), is a "hypothetical construct relating to evaluative judgments of the adequacy of a person's performance [within the context of a social interaction]" (p. 331). Others regard social competence as a combination of knowledge (i.e., cognitions) and translation of that knowledge into performance (i.e., behavior), although this distinction is not meant to diminish the importance of affect, which is featured prominently in conceptualizations of emotional intelligence (see Mayer & Salovey, 1997). In either case, nonverbal and verbal skills are manifestations of that competence. Social interactions (and their subsequent evaluations) include a variety of verbal and nonverbal codes and cues that are predicated on an individual's knowledge of the display rules for a given social and cultural context. To be a competent communicator requires mastery of both nonverbal and verbal streams of communication.

Conceptual Definitions

One of the most enduring concepts in the social sciences is that the capacity to accurately transmit to and acquire information from other individuals is crucial to the functioning of social relations (Buck, 1983). Indeed, early evolutionary theorists like Darwin (1872) posited that the ability to transmit internal states to others is not only an important element of interaction but is integral to the survival of any social species, given that it provides a directive framework for the subsequent behaviors of others (as well as oneself).

The aspects of nonverbal behavior thought to contribute to accurate exchange of social information, however, are highly dependent on scholars' individual orientations toward the importance or role of nonverbal communication. Nonverbal communication skill is typically described (either overtly or tacitly) as individual differences in sending (i.e., encoding) and/or receiving (i.e., decoding) abilities. Unlike the tendency in other writings about communication skill, in which skill is typically equated with the production but not the reception of messages, nonverbal scholars tend to take a broader perspective by also acknowledging the importance of receptive sensitivity to nonverbal cues. However, there also is often a narrowing of perspective by focusing on skills as they relate to the affective features of interpersonal interactions. As Friedman (1979) asserted, the field of nonverbal communication research has its roots firmly implanted in the study of emotions and feelings. As we argue here, nonverbal skills extend far beyond the emotive domain. Conceptualizations also differ according to what nonverbal cues and codes are featured. For example, in some cases (e.g., Ekman & Friesen, 1976) the focus is on facial cues, whereas in others (e.g., Rosenthal, Hall, DiMatteo, Rogers, & Archer, 1979), it is on the voice, body, and face. These differences in code foci notwithstanding, nonverbal skills are typically thought to be manifested when nonverbal sending and receiving abilities "enhance the course of a social interaction and the goals of the interaction are more likely to be achieved" (Feldman et al., 1991, p. 321). That is, consistent with conceptualizations in other areas of communication, scholars embrace a goal-oriented perspective and use as a primary criterion for judging success the extent to which goals are met (although as the above quotation implies, whose goals—sender's or receiver's—and which goals are often unarticulated, making for indeterminacies in what would constitute skillful communication when various goals are incongruent or in conflict). Within this general parameter, several key distinctions have been offered to further delineate what constitutes nonverbal skill.

Sending/Encoding and Receiving/Decoding Abilities. One approach has focused on decomposing nonverbal skills into their constituent encoding and decoding abilities. Nonverbal sending ability—called *nonverbal expressivity* by Rosenthal et al., (1979)— entails the capacity to encode and express emotion and affect in ways that can be received and decoded correctly by others. These abilities may be rooted in a biologically based system of temperament that is further shaped by social learning processes (Buck, 1983). This conclusion is supported by evidence that sending ability is relatively stable across a wide array of situations and strongly associated with tendencies toward internal and external expression (see Buck, 1975, 1977, 1979; Buck, Miller, & Caul, 1974; Buck, Savin, Miller, & Caul, 1972; Crider & Lunn, 1971; Eysenck, 1967; Gray, 1972; Zuckerman, Hall, DeFrank, & Rosenthal, 1979). In contrast, receiving ability—called *nonverbal sensitivity* (Rosenthal et al., 1976)— consists of the ability to decode emotion and affect accurately. This ability has been found to be highly dependent on what Buck (1983) calls *decoding rules*. Analogous to display rules (which are critical in any analysis of sending ability), decoding rules are "cultural rules or expectations about the attention to, and interpretation of, nonverbal displays" (Buck, 1983,

p. 217), with attention being a necessary (but not sufficient) condition of interpretation. In other words, a person may learn to attend to certain nonverbal cues while not attending to others, and such attention can be situationally specific such that some cues are attended to only under certain situations.

Emotional Intelligence. Closely related to descriptions of sending and receiving abilities is the concept of emotional intelligence. Defined by Mayer and Salovey (1997) as "the ability to perceive emotions, to access and generate emotions so as to assist thought, to understand emotions and emotional knowledge, and to reflectively regulate emotions so as to promote emotional and intellectual growth" (p. 5), emotional intelligence is a multidimensional construct. Specifically, the Mayer and Salovey model includes dimensions related to (a) *attention* (perception of the cues), (b) *clarity* (i.e., the granularity of emotional discriminations and emotional knowledge), (c) *knowledge* (which includes facilitation and assimilation of emotions in thinking), and (d) *reflective regulation* of own and others' emotional states (Mayer, Salovey, & Caruso, 1999; Salovey, 1999). Each of these is highly relevant to nonverbal encoding and decoding skills. In addition, there is Goleman's (1995, 1998) typology, which identifies five competencies: (a) *self-awareness* (knowing and following one's own feelings), (b) *self-regulation* (managing one's emotions in a facilitative manner, delaying gratification, and handling distress), (c) *motivation* (striving and persevering toward one's goals), (d) *empathy* (recognizing others' feelings, establishing rapport, taking another's perspective), and (e) *social skills* (handling emotions well and accurately in interpersonal relationships). Whereas the Mayer and Salovey approach tends to be more individualistic and psychological, the Goleman approach includes more interpersonal and social dimensions, distinguishing between personal competence (e.g., self-awareness, self-regulation, motivation) and social competence (e.g., empathy, social skills). Similarly, Bar-On's (1997) dimensions include (a) stress management, (b) interpersonal skills (which also includes empathy), and (c) adaptability (although the latter has strong cognitive connotations in Bar-On's descriptions). Moreover, the concept of generalized intelligence implies some manner of heightened abilities and, in that respect, is closely aligned with the concept of skill or competence.

Moving Forward

Our next reading discusses paralanguage in further detail and reveals how paralanguage can differ across cultures. As you read about the differences in nonverbal communication described in the next reading, think about your own nonverbal interactions with individuals from other cultures. Have you experienced a situation where the use of nonverbals seemed confusing? After you are finished with this reading, continue on to the next selection, which further explores culture-specific nonverbal communication.

PARALINGUISTICS, KINESICS, AND PROXEMICS

Characteristics of vocal communication considered marginal or optional and therefore ex-cludable from the customary linguistic analysis are referred to as **paralanguage**. The most common paralinguistic features have to do with the tone of voice and pacing of speech and are marked by noticeable variations in pitch, tempo, rhythm, articulation, or intensity. For example, highly controlled articulation produces the crisp, precise pronunciation expected of formal pronouncements addressed to large audiences; by contrast, speech so relaxed as to become slurred is heard from those who are very tired, sleepy, or under the influence of alcohol or other drugs. Speakers of English and other languages tend to associate extreme pitch variation with happiness and surprise; high pitch level or fast tempo with fear, surprise, or anger; and low pitch level or slow tempo with boredom and sadness. The rounding of lips imparts to the voice the cooing quality that is frequently used by adults when talking to a baby.

Besides these and other voice qualifiers, there are various vocal characterizers that ac-company speech or, more precisely, through which we talk. These range from laughing to crying and from whispering to shouting, and include such other vocalizations as moaning and yawning. Then there are the so-called vocal segregates represented for the most part by such extralinguistic sounds as the ones graphically rendered in English as *uh-huh* to indicate agree-ment or gratification, *ah* to express a variety of emotions from delight to regret, and *tut-tut* or *tsk-tsk* to show mild disapproval. These optional vocal effects may not carry the same meaning from one language to the next. The breathy or husky tone of voice that in some languages is associated with intense emotion or sexual desire conveys respect or a submissive attitude in Japanese.

Just as any speech that is not completely neutral tends to be accompanied by one or more paralinguistic features, that is, by vocal gestures, it is also likely to be supplemented by visual gestures—facial expressions and other body motions. These are the subject of *kinesics*.

There is no question that bodily gestures serve as important means of communication. Comedians are notably adept at slanting, canceling, or completely turning around the mean-ing of their spoken lines with a well-chosen grimace or gesture of different communicative content, and professional mimes know how to move their audiences to tears or laughter without uttering a single word. But speech-related body motions are by no means limited to performers—they are an integral part of everyone's daily communicative activity.

The basic assumptions that underlie kinesics are that no body movement or facial expres-sion lacks meaning in the context in which it occurs and that like other aspects of voluntary human behavior, body movements, posture, and facial expressions are patterned. Influenced by structural linguistics, Ray L. Birdwhistell (1918–1997) in the 1950s developed a method of studying and describing the body-motion aspects of human communicative behavior by means of units that parallel those employed in linguistic analysis. One such unit, the kineme (analogous to the phoneme), has been defined as the smallest discriminable contrastive unit of body motion.

Observant travelers noticed centuries ago that members of societies along the Mediterranean Sea used many more bodily gestures and facial expressions than, say, those living in Scandinavia or Japan. However, not all Italians, for example, use the same "body language," just as they do not all speak the same dialect of Italian. Birdwhistell offered an interesting example in support of the expectation that kinesic behavior is bound to be just as culture-specific as the corresponding language. He reported that even when the sound is removed from films of the speeches of the late politician and mayor of New York City Fiorello La Guardia, it is possible to tell whether he is speaking English, Yiddish, or Italian, as characteristic body motions are associated with each language (Birdwhistell 1970:102). Although the holistic and contextual approach to communication that Birdwhistell advocated has been uniformly accepted, the extent to which "body language" can be analyzed in terms of his units remains controversial, in part because the detailed transcription he designed is far too complicated and time-consuming.

In the early 1960s the interdependence between communication and culture stimulated Edward T. Hall to develop *proxemics*, the study of the cultural patterning of the spatial separation individuals maintain in face-to-face encounters. The term has subsequently come to embrace studies concerned with privacy, crowding, territoriality, and the designing of buildings, private as well as public, with the view of meeting the different cultural expectations of their prospective users.

According to Hall, the distances individuals maintain from one another depend on the nature of their mutual involvement and are culture-specific. For example, under normal circumstances middle-class American adults of northern European heritage make regular use of four proxemic zones, or distances, ranging from intimate to public, each of the zones consisting of a close and a far phase (see Table 12.1). In the close phase of the intimate distance, the individuals are close enough to be encircled by each other's arms. All senses are engaged: Each individual receives the body heat as well as any odor or scent emanating from the other individual, and the other person's breath is felt; because of the closeness, vision may be blurred or distorted and speaking is at a minimum. As is obvious, this narrowest of all interpersonal distances is suited to lovemaking, protecting, or comforting.

By contrast, business is transacted at the social-consultative distance: The close phase is characteristic of contact among people who work together or are participants at casual social gatherings; the far phase characterizes more formal business transactions, such as interviews or situations where two or more people find themselves in the same space and do not want to appear rude by not communicating. For instance, receptionists who are also expected to type and manage a switchboard must have enough space between them and the visitors to permit them to work rather than to feel they must engage in polite conversation with those waiting to be seen.

The manner in which members of different societies space themselves in each other's presence varies along a contact-noncontact continuum. For example, Arabs, other Mediterranean peoples, and Latin Americans prefer spatially close interactions; northern Europeans prefer to keep their distance, both literally and figuratively.

Moving Forward

Our last reading examines how the use of nonverbal communication is rooted in culture and reveals that there are often culture–specific ways of communicating nonverbally that do not carry over to other cultures. You already have read that verbal communication and nonverbal messages do not always match up with one another; and how when that happens, it can be frustrating when you are trying to determine what someone really means. As you read the following section, consider how culture plays a role in decoding nonverbal communication. Can you think of any examples where nonverbal communication could cause a cultural conflict? Can you think of any gestures that may be universal, regardless of culture?

THE ROLE OF CULTURE IN UNDERSTANDING NONVERBAL COMMUNICATION

Research has shown that the way we form our impressions of other people is far more dependent on the nonverbal behavior (NVB) we observe than on the spoken words we listen to (Argyle, Salter, Nicholson, Williams, & Burgess, 1970; Burgoon, 1994; Mehrabian & Ferris, 1967; Mehrabian & Wiener, 1967; Newcombe & Ashkanasy, 2002). In most instances, nonverbal cues are processed more quickly than verbal messages, and therefore are usually responsible for our first impressions. First impressions/judgments are often based on facial expressions, postures, gestures, use of personal space and distance, general appearance and attire, eye contact and gaze, and so on. Although much of our nonverbal communication is "part of a universally recognized and understood code" (Burgoon, Buller, & Woodall, 1996, p. 5), a great deal is rooted in our culture—and can therefore be culture-specific. This fact is of particular importance in terms of the perception of people from other cultures and the outcomes of intercultural communication, because the standards we apply and the judgments we make are in turn subject to culture-specific interpretations. Matsumoto (2006) concluded that "collectively, the evidence provides more than ample support for the notion that culture plays a large role in molding all of our nonverbal behaviors, which comprise an important part of the communication process" (p. 221). Cultures can differ remarkably with respect to social values and the nature of interpersonal relationships (Hofstede, 1980). These differences are particularly subtle in interpersonal communication and NVB (Kowner & Wiseman, 2003), but the effects can be as substantial as communication breakdowns, ambivalence, or conflict.

In contrast to verbal communication, the central elements of nonverbal communication and their meanings cannot be looked up in a dictionary. Nonverbal signal production, to a large degree, is not rule-based, nor does it follow an explicit grammar. This fact not only complicates cross-cultural communication in practice, but also poses specific methodological problems for the researcher. Cultural differences in NVB are very difficult to describe objectively, and the experimental manipulation of specific nonverbal cues is usually confounded by nuisance variables.

Culture and Nonverbal Communication

Beginning with Efron's pioneering work on gestures (Boas & Efron, 1936; Efron, 1941), a considerable number of studies have demonstrated the cultural variety in the production and interpretation of various NVBs, such as facial expressions (Ekman, 1972; Ekman et al., 1987), emblematic gestures (Ekman, 1976; Friesen, Ekman, & Wallbott, 1979), body postures (Kudoh & Matsumoto, 1985; Matsumoto & Kudoh, 1987), interpersonal distance (Hall, 1976), and eye contact (Hall & Hall, 1990; Kitao & Kitao, 1989). The common thread in all of these approaches is that they address well-described spatiotemporal activity patterns that can easily be isolated from the behavioral stream, or even directly measured, and for which specific functional a priori hypotheses can be formulated. Beyond such "meaningful" units, however, more subtle nonverbal signals can be observed in interpersonal communication, signals that bypass conscious attention and registration but nevertheless have a strong influence on our interpersonal impressions and social relationships. Recent research from human ethology and cognitive neuroscience clearly shows that movement qualities, such as speed, acceleration, and dimensional complexity can carry relevant social information (Grammer, Honda, Juette, & Schmitt, 1999; Krumhuber & Kappas, 2005). The authors of these studies have pointed out that the dynamic qualities of NVB can have an even stronger impact on the observer's impressions than so-called *semantic aspects*, although they might not be consciously processed or identified as a possible cause. It is evident that semantic and nonsemantic aspects of NVB are interwoven in real-life interactions and can hardly be separated by the observer, neither with respect to their physical properties nor with respect to their particular socioemotional effects. Actual conceptions hold that nonverbal communication can be considered as analogous, widely automated, and unconscious in production and in reception (Buck, Losow, Murphy, & Costanzo, 1992; DePaulo & Friedman, 1998). The subliminal nature of nonverbal communication is also underlined by the facts that impressions based on nonverbal cues are formed within extremely short time periods (Dimberg, 1997) and that even very subtle nonverbal variations can have a significant influence on the observer's perception of the sender (Frey, 1999; Frey, Hirsbrunner, Florin, Daw, & Crawford, 1983). The growing knowledge about the "nature" of nonverbal communication has forced researchers to broaden their analytical perspective to capture variations beyond predefined signals, and at the same time to refine the resolution of observation in order to account for more subtle and transient variations.

Although these implications concern the descriptive analysis of NVB, cultural comparisons face further methodological problems when it comes to the investigation of nonverbal communication effects. We know that the evaluation of another person and the perception and interpretation of his or her behavior is often biased by prior categorical judgments, such as stereotypes or even prejudice. For example, white subjects judge the behavior of a black person to be more violent than the same behavior exhibited by a white person (Duncan, 1976). Moreover, not only person perception is affected by this categorization based on culture or race, but also the interaction behavior toward, for instance, a black person. Thus, Dovidio, Kawakami, and Gaertner (2002) showed that skin color has a crucial impact on verbal as well as nonverbal communication patterns of interlocutors. This influence is often unconscious and is exerted by even the most subtle stimulations. For example, Chen and Bargh (1997) showed that subliminal presentations of black faces caused more hostile behavior in white participants than did similar presentations of white faces. From these results, it can be expected that photo or video samples from other cultures more or less automatically activate stereotypes as they convey category-relevant information tied to physical appearance. This fact can cause severe confusion in the analysis of impression effects, making it difficult to separate category-based, top-down processes and behavior-based, bottom-up processes in person perception. These methodological problems are not specific to the analysis of cultural differences, but are instead inherent in the analysis of nonverbal communication in general.

SUMMARY

Nonverbal communication is not simply body language or physical movements. Nonverbal communication is intertwined in every message we send and receive throughout our daily interactions. Nonverbals can complement or contradict the verbal communication we intentionally or unintentionally use. Because our verbal and nonverbal communication does not always match up, individuals often can feel frustrated. With verbal communication, we can look up a word if we do not understand how it is being used. However, with nonverbal communication, there is not a dictionary readily available to provide us with the same insight.

Nonverbal communication is rooted in culture. Our culture defines how we use nonverbal communication. Sometimes, nonverbal messages are specific to a culture and do not carry over to another culture. Understanding how culture plays a role in nonverbal communication brings us one step closer to becoming culturally competent communicators.

In this chapter, we first defined nonverbal communication and explained the different nonverbal codes that are used while communicating. Our second reading focused on the role that nonverbal skills play in communication competence. The last sections examined the role that culture plays in nonverbal communication and how culture can be a factor in decoding and sending nonverbal communication. Continue onward for an opportunity to put your nonverbal knowledge to the test with discussion questions.

DISCUSSION QUESTIONS

1. Describe a situation where the way you acted or dressed affected how others perceived you. Have you ever purposely acted or dressed in a way that did not reflect your true self in order to be accepted by another person or group? Why might this pose a problem when people from different cultures are communicating with each other?

2. Of the different kinds of nonverbal communication (e.g., kinesics, proxemics, haptics), which has the most impact upon you? How would different perceptions about body language, distance, or touch enhance or detract from intercultural communication?

3. How and why does physical appearance encourage or discourage intercultural communication? What competencies are involved in overcoming misperceptions about physical appearance?

4. Can you think of a situation where your first impression of a culturally different person turned out to be inaccurate? When your impression changed, did you modify your communication style? If so, how?

VERBAL COMMUNICATION

CHAPTER 4

STUDY OBJECTIVES

After completing this chapter, you will be able to:
- Describe the Sapir-Whorf hypothesis.
- Discuss the differences in languages across cultures.
- Describe and explain how culture influences verbal communication.

INTRODUCTION

Whenever you communicate with another individual, there is always the opportunity for miscommunication to occur or for other challenges to arise. Worldwide, over 7,000 languages are spoken. As you may have guessed with that figure, language plays an important role in intercultural communication. With multiple languages being spoken around the globe, understanding how culture influences the languages that are spoken is essential. Understanding the role culture plays in verbal communication aids you in becoming a more culturally competent communicator.

In this chapter, we explore verbal communication in intercultural communication settings. Our first reading focuses on linguistic relativity and linguistic determinism through the introduction of the Sapir-Whorf hypothesis. In the next section, we examine how culture influences verbal communication. Here our readings explore the role that personal power can have on how language is used, the concept of cultural grammars, and potential differences between Western and Eastern languages. After you have completed the readings, you will find discussion questions at the end of the chapter for you to apply your knowledge about culture and verbal communication.

Moving Forward

Our first reading is a short selection that introduces linguistic relativity. You may already be familiar with the Sapir-Whorf hypothesis from other communication courses that you have taken. Or the Sapir-Whorf hypothesis may be new to you. Whether you are familiar with this hypothesis or not, this reading provides background and understanding of this instrumental hypothesis and discusses linguistic determinism and linguistic relativity, providing a brief overview of both. As you move through this next selection, think about how language can develop and how it can impact our lives.

LINGUISTIC RELATIVITY

Another cross-cultural area is the study of linguistic relativity, which can be traced to Aristotle's speculations on whether doing philosophy while using Greek as a symbol system would make the knowledge discovered different if, say, Latin were the symbol system (Steinfatt, 1989). Aristotle's answer was that the language in use would not make a substantial difference in the final result—that any thought could be expressed equally well in any language.

This view held sway until the late 19th century, when Cassirer (1953) suggested that the language used to conduct philosophical analyses could influence the resultant knowledge. Cassirer's work was not widely accepted in philosophy, but a young Yale anthropologist, Edward Sapir, began to write and lecture on topics in linguistic anthropology in the late 1800s. Sapir (1921) suggested that thought was potentially relative to language. Prior to 1920 Benjamin Lee Whorf, an undergraduate student in engineering at MIT who was working his way through college as an inspector for an insurance company, began to study Hopi and Mayan cultures. In the 1920s he lectured extensively on his thesis, developed independently of Sapir's ideas, that the language of thought influences its content. Though not Sapir's student at this point, he had heard of Sapir and attended one of Sapir's lectures at Yale late in that decade, eventually joining Sapir's graduate program in anthropology as a student. From this simple meeting was born what has come to be called the *Sapir–Whorf hypothesis*, that language structures thought. Mandell (1931) presents an early view of linguistic relativity; reviews of experimental research may be found in Gibson and McGarvy (1937), Woodworth (1938), Heidbreder (1948), Johnson (1950), Humphrey (1951), (1951), Diebold (1965), and Steinfatt (1988, 1989). Lee's (1996) *The Whorf Theory Complex: A Critical Reconstruction*, provides an excellent discussion of Whorf's intercultural work. Sapir (1921), Whorf (1956), and Cassirer (1953) are perhaps the best known advocates of the notion that language influences thought. They treated linguistic relativity as an interlanguage phenomenon, a process attributable to differences between languages Sapir and Whorf's thesis involves both "linguistic determinism" and "linguistic relativity." Linguistic determinism holds that language shapes thought, but allows that people who speak different languages could still have the same thoughts and think in similar ways. For example, a counterfactual conditional (e.g., "I would take you if I were going that way but I'm not so I can't") is very difficult to express in Chinese. But while the language makes such thoughts difficult to express, linguistic determinism suggests that such thoughts could occur in Chinese, although they would be difficult. Linguistic relativity, a more radical version of linguistic determinism, holds that different languages actually shape thought differently (Glucksberg & Danks, 1975). Linguistic relativity would argue that speakers of Chinese would have great difficulty thinking in counterfactual conditional terms and that thought processes in Chinese would have to follow the structure of the language.

As initially proposed, the *Weltanschauung*—world *view*—thesis of linguistic relativity was very general and thus almost impossible to test. Greenberg (1956), Lenneberg and Roberts (1956), Henle (1958), Fishman (1960), Osgood and Sebeok (1965), and Slobin (1979) all have suggested different ways of organizing the hypothesis. Steinfatt (1989) proposed that three groups of independent variables—phonological, syntactical, and semantic—are possible causative sets in linguistic relativity as the basis for any proposed differences in thought. At least one variable from at least one of these sets must influence at least one dependent measure in one of three variable sets—the logic of thought itself, the structure of cognition and worldview, or perception and areas of cognition—in order for a linguistic relativity effect to be claimed. Beyond looking at differences between natural languages as a source of linguistic relativity effects, Steinfatt (1989) also suggested that substantial phonological, syntactical, or semantic differences in any natural language would have to be regarded as a potential source of linguistic relativity effects. Thus, dialects such as Black-American English, compound bilingualism, aphasics relearning a language, and the deaf, should provide examples of linguistic relativity effects if such effects actually occur. Linguistic relativity should not be limited to the natural language differences proposed by Whorf (1956) and others. Additionally, Steinfatt (1989) suggested that knowledge of the methods by which language is acquired should provide insight into whether linguistic relativity effects are likely to exist.

Moving Forward

Our next selection introduces how culture can influence our verbal communication. Highlighting beliefs about verbal communication, this next selection discusses how our communities, cultures, and societal norms influence the way we verbally communicate. After this reading, we continue our discussion of the cultural impact of verbal communication. As you process this reading, consider how different regions in the United States have different ways of communicating. If you have ever traveled to another area of the world, what differences in your communication styles did you notice?

BELIEFS ABOUT VERBAL COMMUNICATIVENESS

Desire to communicate verbally may be conceived as a continuum that goes from high willingness to low willingness. In order to understand the argumentativeness trait more fully, Rancer,

Baukus, and Infante (1985) utilized Fishbein and Ajzen's (1975) theory of reasoned action, which proposes that human behavior is directly linked to attitudes and beliefs. Further, a predisposition (an inclination to behave in a particular way) is controlled by the set of beliefs that the individual learns to associate with the object of the predisposition (Kim & Hunter, 1993a, 1993b; Rancer, Kosberg, & Baukus, 1992). For example, one way to understand verbal approach versus "avoidance" tendencies is to determine the belief structures people have about arguing: If beliefs control predispositions, a person's level of argumentativeness may be related to his or her beliefs about arguing.

In measuring beliefs about arguing, Rancer et al. (1985) found that more argumentative individuals had predominantly positive beliefs about arguing, whereas less argumentative individuals had predominantly negative beliefs about arguing. Early research in communication apprehension suggested that individuals with high public speaking apprehension would experience high levels of negative thinking, both in anticipation of presenting a speech and in the delivery of the speech (Meichenbaum, 1977). More recent studies support these ideas with respect to both positive and negative thinking (Buhr, Pryor, & Sullivan, 1991; Daly, Vangelisti, Neel, & Cavanaugh, 1989).

Based on these findings, it appears worthwhile to examine how beliefs about arguing are related to verbal communication motivations among individuals of different cultural orientations. Within a given speech community, social values and norms strongly influence the amount of talk and the amount of argument that is considered normal or appropriate. It is possible that among people of high interdependence, arguing is perceived as an unpleasant activity of dubious value that leads to anger and unreasonable behavior. Interdependents may foster negative beliefs about arguing, which may significantly dampen motivation to argue and heighten verbal communication "avoidance."

East Asian tradition appears to value the preservation of the harmony of the social group above the expression of individuals' inner thoughts and negative feelings (Barnlund, 1989). Because of the belief that meaning can be sensed but not phrased, a talkative person is often considered a "show-off" or insincere. The Korean term *noon-chi* ("reading the other person's mind," grasping a situation) and the Japanese term *haragei* (wordless communication) capture the essence of East Asians' positive feelings toward communication without words. For example, a person who "has *noon-chi*" should not ask a favor if he or she knows it cannot be granted, or that granting it would inconvenience the other person.

Several writers have argued that Japanese do not value verbal communication and "avoid" it whenever possible (Gudykunst & Nishida, 1993; Ishii, 1982; Nakane, 1970). For instance, Gudykunst and Nishida (1993) assert that the Japanese concept of *enryo* (a ritualized verbal self-deprecation process used for the purpose of maintaining group harmony) explains these patterns. Similarly, Ishii (1982) claims that it is traditional in the Japanese culture for people to go out of their way to conceal their sentiments, so that they may not disturb the general atmosphere of harmony. Hiroshi Ota argues that *enryo* is an "active" process in Japan, not a "passive" process like reticence (the nearest equivalent concept) in the United States (personal communication cited in Gudykunst & Nishida, 1993). Compatible with this argument, Giles, Coupland, and Wiemann (1992) compared the beliefs of Chinese and Americans about talking. The Americans described talking as pleasant and important, and as a way of controlling what goes on. The Chinese were more "tolerant" of silence and saw quietness as a way of controlling what goes on.

In a more philosophical and complex account' of Chinese relationships, Chang and Holt (1991) argue that Chinese feel no need to develop verbal communicative strategies to maintain their relationships. They note that Chinese cherish the chance of association and allow relationships to develop according to their own course. Chang and Holt further claim that Chinese do not perceive verbal communication as the chief factor in determining relationships. Thus communication "avoidance" should not be interpreted as merely a "passive" form of communication. As Katriel and Philipsen (1981) point out, many North Americans feel that they need "communication" to make a relationship "work." On the other hand, interdependents may hold a considerably less instrumental view of the role of verbal communication in relationships. These inherent differences lead to fundamentally different views of verbal communication.

Takai and Ota's (1994) work also supports the observations of Japanese interpersonal behavior reported above. These researchers describe five factors as essential to Japanese communication competence. Among these factors, at least three (perceptive ability, self-restraint, and interpersonal sensitivity) seem to be closely related to the "low motivation for verbal communication" among Japanese. Takai and Ota describe their first factor, perceptive ability, as sensing the cues in the interaction context and empathizing with the other person, without having the other directly transmit a message using the verbal code. They identify their second factor, self-restraint, as the key value in Japanese communication, in which the "avoidance" of confrontation is often preferred over direct communication of negative feelings or conflict-raising issues. The third factor, interpersonal sensitivity, involves the encoding and decoding of sensitive messages. According to Takai and Ota, being direct and frank toward another person can sometimes be embarrassing to the hearer. Hence, among Japanese, a speaker must be sensitive enough to get his or her message across using hints.

Min-Sun Kim, Excerpts from: "Cross-Cultural Perspectives on Motivations of Verbal Communication: Review, Critique, and a Theoretical Framework," *Communication Yearbook, vol. 22, ed. Michael Roloff*, pp. 70–72. Copyright © 1999 by Taylor & Francis Group. Reprinted with permission.

Moving Forward

Our next selections continue an examination of culture's impact on verbal communication. Language enables us to communicate with one another, and within that language use, the presence of power is evident. The next reading explores levels of power and notes that language cannot be separated from its cultural context. This selection also highlights the differences between Western and Eastern languages. Here, you will begin to see how culture can heavily impact verbal communication. As you move through this reading, also note the differences between Western and Eastern languages, and keep those differences in mind when we later examine the topics of collectivism and individualism. The second reading includes further examples of cultural differences in verbally communicating.

LANGUAGE AS CULTURE AND POWER

Language is an instrument of communication and power. People communicate by means of language. But at the same time, language arises out of the social matrix of power relationships in a given nation (Fuglesang, 1984; Pattanayak, 1986; Rahim, 1986). Linguistic misunderstandings are mainly a result not of linguistic incompetence, but to the difference in social and cultural patterns between communicating groups or individuals. One does "understand" the other, but one does not always comprehend.

In many Asian languages there is a distinction made between so-called levels of speech according to age, social status, and patterns of social interaction. One has to use other titles and forms of addressing when one approaches a younger or elder, a higher- or lower-ranked person. This kind of hierarchical language use has gradually disappeared in the West. Misunderstandings can be of a verbal and of a nonverbal nature. The impact of nonverbal communication forms cannot be underestimated. According to Klopf and Park (1982), only 35% of the social meaning in a face-to-face conversation is imparted verbally, more than 55% in a nonverbal way (i.e., by making use of space and time, body language, and so on).

There is something more involved than just the grammatical competence in the Chomskyian meaning. Of importance are the social use and the social and cultural context in which the language appears. Myung-Seok Park (1979, p. 29) calls this broader notion of linguistic competence the "communicative competence" of a language. A language cannot be separated from its social-cultural context. In different cultures the same words or concepts can have different connotative, contextual, or figurative meanings and evoke idiomatic or metaphoric expressions. The word *fat*, for instance, has a positive connotation in most Asian societies, it shows the person's well-being and wealth. In the West, however, the word is interpreted mainly in a negative way. In the West, the owl is a symbol for wisdom, in the East it is regarded as a stupid bird (for more of these examples, see Klopf, 1981). Rahim (1984) explores the full consequences that these differences have on international communications, while McCreary and Blanchfield (1986) analyze the patterns of discourse in negotiations between Japanese and U.S. companies.

O-Young Lee (1967) concludes that Asian languages have developed on the basis of auditive interpretation (listening) and emotion (pathos) and take into account the "aura" of things. Because of this, Asian languages are more colorful and poetic than are Indo-European languages that are based on visual ascertainment (seeing) and rationation (logos): "A culture of the eye is intellectual, rational, theoretical and active, while a culture of the ear is emotional, sensitive, intuitive and passive" (Lee, 1967, p. 43).

I or We

An essential difference between Western and Asian society is the position of the individual and, consequently, the conception of self. While Western culture is characterized by a strong self-image, in the Asian context, group consciousness plays a much bigger part. Geertz (1973), for instance, in his influential essay on Bali, describes how Balinese act as if persons are impersonal sets of roles, in which all individuality and emotional volatility are systematically repressed. Their notion of self is quite different from the one described by Freud (1951).

Freud demonstrated that one can trace out systematic interrelationships between conscious understandings of social relations, unconscious dynamics, and the ways ambiguous, flexible symbols are turned into almost deterministic patterns of cultural logic. Therefore, Westerners are I-orientated:

> Their behavior is largely determined by their perception of self, a concept we define as the identity, personality, or individualism of a given person as distinct from all other people. For them, the self is a unifying concept. It provides a perspective in thinking, a direction for activity, a source of motivation, a locus in decision-making and a limit to group involvement. (Stewart, 1972, p. 75)

Asians, on the other hand, are we-orientated. They get their identity from the position they hold in the group. In Geertz's study, the Balinese tried to establish smooth and formal interpersonal relationships in which the presentation of the self is affectless and determined by the social group. A typical example is the Asian way of addressing people. A Westerner writes first his Christian name, then his surname, followed by street, town, and country. Asians do it the other way around. Agehananda Bharati (1985), for instance, points out that when one asks for a Hindu's identity, he will give you his caste and his village as well as his name. There is a Sanskrit formula that starts with lineage, family, house, and ends with one's personal name. In this presentational formula the empirical self comes last.

In other words, Asians are submerged, so to speak, in the group, and find themselves lost and powerless as individuals when the link with the group is taken away or does not exist:

> The predominant value is congeniality in social interactions based on relations among individuals rather than on the individual himself. A network of obligations among members of a group is the point of reference, not the self. In Oriental cultures, people's behavior is directed first to maintaining affiliation in groups and congenial social relations. Goals that could be personally rewarding to the individual are only of secondary importance. (Klopf & Park, 1982, p. 30)

Only after the Asian knows someone's status, age, sex, and so on (these are often the first questions that are asked of a foreigner and are regarded as "indiscreet" by a Westerner), he or she will be capable of communicating, of addressing the conversational partner in the "appropriate" cultural way.

Several studies have compared European cultures with U.S. culture. McCroskey et al. (1990) found that adult Swedes and Americans hold substantially different orientations toward verbal communication. Although Swedes see themselves as more competent as communicators than do Americans, they are less prone to initiate communication than are Americans. It is important to consider the fact that verbal communication skills seem to be valued much more highly in mainstream American culture than in the Swedish culture. According to McCroskey et al., this is reflected in the stress that is placed on verbal performance in American schools and colleges, and in the fact that verbal ability, in most colleges, even influences the formal grading of students. Such emphasis is unheard of in Sweden. Another indication is the large quantity of research that has been conducted on speech anxiety and related constructs in the United States, whereas very little interest in this area has been expressed in Sweden, where quietness and reticence are generally looked upon as individual differences rather than problems.

Moving beyond the two-culture comparison, McCroskey and Richmond (1990) summarize data from five cultures that they have studied. Among the participants from the five countries studied (the United States, Sweden, Australia, Micronesia, and Puerto Rico), they found that there were large differences in mean scores. With regard to the Willingness to Communicate Scale, the U.S. subjects reported the highest willingness and the Micronesians reported the lowest. For most of the countries, public speaking drew the least willingness and talking in a dyad drew the most. McCroskey and Richmond conclude that any generalizations concerning the association of self-perceived competence with willingness to communicate must be qualified with reference to culture.

Studies involving various other cultures also confirm the finding that general levels of communication apprehension vary from one culture to another. Chesebro et al. (1992) found that the Hispanic group in their sample included a substantially greater proportion of highly apprehensive students than did either their white group or their black group. Thus ethnicity was highly predictive of the proportion of students classified as highly communication apprehensive. In a study by Hackman and Barthel-Hackman (1993), the New Zealand students sampled were significantly less willing to communicate than were U.S. students in all four contexts (public speaking, meeting, group, and dyad) and with all three types of receivers (stranger, acquaintance, and friend). The authors attribute these results to the collectivist Maori society in New Zealand. Maoris utilize silence rather than verbal expression when they are uncomfortable or are attempting to gather their thoughts. Also, Olaniran and Roach (1994) found that the average CA scores for the Nigerian high school students in their sample seemed to be lower than the average CA scores for American high school students.

Moving Forward

Our last selection furthers our exploration into how culture can impact verbal communication. In the following reading, culture grammars are examined. Here, the way we think, feel, speak, and interact is governed by subconscious rules set forth according to our culture. This selection acknowledges the role high-context and low-context cultures play when it comes to translating across differing cultures. When translating between languages, clarity is extremely important, and back translating aids in making sure the original content and meaning remains as intended in translation. As you move through this reading, consider what you know already about cultural impact on language and verbal communication and connect your knowledge to this selection.

CULTURAL GRAMMAR

Ethnographers have talked about the creation of a 'cultural "grammar"' (see Duranti 1997: 27; Goodenough in Risager 2006: 45), which Wierzbicka (1996: 527) describes as 'a set of subconscious rules that shape a people's ways of thinking, feeling, speaking, and interacting'.

The values and beliefs that form the basis of the subconscious rules can be teased out in two particular ways, emically and etically.[3] Wierzbicka's emic ethnographic approach (e.g. 1996, 2006) is to spell out subjective beliefs about appropriacy using semantic universals to provide 'cultural scripts'. The 'universals' contain a strictly limited use of language, free of cultural baggage, such as the adjectives 'good' and 'bad'. Table 4.1 is an example of her analysis of the difference between the 'vague, undefined' Japanese 'effacement' and Anglo 'self-enhancement'.

Table 4.1 Japanese 'Effacement' and Anglo 'Self-Enhancement' Scripts

JAPANESE 'SELF-EFFACEMENT' SCRIPT	ANGLO 'SELF-ENHANCEMENT' SCRIPT
It is good to often think something like this: 'I did something bad I often do things like this Not everyone does things like this Other people don't often do things like this'	It is good to often think something like this: 'I did something very good I can do things like this Not everyone can do things like this Other people don't often do things like this'

Source: Adapted from Wierzbicka (1996: 537)

Alternatively, either through ethnographic fieldwork or through extensive questionnaire research, attempts have been made to distil the subjective scripts into etic classifications to model the basic orientations, such as 'self-effacement'. Kroeber and Klockhuhn (1952) were the first to introduce value orientations, suggesting that there were a limited number of responses to universal human needs or problems and that cultures tended to prefer one response over another (for a summary see Katan 1999/2004). E.T. Hall (1976/1989), for example, through his 'contexting theory', distinguished between a culture's preference to communicate in a WYSIWYG way ('low context') or through more context-based channels ('high context'). This general cline of preference helps to clarify the relative values of verbal/written contracts across cultures (Hampden-Turner and Trompenaars 1983: 123–4), website design differences (Wurtz 2005), the relative importance and detail of public signs (e.g. the 'Caution HOT!' takeaway coffee cups – a necessity in low-context communication cultures) and, indeed, the Anglo concern for clarity in translation (Katan 1999/2004: 234).

In a study of insurance brochures offered by banks in Britain and Italy, Katan (2006) analysed the frequency of words that logically indicate orientation alternatives, as outlined by Hofstede (1991, 2001). The frequency of terms, appertaining for example, to 'security/ *sicurezza*' and to 'comfort/*tranquillita*' was significantly different, as were the use of time markers and interrogatives/declaratives, to the extent that 'Basically it would seem that the British reader is being sold an independent and comfortable life, whereas the Italian reader is being sold security and certainty' (Katan 2006: 69). See also Mooij's (2004b) work on advertising, and Manca (forthcoming) for a corpus-driven perspective.

David Katan, Excerpts from: "Translation as Intercultural Communication," *The Routledge Companion to Translation Studies, ed. Jeremy Munday,* pp. 86–87. Copyright © 2009 by Taylor & Francis Group. Reprinted with permission.

SUMMARY

Many languages are spoken in today's world. Whenever verbal communication occurs using languages that differ from each other, communication challenges follow. Knowing how culture affects language can help minimize the potential challenges and prevent miscommunication.

In this chapter, we examined the role of culture on verbal communication. Our first reading explored linguistic relativity and introduced the Sapir-Whorf hypothesis. The final selections concerned how culture influences our verbal communication. These readings examined the role power can play in communicating interculturally, the differences between Western languages and Eastern languages, and cultural grammars. Continue onward to apply your knowledge about culture and verbal communication using the discussion questions.

DISCUSSION QUESTIONS

1. If you were debating the role of language in our communication, what would be some of your arguments supporting the position that the words you use determine the way you view the world (linguistic determinism)?

2. What would be some of your arguments supporting the position that the way you view the world determines the words you use (linguistic relativism)?

3. How does the variable of culture affect communication between individuals with differing verbal communication strategies ranging from passive to aggressive?

4. Can you think of situations where language has been used as a tool of power to control the communication of individuals from different cultures?

DESCRIBING, INTERPRETING, AND EVALUATING CULTURAL PERSPECTIVES

CHAPTER 5

STUDY OBJECTIVES

After completing this chapter, you will be able to:
- Describe cultural perspectives and communication in a scholarly fashion.
- Interpret cultural perspectives and communication in a scholarly fashion.
- Evaluate cultural perspectives and communication in a scholarly fashion.

INTRODUCTION

We conceive of culture in its broadest sense as the accumulated knowledge and belief of specific portions of humanity. Thus defined, the fundamental nature of culture is phenomenological: culture exists fundamentally in the hearts and minds of people. Cultural artifacts such as paintings, sculpture, machinery, and construction projects are products of the knowledge and beliefs that constitute culture. While cultural artifacts provide clues to culture, culture itself can be passed on to other persons and future generations only through communication. No study of culture's artifacts, no matter how deep or extensive, can describe, explain, predict, or even transmit culture from one person or generation to another without communication about cultural meaning. Intercultural communication involves communication between people from different cultures, leading to several questions: What constitutes a "different" culture?

Do intercultural differences necessarily involve different languages? Different ways of thinking? Different world-views? Different beliefs, attitudes, and values?

Thomas M. Steinfatt and Diane M. Millette, Excerpt from: "Intercultural Communication," An Integrated Approach to Communication Theory and Research, ed. Don W. Stacks and Michael B. Salwen, pp. 300. Copyright © 2009 by Taylor & Francis Group. Reprinted with permission..

The following chapter strays away from the format you have become accustomed to in this book and provides you with just one selection to read. This selection provides a framework for how to examine and improve upon intercultural communication. This reading details a way to describe, interpret, and evaluate communication through a number of categories and provides examples along the way. Being able to describe, interpret, and evaluate enables us to answer questions regarding intercultural communication and other subjects. The elements in this chapter can be extended to other scenarios outside of communication. As you read, consider how you can use these approaches in your upcoming assignments in this class or in other classes. At the end of the chapter, you will find discussion questions that will test your ability to describe, interpret, and evaluate.

USING A TAXONOMY TO UNDERSTAND INTERCULTURAL COMMUNICATION

The Value of A Taxonomy

The communication scholar is faced with a problem similar to that of the botanist, zoologist, or entomologist. Each has a tremendous number of individual items to study and explain in his efforts to plan and predict future behavior. If the botanist would attempt to do this with each individual plant, it would seem hopeless. If the zoologist would attempt to develop principles for each individually unique animal, it would be an overwhelming task; and the entomologist with the vast number of insects would have an impossible task if he approached each as though it were completely different from all the others.

Each of these groups of scholars has developed a systematic scheme for classifying the objects of their study. These are conceptually rigorous systems, taking into account variables which make a critical difference in the growth and development of each of the objects of study—plants, animals, or insects, as the case may be. Such a conceptual scheme allows more parsimonious theory development, hypothesis testing, and the generation of principles for the efficient propagation and care of beneficial plants, animals and insects, and for the eradication of those which man finds detrimental to his own growth and development.

If we can identify those elements which make a critical difference in the effectiveness and efficiency of communication among different types of persons in different types of situations, we can develop a systematic scheme for classifying communication events for study and management. The purpose of this chapter is to present the *beginnings* of such a system for communication. This system will be applied to our study of intracultural and intercultural communication. The hope is to produce a set of principles which can be used to improve the effectiveness and efficiency of all communication, and especially intercultural communication.

Efficiency, to me, implies the optimum balance between effectiveness and cost. The cost may be in dollars, time, or impediments to future communicative efforts. Effectiveness here is defined as the extent to which the participants achieve the intended outcome of the communication event.

The botanist, for example, will have a set of practices that apply to controlling growth for a category of plants which he labels legumes. One important characteristic of legume plants is the requirement of non-acid soil. Another category of plants will grow effectively only on acid soils. If it is known that a plant fits in the legume category, a program of treatment can be prescribed to produce optimum growth for it and all plants in that category. Such a system offers both parsimony and precise specifications for treatment.

The taxonomic scheme allows classification at a number of levels and with varying degrees of precision. With trees, e.g., one may start with the distinction between deciduous and evergreens. From this one may identify subclasses of each depending on their tolerance of or requirements for water, acidity, light, soil type, temperature ranges, chemicals, etc.

For the taxonomy to be theoretically, and operationally useful, the variables that "make a difference" must be identified and combined to establish functional categories of objects and events. This is the primary challenge of the communication scholar in developing a rigorous taxonomy, for classifying communication events.

The refinement of such a system is continuous, in that a first approximation may be developed with existing knowledge, then modifications may be made with each new bit of knowledge. Generalizations about communication will be derived for categories of events, i.e., people behaving in certain ways in certain situations to achieve certain outcomes. These generalizations would then be subjected to test for their validity and refined as indicated by the results obtained. This process will help determine whether the appropriate variables are being used to classify the events; whether the communication principles assumed are the appropriate ones to produce the intended outcome; and whether the principles are being applied appropriately to produce the most effective outcomes.

Consciously or unconsciously, participants in a communication event make several decisions. Among these are: physical location; the persons included and their beliefs, language and other characteristics; the use or non-use of interposed channels—electronic, print or other devices; the codes to use, either individually or in combination, judgments about the similarity or dissimilarity, among several dimensions, especially between self and the others who are involved; the intent of self and others; the preceding sets of events which impinge on the present situations; the positiveness, negativeness, or neutrality of the relationship among the participants; amount of time available; the "timing" of the communication in relation to the total context of events; individual feelings of comfort, stress, satisfaction, fear, sorrow, happiness, etc.; and judgments of the presence or absence of communication disorders, either physiological or psychological.

The number of combinations of those variables becomes staggering to comprehend and deal with. Yet, we do deal with them in some way every time we communicate, even though the "dealing with" may mean ignoring some of the factors mentioned.

The Scheme for Categorizing

Approaches

One approach to generating categories for a communication taxonomy is to make a list of a large number of communication situations, then put together those which share the same characteristics. This is essentially the process of factor analysis in which those elements are identified which constitute a common factor.

An example of this approach would be to select from a listing of communication events those which involve only two persons in a private setting, using the same language, working to achieve a common goal, and where the participants had been close friends and had worked together for five or more years. This could be contrasted with a set of events which involved 10–20 persons in a public setting, using two or more different languages, facing a common problem but with different plans for solving it, involving persons who had never met before and where prior knowledge and beliefs differed and led to somewhat antagonistic and suspicious feelings toward one another.

In the example, the variables which would distinguish between the two sets of events are:

public vs. private

number of persons involved

intimacy of prior relationship and similarity of beliefs

similarity of language

similarity of goals

Among the five variables listed, it will be noted that the last three could easily be used to assess the level of homogeneity-heterogeneity among the participants. That would offer the possibility for classifying the first of the two cases above as highly intracultural, and the second of the two cases as highly intercultural.

This process of listing and separating the events into sets with common characteristics could proceed until a judgment was made that some optimum collection of meaningfully different sets of events had been established. The discriminating variables could be identified; then principles could be derived for dealing with communication in each of the various sets.

A second approach to generating a category scheme would be to list what are assumed to be the critical variables which influence communication outcomes and would thus be useful variables in categorizing communication events. These variables would be selected from those which have produced most notable results in prior studies. They also might be selected from those which come from speculation about the communication process; or a combination of those from speculation and those which past studies have indicated as useful in predicting and explaining communication outcomes.

A third approach is to work back and forth between the two approaches above, striving to develop an increasingly rigorous system through successive approximations.

I will start with a set of variables which I believe will be useful in categorizing communication events. From those. 1 will construct a general system for classifying these events, a rather crude taxonomy. Then I will take some situations and fit them into the system. The test of the system will be whether a particular communication is adequately described by one of the categories.

Any restructuring of a set of elements may be expected to provide a different way of looking at that part of the world. An outcome of a taxonomic system should be its power to generate an expanded set of generalizations and questions to guide communication behavior and study.

The Key Variables

Seven sets of variables will be used in developing the taxonomic system. These include:

Number of persons involved in the communication

Type of channels used

Perceived relationship among the participants

Perceived intent of the communicators

Code systems, including both verbal and nonverbal

Normative patterns of beliefs and overt behaviors, with special consideration of values and roles

World view as a special category of beliefs

It will be noted that variables a and b are situational variables which always influence the communication process, but influence it somewhat differently for different levels of interculturalness. Variables c and d also change from situation to situation; however, they are heavily influenced by the characteristics and behaviors of the participants themselves. Variables e to g inclusive are those which would be used to identify the level of homo-geheity-heterogeneity of the participants.

It is not claimed that these variables are independent of one another in their effect, as has already been noted. It is believed that some understanding of each and its effect on the communication process will help communicators to better predict and explain the outcomes of their communication efforts. With that in mind, each of the variables will be discussed briefly here.

With only two values for each of the variables there are 128 potential combinations for the seven variables. The potential number of values is obviously much larger than two. With only three values for each variable the number of potential combinations is 2,187; with four values, there are 16,384 potential combinations. Numbers such as these dramatize the magnitude of possible variations in communication and some of the complexities involved in studying the process.

To keep the taxonomy and the discussion of intercultural communication within some reasonably manageable frame, a limited set of values of the variables will be used. It will not be the same number of values for all variables; and some of the variables will be combined prior to building the taxonomy. As the explication of the variables develops, the basis for the combinations hopefully will become meaningful.

Number of Participants

Number of participants is a continuous variable ranging from two persons to an extremely large number. With worldwide coverage by electronic media, it is potentially possible to have the largest number of participants equal to the total population of the world. As this statement already suggests, number of persons is not independent of channels used in the communication process.

A tendency toward increased difficulty of communicating effectively is expected with an increase in number of persons involved. That increased difficulty is expected to be greater as the number of persons involved requires the use of channels which reduce either the immediacy of feedback or the number of sensory channels available. It also is expected that the increase in difficulty accompanying either more persons or less direct channels will be greater as the interculturalness of the communication situation increases.

Studies of consensus formation illustrate the increased time required to reach agreement on an issue as the number of persons in the group increases. Also, as the size of an organization increases, the complexity of the communication flow increases with an attendant greater probability of communication breakdowns.

It is conceivable that adding another person to a transaction may facilitate communication. This would obviously be true if two persons with two different languages were attempting a transaction and a third party is added who knows both languages. The third party may become an active participant in the transaction, or may serve mainly as translator.

The addition of another person or persons also may facilitate the communication when the added parties bring new information. This is especially true when the additional information is needed to achieve the goals of the participants.

We must be careful to recognize that the need for additional persons to achieve coordinated action and accomplish a complex task is not confused with the potential for communication breakdown. It is the added variation and the increased potential for distortion of messages which comes with the added variation that is being considered when the claim is made that there is a tendency for increased communication difficulty with increased numbers of persons involved. Furthermore, the sheen potential for each-person to produce messages to which all the others may attend declines as the number of participants increases.

Channels

It is readily apparent that the number of persons involved is not independent of the *channels* used. Especially in communication involving so many persons that a speaker could not be heard or seen, there is need for some form of *interposed channel*. An *interposed channel* is one in which some mechanical device or some personis between the primary participants to relay the messages. Interposed as used here most often will refer to telephone, broadcast media, or print media.

Direct channels are .those in which the participants are in the physical presence of one another.

Channels for one-to-one communication may be either direct or interposed. A *direct channel* offers the most immediate feedback and the greatest choice of codes, potentially involving all sensory channels. An *interposed channel,* whether it is another person or some mechanical device, introduces some limits on the codes which may be used. Any *interposed channel* also is necessarily more restrictive of the context available for the interpreter of messages to use in his interpretation. On the other hand, new technology is making possible immediate feedback with 2-way simultaneous transmission via television, or phonevision. Citizens Band radio also is adding a new dimension to communication with ramifications as yet unknown. These still leave the problem of the more restricted context for interposed channels than for direct channels.

As noted earlier, the need for access to all possible code elements and for immediate feedback is greater as the heterogeneity of the participants increases, i.e., in the more intercultural communication situations. The feedback allows for more self-correction during the communication process; and the additional code elements permit each person to check for consistency among the codes employed by the other.

In the *direct channel* situation, one may use any of the five sensory modes, singly or in combination. One of the main advantages of the *direct channel* is the opportunity for using multiple sensory modes simultaneously. Which combinations are used, of course, is dependent on which senses are most appropriate to experience the aspect of the event one hopes to share with the other, e.g., hot-cold requires touch; sweet-sour requires taste, etc.

The choice of *interposed channels* again is dependent upon the aspect of an experience or event to be shared, the fidelity desired, the resources one is willing to commit, and the time and distance to be spanned Both intuitive judgments and those based on empirical data, lead one who is seeking optimum effectiveness to use channels that can handle multiple sensory modes.

Perceived Relationships

Perceived relationships between or among persons in a transaction will influence the level of trust or suspicion, anxiety or confidence, and the eagerness or reluctance to initiate the transaction. Three factors will be considered here which contribute to trust, confidence, and desire to communicate. These are: (a) the positiveness or negativeness of feeling toward the other; (b) the extent to which they believe their individual goals are compatible and mutually shared with one another, or are incompatible and possibly conflicting; and (c) the extent to which they believe the relationship is hierarchical or equal.

One side of the perceived relationship is based on the view people generally; the other side is based on knowledge of the specific participant. Some persons see other people as generally trustworthy, well-intentioned, worthwhile, and genuinely concerned about the well-being of those around them. There are others whose general view of people is so dominated by fear and suspicion that it borders on paranoia. This latter type believes that people can't be trusted; that people seek to manipulate and injure others whenever possible; and they believe people generally tend to be destructive, having evil intentions toward everyone and everything. Persons in this latter category tend to look at the relationship with others as one of "get the other guy before he gets you." This general view is a composite of judgments from one's experiences with people throughout his life.

A careful observe will be able to identify some persons in each of the two categories just cited; and they will recognize that there are many shades in between. It's likely, too, that most individuals will vary along this continuum as conditions around them change, suggesting that the perceived relationship between or among specific persons may change from time to time.

The positive or negative feelings a person has about himself often are projected onto other persons with whom he engages in transactions. I have found in my own introspections, perhaps you have too, that when I'm feeling unhappy with my own performance, I'm more likely to be impatient and critical of those around me.

For any given transaction, the participants will have as their basis for perceiving the nature of the relationship, their general orientation toward people combined with what they know about the specific persons involved with them. If they are engaged in a transaction with a person of another skin color than their own and all their prior experience with those of that skin color has been one of being dominated, they will have difficulty believing that the other person wants to operate as equals. Further experience with person A can confirm for person B that person A does intend to enter their transactions as an equal; then B can decide that it is safe to behave as an equal with person A with very satisfying results.

In intercultural situations, less specific data are available to the persons in the transactions regarding the other party. That leads to more reliance on the beliefs about people generally, and stereotypic beliefs based on whatever composite of experiences one has had with persons who appear similar to the other in the transaction. The perception of the relationship may be adjusted during the transaction depending on the nature of the mutual responsiveness, the congruence of functional identities and the shared focus which emerge.

The variable, *perceived relationships* (PR) between participants, is intended to be a composite of general and specific orientations toward one another. Under this variable, the positive-negative feeling dimensions will be categorized on a continuum of strongly positive feelings toward the other (F_1)[1] to strongly negative feelings toward the other (F_2).

The goal orientation dimension will be labeled on a continuum from mutually shared and compatible goals (G_1) to not compatible, not shared, and conflicting goals (G_2); and the hierarchical dimension of the relationship will be categorized along with the Watzlawick et al. (1967) continuum of symmetrical; i.e., not hierarchical (H_1) to complementary, i.e., strongly hierarchical (H_2).

Note that the labels for each of the dimensions of the perceived relationship variable identify opposite ends of a continuum.[2] At one end are those which express perceptions

---

1 The letters with numerical subscripts in parentheses beside the labels used in describing the variables are a shorthand which will be used in the statements to show the various combinations of variables in the taxonomy. The subscript of *one* (as in F1) is intended to suggest homogeneity and ease of communication; and a subscript of two or more is intended to identify the level of variables where communication is expected to be more difficult, and involves heterogeneous participants.

2 In selecting terms to designate polar ends of a continuum, often there are questions as to what are truly polar terms. Terms such as positive and negative generally are less troublesome than some other terms, with not positive and not negative being considered mid or neutral points on the continuum. Terms such as friendly and hostile are considered polar terms by some, with not friendly and not hostile being the neutral midpoint. Others may believe

which would encourage sharing of information ($F_1G_1H_1$); and at the other end are those which express perceptions which would tend to discourage sharing of information ($F_2G_2H_2$).

It is possible, of course, for both persons to perceive a relationship in the same way—positive feelings—sharing goals—symmetrical (F_1G1H_1). Another possibility is that one person may expect the relationship to be an F1G1H1, while the other may see it as an $F_2G_2H_2$ relationship (negative feelings, conflicting goals, and hierarchical). Still another alternative is that both participants would see the relationship as $F_2G_2H_2$. It's also possible for there to be congruence on the nature of the relationship on one dimension, but not on the other dimensions.

When I perceive the relationship to be highly favorable on all dimensions, I expect that the other will attend to me, have some concern with helping me achieve my needs, will be kind, sympathetic, and understanding. When I perceive that the relationship is very unfavorable, possibly antagonistic, then I expect the other person to be angry, unsympathetic, and unkind or cruel with me, and that he will interfere with my efforts to satisfy my needs.

A symmetrical transaction is one in which the parties involved are carrying out transactions as equals. Complementary (hierarchical) transactions are those in which one party is in a superior position and the other is in a subordinate position.

If there is mutual satisfaction with a complementary relationship, the communication may go smoothly; if there is dissatisfaction with the complementary nature of the relationship, the communication may produce crossed transactions and game playing of the type described by Eric Berne and others. In the negotiating situation there tends to be a desire by each of the parties involved to control the complementarity of the relationship in a highly competitive environment so as to put oneself in the favored or dominant position. The desire to establish relational dominance may be so strong in a transaction that all other messages are lost, i.e., not attended to by either party.

The competitive-cooperative relationship involves the relationship among the goals of the parties involved. In the competitive situation, the goals of the parties are conflicting so that if one achieves his goal, the other cannot and vice versa. In the cooperative situation, all parties are directing their combined energies to achieving a common goal.

The combinations of elements under this dimension would range from strongly positive feelings-cooperative-symmetrical ($F_1G_1H_1$), to strongly negative feelings-competitive-complementary ($F_2G_2H_2$) at the other end of the continuum. The contention here is that the last combination—strongly negative feelings-competitive-complementary ($F_2G_2H_2$)—would be the one in which the least probability exists for effective communication, the least probability for either party to achieve the desired outcome. Conversely, the first listed combination—strongly positive feelings-symmetrical-cooperative ($F_1G_1H_1$) would offer the highest probability of both parties achieving their desired outcomes from the communication.

---

that these two terms are not on the same meaning dimension, with friendly and not friendly being a polar pair of terms and hostile and not hostile being another polar pair.

The pairs of terms used in this text to designate the homogeneous and heterogeneous poles of the variables have been checked by asking five to ten persons to name opposites in response to a question: What is the opposite of —?

Perceived Intent

Intent (I) of the participants in the communication is another of those variables which we take into account in our communication. Sometimes the intent of a communicator is conscious, definite, and explicit; sometimes it is implicit, indefinite, and ambiguous. There are persons who believe that the alternatives in communication are to control or be controlled. Darnell and Brockriede (1976), in dealing with intention and control in their discussion of choice and choice attribution in communication, offer a shared-freedom-of-choice model as an alternative to the control-or-be-controlled model.

I have approached the intent of participants in a transaction from introspection about my own intent in various situations. From this I have, for now, settled on the following categories of intent:

To share (s) experiences, beliefs, feelings, and materials.

To help (h) with a task, including dealing with feelings, questions, etc.

To ignore (ig) or avoid the other person, including his messages.

To disrupt (di) a transaction, or the efforts to establish interdependent activity.

To dominate (do) the relationship through "put downs", manipulating power, status, etc.

To injure (in) the other person or group physically, socially, or psychologically. This would include attacks on status, integrity, self-concept, etc.

I find that those categories encompass the more specific content of my own intent in a range of situations. Among those situations would be such desired outcomes as: to have you open the door (helping); to receive your suggestions about the usefulness of this taxonomy (share-help); to get answers to questions (share); to avoid a superior's attempts to embarrass me (ignore); to get the salesman to sell me a car at less than the usual price (dominate); to fire an employee (dominate); or to be flippant in a discussion where serious analysis might embarrass me (disrupt).

It becomes threatening to my self-concept to believe that I would deliberately communicate to injure another. However, an example of that might be the deliberate spreading of stories of indiscrete behavior of an opponent in a political campaign, or regarding someone I did not want in a responsible position in an organization.

Perhaps these are enough examples to suggest the base for the categories of intent of the participants which will be used in this taxonomy. In a transaction involving two participants or two groups of participants there would be 21 different possible pairings of those dimensions; i.e., sharing-sharing, sharing-disrupting, sharing-injuring, etc.

The greatest contrast would seem to be between a pair of participants who wish to share experiences, and a pair of participants who wish to dominate or injure each other. The interaction would likely be quite intense in both cases. In contrast, if the intent of both is to ignore the other, the transaction may be of relatively low intensity; it may not even achieve the first phase of an "opening", i.e., reciprocally acknowledged attention.

Some of the more frustrating communication may occur where one participant intends to share and the other intends to disrupt or ignore. It is suggested that when both parties have the same positive intent in engaging in a transaction, the intent is more likely to be realized. When the parties do not have the same intent in approaching the transaction, or where the intent of both is negative, there is a fairly high probability that the intent of one and often both participants will be frustrated.

The intent of the participants is more likely to be known in the highly intracultural communication than in highly intercultural communication. This claim follows from the contention that meanings are more likely to be shared when there is a homogeneity of code, world view, values, role expectations, and other normative beliefs.

In most, transactions, intent is not explicitly stated. It generally is inferred from prior and present cues emitted by the other party. The meaning derived from those cues then forms the basis for the *perceived intent,* which in turn sets the tone for the communication.

If trust exists among the participants, an explicit statement of intent may reduce confusion regarding intent and facilitate effective communication. If trust does not exist, suspicion of intent likely will exist and be difficult to dispel; and the possibility of effective communication will be seriously impeded. Even in the latter case an explicit statement of intent may facilitate further communication.

Code Systems

The *code* (CS), both verbal, and nonverbal, which each participant uses to elicit meanings in the other(s), is undoubtedly one of the most critical variables in all communication situations, at any level of intraculturalness and interculturalness.

One of the axioms of communication is that meaning elicited by a code—word, gesture, picture, etc.,—is unique for each individual in each context in which it occurs. The extent to which there is a consensual, similar or conflicting meaning elicited will depend on the extent to which participants have shared similar experiences in relation to the code and situation. This probably is the point at which heterogeneity of participants has the greatest impact in communication. The more heterogeneous the participants, the fewer experiences they will have shared in common, and the fewer experiences shared, the lower the probability of congruity of meaning elicited by a message available to both.

Not only are experiences different among heterogeneous participants, but those experiences likely will be categorized (conceptualized) differently. This makes it virtually impossible to have a one-to-one translation of words (and other codes) between language groups.

An experience from a study of dimensions of source evaluation among persons from two different countries (Sarbaugh, 1967) will illustrate this point. Some of the respondents from each country had been to the USA; the others had not. Those participating in the preliminary phase of the study were asked to list adjectives they would use in describing the best possible source of information for a question they had in their field of work. They were then asked to list adjectives used to describe the worst possible source. From 200 participants, 165 different adjectives were obtained. These were then translated into each of the languages, then back into English and back into the other languages.

The translators frequently pointed out the difficulty of finding suitable words to translate from one language to the other. One example was "scientific." The Ibo translators finally determined that the closest Ibo words when translated back to English would be "of this world." The Ibo words selected as closest to "unscientific" translate back into English as "not of this world." This is illustrative of the translation problem. The result was a set of 66 adjectives on which there was reasonably high agreement among three bilingual translators for each language.

Another illustration was shared with me by one of my students from Ghana. She told me that she has difficulty finding a suitable English translation from the Ghanian concept of "Asem No Apae." It's one of those situations where the equivalent notion is not common in "Western" cultures. It labels a situation where one person has offended or done some wrong to another. The situation is brought to the chief or a court of elders. Literally, the words translate into: "The matter has divided into two equal parts." There are no guilty parties. It is to be settled between the parties themselves by agreeing that they both should forget and proceed as though it never happened. This case also illustrates those situations where the language is not readily translatable due to differences in norms and role expectations between the two language groups.

To be an effective translator of codes between two distinct cultural groups, one .would fleed to have been immersed in both cultures. Such a translator would have an appreciation for the subtleties of meaning elicited by the codes and would select codes in the second language which would elicit meanings closest to the meanings intended by the person whose code he is translating. Four combinations of knowledge of codes which may exist between persons who are communicating are used here:

Both (or all) individuals in the situation share a common code, i.e., Person A and Person B know and share a common code system. In the shorthand, this will be CS_1.

Person A knows code 1, but not code 2; Person B knows code 2 but not code 1. This type of situation will be labeled CS_3.

Person A knows codes 1 and 2; Person B knows only code 2. The reverse of this where Person B knows both codes and Person A knows only one would operate in the same way. The situation falls between *a* and *b* and will be labeled CS_2.

Both sharing two codes is an elaboration of situation *a* above and also will be identified as CS_1.

Situation *a* or *d* is necessary for those communications we would label intracultural, However, as has already been suggested earlier, sharing a common code may not be sufficient to provide communication "that we would label intracultural. Differences between the participants on dimensions other than code may be great enough to interfere with achieving a desired state of interdependence. In that case, even though the participants know the same codes, the communication will be near the intercultural end of the continuum.

Situation *c* may be only minimally intercultural. The person who shares both codes may communicate with the other using the code which is common to both. If they are relatively homogeneous on the other dimensions presumed critical in effective communication, then the code would not be a critical deterrent in this situation. There may be some nuances of meaning on the part of the person with the two codes which could not be shared since one person lacks one of the systems for categorizing some aspects of reality which the other has available for use.

Situation *b* would be the one which would cause the most difficulty in communicating. A third party translator could help bridge the code gap. However, if we accept a whorfian (Whorf, 1956) position that one's code influences the way one structures reality then we would expect differences on some of the other variables. If by chance, there is relatively high homogeneity on the other variables, a third party translator likely could help the persons overcome the code difference and communicate effectively. In the highly intercultural situation, if the translator has been immersed in both cultures, the heterogeneity gap between the parties wishing to communicate may be handled reasonably well; however, it will require considerably more time and energy to achieve effective communication.

Without the aid of the translator, the parties may find some points of commonality which will permit some interdependent activity. It will require more time and energy and the level of certainty of what has been shared will be very low, in most cases.

One of the memorable experiences my wife and I had during a visit to Venice, Italy, was buying a shirt for our daughter from a shopkeeper who spoke no English. Our 100-word Italian vocabulary did not include words to refer to the characteristics of shirts which we wanted to know about before buying. With the aid of a pocket dictionary and much sign language we learned that the fabric was machine washable, did not require ironing, that it was a synthetic fabric (a type unknown to us) and we managed to get the correct size. This transaction required 20–30 minutes to complete. It's an example of a highly heterogeneous code combination, CS_3.

The four combinations of knowing codes cited above presume reasonably high proficiency in the codes known by the participants. If the varying levels of facility and sophistication with a code are added to the dimensions cited, the number of levels of similarity-dissimilarity increases fantastically. That's a further refinement that could be handled after the first assessment of homogeneity-heterogeneity.

For relatively simple transactions dealing with fairly concrete acts, the parties can achieve mutual satisfaction of their needs with lower language facility than when the transactions deal with highly complex and abstract notions. We satisfactorily bought the shirt from the Italian shopkeeper; but we would not have had much success attempting to discuss the ramifications of the divorce referendum which was being voted on in Italy at that time.

The more abstract the communication content, the higher the level of uncertainty at all levels of interculturalness but the uncertainty will be much higher in the highly intercultural communication and the probability of satisfactorily reducing that uncertainty will decline as the heterogeneity increases.

Normative Beliefs and Overt Behaviors

Norms are the standards for beliefs and behaviors that develop within any group which we consider a culture or subculture. For our purposes the normative continuum for behaviors and beliefs ranges from *"must do"* to *"must not do,"* with those in the middle range *being "allowed."* The behaviors and beliefs at the two ends of the continuum are highly obligatory, with maximum flexibility and freedom for those behaviors and beliefs at the midpoint.

There are *norms* for what one wears on what occasions, how close one stands or sits to other persons for given activities, when to speak or not speak, which words to use when and where, what to eat and how, what time to arrive for visits, how long to stay, how one works, etc.

The content of values is normative in nature. There are certain values that one must hold to be a member of a culture; and there are values that must be rejected, as well as some that are allowed. Hence, values are part of the normative structure; and they will be discussed later in this chapter.

Taboos ate norms of the very strong "must not do" type. Gantz (1975) has developed one of the more precise ways of looking at taboo communication. He lists three types of taboos—overt behavior, coimnumcative, and both communicative and overt behavior. He also points out that taboos are bound by time, setting and participants. It should be recognized that what is taboo in one culture may be common practice in another; e.g., the eating of pork or beef.

A more specific statement of *types of taboos* would include:

Behaviors which are neither *talked about nor done* (e.g., sex relations with one's parent).

Those which are *talked about* but *not done* (e.g., eating of some foods such as snakes or ants in some cultures).

Those which may be *done* but are *not talked about (e.g.,* sex relations between marital partners).

Those which may be *talked about in one setting*, but *not in another* (e.g., your physician may talk with you in his office about your urination problems, but not at a party).

Those which may be *done in some settings* but *not in others (e.g.,* in the USA it is permissible for a male to be in a room nude with his wife or his brother, but not with both present).

Many taboos develop around sexual behaviors, other biologic functions, and around patterns of interpersonal relations. They tend to relate to those behaviors which affect the well-being and stability of the society.

One of the grave risks in intercultural communication is that of violating taboos. Knowledge of and adherence to norms, especially those of the obligatory "must-must not" levels, is one of the very important requirements for effective communication.

In communication, between homogeneous participants, both, by definition, will know and adhere to the norms. The levels of knowing and adhering to norms used in this text will be outlined in the next chapter.

Norms form the standard set of rules for belief and overt behavior for all persons in a given society. To the extent that norms are known and adhered to among a given set of persons, their beliefs and behavior become more predictable.

Values, in keeping with the theme of this text, are of concert relation to their similarity or dissimilarity among the participants in the communication. This similarity would apply to both the content and structure (Kohlberg, 1975) of the values.

There are numerous definitions of values, as with most social science concepts. Values, as used here, will be that set of beliefs about what is important or unimportant, good or bad, right or wrong. It's the set of beliefs that strongly influence what one does or refuses to do; and when, how, and with whom one does those things.

Knowing and accepting the values of the other would contribute to the homogeneity of the participants, while not knowing and not having similar value would contribute most to the heterogeneity of the participants. Presumably the first situation would be the most conducive combination for effective communication, while the latter situation would be least conducive. Where participants have similar values, but don't know that they do, it is assumed that the participants could discover through their transactions that they do indeed share similar values; then they could proceed with their communication from a common frame of reference.

The reasoning is that when the values of the other are *not* known, many more untested assumptions are operating within the communication. Not knowing increases the risks of inappropriate decisions in starting and carrying out transactions. More time is required in testing these assumptions before the intent of the transaction can be approached, unless the intent is merely to test the assumptions of similarity or dissimilarity. Keep in mind that honesty may be a value for both participants, but what constitutes honesty may differ between them.

The extent to which differences in values of the participants will be a barrier to communication will depend on whether they share a value which holds that one ought to tolerate and adapt to differences in persons with whom one is involved in a transaction. This tolerance offers some potential for establishing interdependent activity. Of course, this tolerance itself indicates some level of shared values. Where the values are different and the tolerance of difference in values is lacking, there may be little desire to communicate; and where communication is required, it is not likely to be effective or satisfying.

Where it is merely a matter of the values not being known, this may be overcome by communicating. Values of other participants also may be learned from sources who know the values of those with whom you will communicate. Obviously, an inventory of values of all the various cultural groupings and subgroupings would be overwhelmingly encyclopedic. On the other hand, there are some broad classifications which provide a useful starting point in knowing the values and other characteristics of persons from another culture. Such a starting point can facilitate that initial communication intended to increase the knowing.

Sitaram and Cogdell (1976) provide a useful comparison of values generally held by members of five different "cultures"—Western, Eastern, Muslim, African, and American blacks. Their tabulation of 28 societal values, such as individuality, equality of women, education, modesty, peace, authoritarianism, etc., focuses on values content as do most writings on values clarification. Such classifications are helpful to a person who will engage in communication with a person from one of those broad cultural areas. It will provide a basis for an initial assessment of the similarity or dissimilarity, and the nature of the dissimilarity, where it is dissimilar.

What Kohlberg refers to as the structure of value is another aspect which will influence the effectiveness of the participants in a communicative efforts. For Kohlberg, there are three levels and two stages within each level from which one approaches moral judgment. These levels identify the structure. They are an outgrowth of his effort to validate, through longitudinal studies, levels and stages of value development set forth by Dewey and Piaget.

Level one for Dewey and Piaget was a *premoral or preconventional* level. For Dewey, behavior at this level was motivated by biological and social impulses; for Piaget, level one persons had no sense of obligation to rules. Level two people for Dewey were at *a conventional* level in which the individual accepts the standards of his group with little critical reflection. Piaget's level two is labeled a *heteronpmous stage* where"right" is a literal obedience to rules and obligation is equated with power and punishment. Level three for Dewey is an *autonomous*, level in which conducts guided by the individual thinking and judging for himself whether a purpose is good. Piaget's level three also is labeled *autonomous*. Here the purposes and consequences of following the rules are considered, and obligation is based on reciprocity and exchange.

Kohlberg (1975) labels his three levels (a) *preconventional*, (b) *conventional*, and (c) *postconventional, autonomous, or principledr*. At the *preconventional level*, the person is responsive to rules and labels of good-bad, right-wrong, but interprets these in terms of physical or hedonistic consequences, or the power of those who set forth the rules and labels.

Stage one of the preconventional level is a punishment-obedience orientation; avoidance of punishment and unquestioning deference to power are valued in their own right. *Stage two* is an instrumental-relativist orientation; right action is that which satisfies one's own needs; reciprocity is a matter of "you scratch my back and I'll scratch yours."

At the *conventional level*, the maintenance of the expectations of the family, group, or nation is valued in its own right. There is not only conformity to personal expectations and the social order, but loyalty to it. *Stage three*, the first stage within this level, is a "good boy-nice girl" orientation in which good behavior is that which pleases or helps others and is approved by them. *Stage four* is a law and order orientation. This is an orientation toward authority, fixed rules, and maintaining the social order. Right behavior consists of doing one's duty, respecting authority, and maintaining the social order for its own sake.

Level three, the *postconventional, autonomous, or principled level* is one where there is an effort to define moral values and principles apart from the authority or identification with any particular group. *Stage five*, the first stage within this level is a social contract, legalistic orientation. Right action tends to be defined in terms of general individual rights and standards which have been critically examined and agreed upon by the whole society. There is an emphasis on a legal point of view but with the possibility of changing law within a framework of rational consideration of social utility.

Stage six is the universal-ethical principle orientation Right is defined by a decision of conscience in accord with self-chosen ethical principles appealing to logical comprehensiveness, universality' and consistency. Examples are the Golden Rule, or Kant's categorial imperative ("Choose only as you would be willing to have everyone choose in your situation;" and "act always toward the other as an end, not a means"). These contain the dual criteria of universality and respect for the human personality.

An illustration may help to distinguish between the content and the structure of values. I have a value which says it is wrong to steal anything from another person or organization. The content is: "It's wrong to steal." The structure will indicate the level at which I operate in following that value. Level one would say I might be caught and punished, so I won't steal if there's a risk of being caught. Level two would say it's not in keeping with the rules of society and as a loyal member of society, I won't steal because it's not good for society. Level three would ask, would I choose to have someone steal from me if the situation were reversed. It also would ask what the consequences are for me and for other persons in the short-range and in the long-range. Are there conditions under which stealing might be acceptable; e.g., if it were the only way to save a person's life? What is the higher principle that would determine the decision and the conditions under which one might steal, if ever?

If two persons, or two groups of persons are operating with different value orientations, either of content or structure, their communication would be much more difficult and more subject to breakdown than if they were operating at the same level. One who is aware of the different value levels would have some advantage over the person who is unaware; but even awareness of the levels would not seem to be enough to overcome the barriers introduced when the other participant is operating at a different level of values.

The contention here is that the similarity or dissimilarity of value structure (the levels) among the participants, in addition to the values content, will influence the outcome of the communication. It is another of the dimensions which establishes level of homogeneity-heterogeneity, hence, the extent to which the communication is intercultural.

Roles, as *sets shared expectations* about how one behaves in a given situation are another critical aspect intercultural communication. The participants in a communication constantly adjust and readjust their behavior toward one another. This is what Mead (1934) and others call "taking the role of the other." To do that in a way that leads to effective communication, one must have a reasonably accurate knowledge of the expected behavior for both parties in the situation.

In the homogeneity-heterogeneity model being developed, the homogeneous participants would be those who know the expected role behaviors in the situation and can respond appropriately to the behavior. The extreme of heterogeneity exists when the participants do not know the expected role behaviors and their "guestimates" are inaccurate. The result in the heterogeneous (intercultural) case is likely to be noninterpretable or misinterpreted adjustments to one another and an inability to achieve intended outcomes.

Mead's generalized other is the generally uniform set of behaviors which one member of a culture (homogeneous group) expects of other members of that culture in given situations. Based on my playing of the roles in which I operate day-by-day and on the way I observe others in similar positions play those roles, I arrive at this generalized picture of the expected behavior in the various situations in which I find myself. I then develop the expectation that all persons occupying similar positions in my society will play those, roles in much the same way, or at least within some reasonably well-defined boundaries.

In a given week, I play the roles of husband, father, teacher, administrator, neighbor, choir member, shopper, member of selected organizations, committee member, etc. To the extent that I and others share the same beliefs about how I should behave in those roles, we will be able to communicate more effectively than if we held divergent beliefs about the expected behavior.

It is fairly obvious that roles come in pairs. For me to be a father, there is a son or daughter; for me to be a husband, there is a wife, etc. It is the set of reciprocal relationships which are created by communication and in turn affect the communication which occurs.

The various combinations of knowing and adhering to the same or different definitions of roles and other normative beliefs will be presented in Chapter 3.

World View

World View (*WV*), a variable considered helpful in assessing homogeneity-heterogeneity among participants, is used here to refer to one's view of the *purpose of life* (PL), the *nature of life* (NL), and the *relation of man to the cosmos* (RMC). It would include the belief or nonbelief in a deity; and if a belief in a deity, the nature of the deity.

The *nature of life* (NL), for some people, is continual drudgery, pain, and suffering. It's something to tolerate rather than enjoy. For some, this comes out of a set of religious beliefs which claim that man was born in sin and condemned to continual suffering; that the purpose of life is to prepare for some utopian life after death. For others life is a continual process of growth, full of anticipation, discovery, and the possibility of improving the comfort and enjoyment; life is a cyclical process of regeneration, maturation, decline (deterioration), regeneration, etc. Questions of mind, body, and soul are aspects of the beliefs about the nature of life.

For the physiologist, the nature of life may be described in terms of cells and the processes by which cells combine, divide, grow and die. It may involve questions regarding the set of conditions for life to begin and life to end, and the search for a definition of "life."

Some persons view life and the various events in the world as deterministic and quite predictable. For other persons, life and all aspects of the universe are in a constant state of flux, and any predictions are more or less probable of being confirmed. Different perspectives on the nature of life between or among persons contribute to different world views among those persons.

The *purpose of life* (PL) for one set of persons may be to control as many things and to accumulate all the resources possible for their own pleasure, irrespective of other persons now or in the future. For another set of persons, the purpose is to live modestly, to strive to know God's will and live as God directs, recognizing that everything is in God's hands. For still another set, there may be a recognition of some all encompassing force, and the purpose of one's life is to develop scientific laws which specify the relationships among forces emanating from that all encompassing force; strive to have all persons understand the long-range consequences of various courses of action; then select those courses of action which will benefit most persons now and in ages to come. These and other different views of the purposes of life would identify another aspect of heterogeneity and an aspect of intercultural communication.

The *relation of man to the* cosmos (RMC) could be one of being subjugated to the cosmos, hence helpless; or one of working with nature to preserve and improve the products of the cosmos for the ultimate benefit of man and other elements in the cosmos in a continuing state of balance and renewal; or one of man controlling nature for his own benefit, assuming that unlimited resources will continue to be available to man to use.

When persons who have different views of this relationship of man to the-cosmos attempt to communicate, they will be expected to experience communication difficulties. They will be looking at the world from different perspectives and may have difficulty appreciating the different assumptions from which the other is operating.

Time orientation is an important aspect *of world view* (WV) which impinges on communication and other coordinated activities among persons. For some persons, the past is the most meaningful aspect of life and the preservation of past traditions is highly valued. For another, the anticipation of the future offers a very satisfying excitement; and preparation for the future includes efforts to modify ther past, consuming much energy of both thought and overt acts. For still others, the emphasis is on the present; some in a self-indulge way that attempts to ignore future or past. For still others, there is an orientation which some have labeled the self-actualizing orientation (Johnson, 1972); it emphasizes living in the present with a strong appreciation of and involvement in both past and future orientations.

Time orientation, as viewed here, Becomes intertwined with views of the nature and purpose of life and of man's relation to the cosmos.

Some people may seek to avoid thinking about the nature and purpose of life and man's relation to the cosmos. They might find any reflection on questions of that sort very frustrating and disturbing. Others might enjoy such reflections and seek discussions with others about such topics. One might focus almost solely on physical gratification; another would focus on self-denial in regard to physical gratification and see the purpose of life as achieving some ultimate state of self-denial. Some would say that it is not for man to know either the nature or purpose of life.

Some people might believe that the spirits of their ancestors are within them and control their behavior. Others feel a nearly complete independence of ancestors and are proud of their difference from their ancestors.

All of the possibilities suggested above represent some of the dimensions along which participants in a transaction may differ on the variable which I've called *world view* (WV).

Stability of the Variables

Among the variables: Which pertain to characterises of the participants, two seem most likely to be dynamic and changing. These are the perceived relationship among the participants and their intent. As the participants engage in communication, they may find the relationship of each to the other changing and they may clarify or agree to change their intent.

Beliefs pertaining to world view and values are expected to be the most stable, most enduring, and slowest to change of any of the variables. These beliefs are built up slowly and continuously, with repeated reinforcement, throughout one's lifetime. It is recognized that they do change, but they represent generally highly ego-involving beliefs; and it is recognized that the greater the ego-involvement with a belief, the more resistant to change it is likely to be.

Codes, role prescriptions, and normative beliefs, other than values and world view, are relatively stable: but they are expected to be more likely to change than are world view and values. There is evidence all around us, especially from generation to generation, of changes in language—both verbal and nonverbal. As new technology develops, it brings new codes, new positions and roles, and new knowledge to assimilate if our belief system.

This view of the stability of the variables would suggest that if one wanted to modify a communication situation so that it would beat a more efficient level, the first variables to manipulate would be the channel and number of persons. The next level which one might affect would be perceived intent and relationship.

As we seek to modify those variables which deal directly with the homogeneity-heterogeneity of the participants, the code and role expectations would be easiest to affect. Values and world view would seem to be the most difficult to modify. Over an extended time, repeated transactions would likely lead to greater homogeneity in values and world view among initially heterogeneous participants. This latter possibility offers the potential for highly heterogeneous communicators to increase the effectiveness and efficiency of their communication.

SUMMARY

In responding to a question or in conducting research, taxonomies can be useful as you consider all of the elements involved in intercultural communication. This chapter provided a taxonomy examining intercultural communication enabling you to describe, interpret, and evaluate human interaction. As you move forward in this book and in class, refer to this chapter often and to the elements included when embarking on classroom assignments or larger papers. Continue on to the discussion questions to put your skills of describing, interpreting, and evaluating to the test.

DISCUSSION QUESTIONS

1. How does knowing the intent of a culturally different person (e.g., helping, indifferent, hurting) affect your willingness to engage in communication with that person? If the person is a stranger, does that change your willingness to engage in communication?

2. Some people refuse to communicate with individuals from different cultures because they have pre-existing knowledge of the other culture and are unwilling to accept the different beliefs and values; while others are willing to communication with individuals from other cultures even if they do not know their beliefs and values. Is it really possible for people who do not share common beliefs and values to accept those with different perspectives and have meaningful conversations with them?

3. How should individuals with different worldviews approach subjects such as global warming, economic development, or population control?

CULTURE
CHAPTER 6

STUDY OBJECTIVES

After completing this chapter, you will be able to:
- Define the meaning of culture.
- Describe and explain how culture is created.
- Identify and describe the different dimensions of culture.

INTRODUCTION

The world would be a boring place if everyone and everything were homogenous, or the same. Imagine traveling abroad and finding that everything was similar to what you experienced at home: the food was the same, the fashion was no different, and everyone spoke the same language as you. Our guess is that you would not experience anything new on that trip. One of the cool things about traveling is experiencing different cultures and scenarios with which you are not familiar. Fortunately, the world is not homogenous, and culture is everywhere. You do not need to travel someplace far; you are surrounded by culture everywhere you go!

Culture is dynamic and at the core of intercultural communication. In fact, culture is such an important piece of intercultural communication that it appears in the very first word! As important as culture is, chances are you probably do not think about your own culture very much. Most of the time, it is hard to explain or identify your own culture unless you are exposed to someone from a different culture. When we meet someone from another culture, we are able to identify similarities to and differences from our own culture.

Learning, defining, and understanding culture are key steps in becoming a competent intercultural communicator. In this chapter, we look to the field of anthropology to explore the meaning of culture and examine how culture is formed. This will provide us with the foundation to what we learn about culture. As you progress through the chapter, we return to the field of communication to examine different dimensions of culture. As you read about cultural differences, keep in mind what you previously learned about how culture is created. At the end of the chapter, there are discussion questions to guide your learning experience and aid you in applying your knowledge about culture.

WHAT IS CULTURE?

The capacity to create culture is a fundamental human trait. Although some animal species, especially other primates, possess similar cultural capacities for categorizing and symbolizing, no species elaborates culture to the extent that human beings do. Humans do not just eat; they create cuisines and rules that forbid the eating of certain perfectly good sources of vitamins and protein like pork or beef or worms or insects. Humans don't just mate; they marry, elaborating the process with rituals, expenses, rules about who can and cannot mate, and tying the process to religious values. Humans do not just produce offspring; they create families, naming their relatives and assigning them roles and different rights and responsibilities. Humans do not just die; they revere their dead through mortuary rites and practices of remembrance.

To be human is to need to live in a world of meanings. To be able to act effectively in the universe, humans must construct models of how the world works, values that help them decide what goals are worth pursuing, and plans of action to help them achieve those goals. Yet all humans do not live in the *same* world of meanings. Groups of humans generate and elaborate different systems of meanings, and to the extent that these systems are shared, they define groups as communities. Individuals in communities create their own unique ways of acting, but they do so within the horizon of meanings defined by the community. Culture, then, is this learned system of meanings through which people orient themselves in the world so that they can act in it. As such, culture is symbolic, shared, learned, and adaptive.

Culture is Symbolic

Humans live in a physical world, and they understand and manipulate that world through symbols. Everything humans produce—from words to gestures to clothes to housing to complex technologies—are symbols. A symbol is *something* that stands for *something else* to *someone* in *some respect*. The use of words in language is a good example. A *word*, such as *horse*, is a something (the technical word is *signifier*) that stands for something else (its *referent*)—in this case, a particular animal—to speakers of English.

When we define a symbol as a signifier standing for a referent to someone *in some respect*, we are drawing attention to special features possessed by symbolic systems. One of the most important is that signs have no intrinsic or essential relationship to their referent. There is nothing in the phonetic sounds of the words *horse*, *hassan*, *equus*, or *cheval* that connect them with the particular animal to which all these signs refer. Their relationship is arbitrary—we know the meaning of the word only if we've grown up in a community that shares the knowledge of which signifiers refer to which referents.

To say that a symbol means something only to a *someone* is to emphasize that culture is expressive. Our words, our actions, and our artifacts communicate things to others about us. Not only what we say but how we say it—intonation, volume, and pitch—communicates important information about us and what we may be thinking, feeling, or about to do. The same is true of the kinds of clothing we wear, how we cut our hair, how close we stand to people, and how we eat our food. Even the most practical of actions possesses a symbolic, communicative element. It is because we share a common set of understandings about what symbols mean that we can understand and predict one another's actions, and so cooperate as a community.

Culture is Shared

Culture, then, involves shared understandings of symbols and their meanings that allow us to communicate, to cooperate, and to predict and understand one another's actions. Yet while culture is shared, it is not equally distributed among all the peoples of a society. Different distributions of cultural knowledge usually serve to produce and maintain differences in social positions such as gender, race, caste, or class. But in highly complex and diverse societies, differences can also distinguish people on the basis of education, occupation, or even leisure. In most societies, rights, responsibilities, and control over resources are unequally distributed to people on the basis of these social categories. The mobilization of cultural symbols to create, sustain, or resist such social inequities is called ideology.

Shared culture includes knowledge of history and also the whole realm of convention and belief we call tradition. Slavery is part of a shared heritage in the United States, but what it means to people differs according to their social positions and other aspects of their belief systems. These areas of similarity and differentiation intertwine in complex ways. Because of this, specific symbols may have very different meanings to different people within the same general culture; the meaning of the Confederate battle flag emblazoned on T-shirts, belt buckles, or bumper stickers and flown in front of courthouses differs in relation to people's understandings of the meanings of the common heritage of slavery.

Because culture is shared but unequally distributed, every society must have mechanisms to deal with two processes: the generation of similarity and the organization of difference (Wallace 1961). The generation of similarity involves those institutions and processes that teach and reinforce common beliefs, values, orientations, and models for action among members of a community. Family, school and peer groups, and mass media, among others, generally serve as key institutions for enculturating members of a society into the most deeply and widely held cultural symbols. But shared, uniform beliefs and values are not necessary for many cooperative activities. People from many different backgrounds can share a bus in a multiethnic neighborhood in Los Angeles; they simply need to know the rules for bus riding. Institutions concerned with the organization of difference include most political and social organizations with the power to regulate behavior and reward or punish behaviors.

Culture is Learned

The fact that not all cultural knowledge is equally shared by all members of a society draws our attention to the fact that we do not simply possess culture by virtue of being born into a society, we learn our culture as we live, work, and grow. Which aspects of our society's total cultural repertoire we learn depends to a large extent on our unique experiences growing up. Yet those experiences are in turn shaped by society. Insofar as we are raised in similar ways and pass through similar institutions (like hospitals, schools, weddings and funerals), we share common sets of cultural knowledge, values, and assumptions. Insofar as our experiences differ—because of unusual family structures, differences in wealth, and exposure to different areas of society—our cultural knowledge is different.

The processes by which members of a society pass on culture to new generations is called enculturation. One aspect of enculturation is formal learning, the acquisition of cultural knowledge that takes place within institutions specifically designed for this purpose, such as schools, apprenticeships, and on-the-job training. Each society has institutions that exist primarily to pass on to children specific skills needed as adult members of that society.

Formal learning makes up only a small part of enculturation, however. Most enculturation takes place through processes of informal learning—the learning we engage in simply by watching, listening, and participating in everyday activities. Consider how you learned to speak, your taste in clothes, or your eating habits. These things are usually learned through observation, imitation, and gauging the responses of those around us.

Our deepest cultural learning often shapes our bodies and unconscious behaviors: how we speak, how we move, how we eat, how close we are comfortable standing to people. This kind of enculturation is called embodiment. An example of embodiment is accent. As we learn the language of our community, we train our whole vocal apparatus to easily and automatically produce a certain range of sounds. When we try later to learn a second language, we find it difficult to produce the new sounds, resulting in a foreign accent. Even though we are physically capable of making the same sounds as any other human, we have trained our bodies so as to privilege certain sounds over others. Similar embodied patterns can be shown to exist for proximity, gesture, how we walk or sit, what we wear (or don't), and many other elements of our everyday life. Embodied culture is especially important because it feels completely natural to us. It is not only difficult to change, it is difficult for us even to become aware of.

Culture is Adaptive

And yet, culture is not only capable of changing, it is always in a process of change. Enculturation does not refer only to the process whereby children become socially adept members of a community. Cultural learning is a lifelong process, because cultural systems adapt to changing environmental, economic, political, and social conditions. All cultural systems change over time in response to shifts in context. Cultures change as they adapt to internal or external pressures. Cultures do not, however, all adapt to the same pressures in the same ways, nor do there seem to be stages that all cultures pass through. One important corollary of this is that there are no primitive or fossil cultures. Studies of foraging societies have been important in helping us understand how all humans must once have lived, but contemporary hunter-gatherers nonetheless have their own unique histories. The Ju/'hoansi !Kung people of the Kalahari desert, for example, have a centuries-long history of being pushed south by fiercer peoples. How they hunted and what they gathered changed as they were pushed into increasingly inhospitable environments and had to adapt by developing new skills and technologies (Lee 2002).

Culture adapts to changing conditions in a number of ways. Creativity is a fundamental human trait, and all societies have mechanisms for generating innovation from within. At least equally important is the capacity of communities to borrow cultural innovations from other societies and adapt them to their needs. The diffusion of ideas, technologies, and practices occurs through direct contact, such as migration or conquest, as well as through indirect contact, such as trade and mass media.

It is important to recognize that culture does not cease to be culture because it borrows and adapts. When the Plains Indians adopted the horse and the rifle from Spanish conquerors, traders, and settlers, they completely transformed their society. They did not, however, become Spaniards. Today it is not uncommon to see Coca-Cola franchises in Cairo or New Delhi and interpret them to be evidence of an emerging global culture, or globalization, a process some have even referred to as *McDonaldization*. But the McDonald's of Egypt is not the McDonald's of the United States. In the United States, McDonald's is a low-status, inexpensive, and convenient restaurant designed to serve frantically busy lifestyles, low budgets, and the desire for places children can go with their parents. In Egypt, McDonald's is a high-priced, high-status restaurant that delivers food, caters parties, and is a favorite place for young cosmopolitan Egyptians to hang out. Although the restaurants share many of the same physical characteristics, those characteristics mean very different things in their different contexts. Understanding how apparently identical things can mean very different things in different contexts is an important aspect of international studies.

Moving Forward

Now that we know how culture is defined and how culture is formed and created, let us explore how cultures can vary from one another. In this next section, short excerpts from several sources explain the different dimensions of culture. As you move through this section, think about how you communicate with your family and friends: do you use low- or high-context communication? Do you belong to an individualistic or collectivistic culture? Answer these questions and keep in mind your responses to both as you continue reading about the following dimensions of culture: uncertainty avoidance, power distance, and masculinity and femininity in cultures.

CULTURE VARIES

Collectivistic vs. Individualistic Cultures

Individualism versus collectivism is one of the most basic cultural dimensions. According to Tomkins (1984), an individual's psychological makeup is the result of this cultural dimension. For example, he reported that human beings in Western Civilization have tended toward positive or negative self-celebration, and in Asian thought harmony between humans and nature is another alternative that is represented. Whether people live alone, in families, or tribes depends on the degree of individualism-collectivism in a culture (Anderson, 1985). An emphasis on community, shared interests, harmony, tradition, the public good, and maintaining face characterize collectivistic cultures. Collectivism "pertains to societies in which people from birth onwards are integrated into strong, cohesive ingroups, which throughout people's lifetime continue to protect them in exchange for unquestioning loyalty" (Hofstede, 1991, p. 51). Societies in which people look after themselves and those in their immediate families and where ties are loose characterize individualistic cultures (Hofstede, 1991).

In individualistic Western cultures, people rely on personal judgments (Triandis, 1994), whereas an emphasis on harmony among people, between people and nature, and on collective judgement can be seen in people from Eastern cultures (Gudykunst et al., 1996). People living in the United States, for example, tend to place a very high value on individualism (Bellah, Madsen, Sullivan, Swidler, & Tipson, 1985; Kim, 1994). More traditional and collectivist cultures place value on the interdependence among individuals and conforming to social roles and norms whereas individualistic and less traditional cultures stress independence in the pursuit of personal goals and interests and self expression. The best and worst in U.S. culture can be attributed to individualism. If we think of some of the positive elements, we may consider individualism as the basis of freedom, creativity, and economic incentive. The majority of Americans believe "that a man [or woman] by following his [or her] own interest, rightly understood, will be led to do what is just and good" (Tocqueville, 1945, p. 409).

On the other hand, individual consciousness may disrupt the systemic nature of life on earth by pulling humans out of their ecological niche, that is separating humans from nature with the increasing isolation and industrialization (Bateson, 1972). The downside of individualism includes alienation, loneliness, materialism and difficulty interacting with those from less individualistic cultures (Condon & Yousef, 1983; Hofstede, 1991). Thus, our individualism leads us to value creative ways of expressing ourselves (e.g., the person who is the "life of the party") but may challenge our ability to work together as a team (e.g., sacrifice for the common good).

Even though the United States is the most individualistic country (Hofstede, 1984/1990), certain ethnic groups and geographic regions vary in their degrees of individualism. For instance, African Americans place a great deal of emphasis on individualism (Collier, Ribeau, & Hecht, 1986; Hecht et al., 2003; Hecht & Ribeau, 1984: Kochman, 1981), whereas Mexican Americans place greater emphasis on relational solidarity and their families (Hecht & Ribeau, 1984; Hecht, Ribeau, & Sedano, 1990). This translates into a general tendency for African Americans to "tell it like it is" in conversations in order to preserve authenticity and Mexican

Americans to focus on the relational with others in conversations, sometimes avoiding negative information in the process. There is a tendency to relay on *simpatia*, a preference for harmony in interpersonal, relations such that negative comments may be ignored in a conversation.

Of course, the very notion of individualism suggests that a person's own values may transcend his or her cultural group membership. In fact, there is evidence that personal individualism may transcend cultural differences for certain variables. Singelis (1996) urged us to examine the connection between context and individual variables. Schmidt (1983), for example, compared the effects of crowding on people from the United States (an individualistic culture) and Singapore (a collectivist culture). Schmidt hypothesized that similar psychological variables would underlie people's stress and annoyance responses to crowding. He studied students at a U.S. university bookstore during the first 3 days of the quarter (a typically crowded time) and Singaporean high school students in their places of residence and found similar perceptions for both cultures on the relationships among personal control on annoyance and stress about environmental crowding. What we conclude is that no culture or individual is completely individualistic or collectivistic. All have some conception of the person as well as the group. What differs is the relative value placed on each and how people work out the competing pressures (e.g., the role of sacrifice).

HIGH CONTEXT VS. LOW CONTEXT CULTURES

Cultural background and context is an important predictor of behavior. For example, there is a distinction in communication between so-called high-context and low-context cultures (Tajaddini & Mujtaba, 2011; Mujtaba & Balboa, 2009; Salleh, 2005). In high-context cultures such as Vietnam, Taiwan, Thailand, China, Japan, Iran, Afghanistan, or India, there is a less verbally detailed communication and less written/formal information. Instead, there is a more common understanding of what is being communicated through general context. Often what is left unsaid is as important as what is said. Low context cultures put more emphasis on the written or spoken words as communication is more explicit. Context indicates the level in which communication occurs outside of verbal discussion (Mujtaba & Balboa, 2009).

Low- and high-context communication is used in all cultures. One form, however, tends to predominate. Members of individualistic cultures tend to use low-context communication and communicate in a direct fashion. Members of collectivistic cultures, in contrast, tend to use high-context messages when maintaining ingroup harmony is important and communicate in an indirect fashion (Gudykunst & Ting-Toomey, 1988).

Members of individualistic cultures who use low-context communication often assume that indirect communication is ineffective. This, however, is not necessarily the case. High-context communication can be effective or ineffective like low-context communication. Most high-context communication is effective. The effectiveness comes from listeners knowing how to interpret speakers' indirect messages in specific contexts.

UNCERTAINTY AVOIDANCE

Uncertainty avoidance is "the extent to which people feel threatened by ambiguous situations and have created beliefs and institutions that try to avoid these" (Hofstede & Bond, 1984, p. 419). This dimension is related to how people deal with conflict and aggression, how they release energy and use formal rules, and the tolerance they have for ambiguity. Members of high uncertainty avoidance cultures try to avoid uncertainty, but at the same time show their emotions more than members of low uncertainty avoidance cultures do. Differences in the uncertainty avoidance dimension should be related to expression of emotion in relationships; that is, members of cultures high on uncertainty avoidance should express more emotion in relationships than do members of cultures low on the dimension.

High and low uncertainty avoidance exists in all cultures, but one tends to predominate. Cultures that tend to be mainly high in uncertainty avoidance include Japan, Mexico, Greece, France, Chile, Belgium, Argentina, and Egypt. Cultures that tend to be mainly low in uncertainty avoidance include Canada, Denmark, India, Jamaica, Sweden, and the United States.

MASCULINITY-FEMININITY

Masculinity predominates in countries where the dominant values "are success, money, and things," while femininity predominates where "caring for others and quality of life" are predominant values (Hofstede & Bond, 1984 pp. 419–420). Cultures high in masculinity differentiate sex roles clearly, while cultures low in masculinity (high in femininity) tend to have fluid sex roles. The rationale for the influence of masculinity-femininity on perceptions of communication behavior associated with relationship terms is straightforward; it should influence how same-sex and opposite-sex relationships are perceived. Specifically, because of differentiated sex roles, members of high masculinity cultures should perceive opposite-sex relationships as less intimate than members of low masculinity cultures.

Masculinity and femininity exist in all cultures, but one tends to predominate. Cultures that tend to be mainly masculine include Arab cultures, Austria, Germany, Italy, Japan, Mexico, New Zealand, Switzerland, and Venezuela. Cultures that tend to be mainly feminine include Chile, Costa Rica, Denmark, eastern Africa, Finland, the Netherlands, Portugal, and Sweden (the United States is below the median).

POWER DISTANCE

Power distance, Hofstede's (1980) final dimension, involves the degree to which members of a culture accept the unequal distribution of power in the society. High power distance cultures assume that inequality should exist, that most people should be dependent on others, and that hierarchy results from existential inequality. Lower power distance cultures, in contrast, assume that inequality should be minimized, people should be interdependent, and that hierarchy results from role inequality and roles are established for convenience.

Low and high power distance exists in all cultures, but one tends to predominate. Cultures that tend to be mainly high in power distance include Egypt, Ethiopia, Ghana, India, Malaysia, Nigeria, Panama, Saudi Arabia, and Venezuela. Cultures that tend to be mainly low in power distance include Australia, Canada, Denmark, Germany, Ireland, New Zealand, Sweden, and the United States.

SUMMARY

Culture is at the core of intercultural communication, and it surrounds you everywhere you go. In this chapter, we examined the meaning of culture and how culture is created. We learned that culture is dynamic, symbolic, learned, shared, and adaptive. Culture is everywhere and helps us define who we are. We also identified that culture is multi-dimensional and it contributes to cultural variety. People from individualistic cultures communicate differently and value different things than collectivistic cultures. In addition, individualism and collectivism directly impact other dimensions of culture. Determining whether a culture is individualistic or collectivistic will clarify (1) whether that culture is comprised of low- or high-context communicators, (2) is low or high in uncertainty avoidance and power distance, and (3) whether the culture can be characterized as masculine or feminine. Continue to the discussion questions to test your knowledge on culture and the dimensions of culture.

DISCUSSION QUESTIONS

1. What rituals have you enacted in your home? When you visit friends or extended family, have you encountered different rituals? How do you communicate about these differences in a way that preserves your friendship or keeps peace in the family? Why should we be concerned about this issue?

2. Can you describe the culture of a college student? A worker in the oil patch? A healthcare provider in a public clinic? How are they similar? What are the differences? How does the culture of each context affect the communication of people who life and work there?

3. What are the characteristics of a culture where the individual is most important? What are the characteristics of a culture where the community comes before the individual? How does conflict between these two orientations affect communication between the groups?

4. What strategies can communicators use when seeking to reduce uncertainty about interacting with individuals from different cultures?

POPULAR CULTURE

CHAPTER 7

STUDY OBJECTIVES

After completing this chapter, you will be able to:
- Define popular culture.
- Describe the effects of Americanization on popular culture worldwide.
- Explain why it is important to understand popular culture in the context of intercultural communication.

INTRODUCTION

Popular culture is everywhere. Often, we derive images of places we have never been from the media that we consume. If you have never been to Disney World, chances are you are still familiar with its iconic Cinderella castle that stands in the middle of Magic Kingdom. If you can visualize the castle and have never been there, you can thank popular culture for your ability to picture this image. Another example is the Eiffel Tower in Paris, France. When someone mentions this building, you are able to visualize it thanks to the consumption and spread of popular media and culture.

Popular-culture-producing industries exist, and sometimes popular culture may not accurately depict an image. While popular culture reinforces certain stereotypes of cultures, at other times, popular culture may contest those stereotypes. The United States widely produces and distributes popular culture around the world. While the United States may be the top distributor of popular culture, Americans also consume popular culture. In fact, several images and characteris of popular culture from other countries have flourished in the United States. For example, Dr. Who, Sherlock Holmes, American Idol, and the Office are all television shows originating outside American borders that are popular in the United States.

This chapter focuses on popular culture and popular media through three selected readings. Our first reading examines Americanization and the United States as a popular-culture distributor world-wide. This reading explores the acts of consuming and resisting popular media and the power behind popular culture. The second and third readings involve stereotypes and perceptions of cultural groups derived from popular media. The second selection concerns flexible and inflexible stereotyping, arguing that since stereotyping is inevitable, we need to learn how to manage it. The final reading includes both positive and negative stereotyping and presents two arguments: First, that stereotyping is harmful and misguided; and second, that while stereotyping is often harmful, it has its uses.

At the end of the chapter you will find a number of discussion questions. These questions will aid you in applying your knowledge about popular culture and intercultural communication. Make sure to contemplate and answer each question carefully before progressing to the next chapter.

Moving Forward

Our first reading discusses the role of the United States in distributing popular and cultural media around the world. Popular media is powerful. Many items are popular internationally only because they are from the United States. In fact, the following reading references several advertisements running in other countries that highlight how well an item is selling, or how popular the item is in the United States. The advertisements do not speak to the items' quality or usefulness; instead, such products are sold solely on the idea of the popularity they experience in the United States.

Just because advertisers highlight how well an item is selling in the United States does not mean that the target audience will become consumers of that item. When it comes to popular culture and media, an individual has the option to consume or to resist. However, as we will find out in this reading, resisting is not always the best path to take. As you move throughout this reading, consider how much the United States influences other countries culturally, and think of a few examples of how the United States does this. Additionally, think about the following questions. How would you define Americanization? What is the megaphone effect? What is an example of a time the United States consumed another country's popular culture?

AMERICANIZATION

Fears of globalization are frequently referred to as fears of Americanization, and the two are often used interchangeably. At a lecture given at the University of Toronto in December 1997, Pulitzer Prize winner and author Thomas L. Friedman put the matter succinctly when he said, "Globalization is so much Americanization. It wears Mickey Mouse ears and it drinks Coke, and it eats Big Macs and it works on an IBM computer with Windows 95" (Stoffman, 1997, p. 1). It is American products, business practices, and the values associated with them, more than those of any other culture, that are evident around the world. As one American journalist (Zachary, 1999) has put it:

> Free market capitalism and high-tech communications have, for better or worse, turned
> the world on to just one culture—ours ... U.S. power stands at a new pinnacle, only this
> time victory isn't measured in the defeat of an ideological foe but in the influence gained
> over the world's wealth, culture, and individual identity. (p. 1)

The claim that we live in a world increasingly characterized by Americanization has been put forth repeatedly (e.g., Ritzer 1998). Beyond this, Kuisel (1993) has claimed that what is referred to as Americanization "has become increasingly disconnected from America" (p. 4). Rather than associating this trend with any particular nation, "It would be better described as the coming of consumer society" (p. 4). Moreover, as Campbell and Kean (1997) note, fear or delight at the potential effects of Americanization has been widely addressed and frequently linked to the debate on the merits of popular culture (e.g., Duignan & Gann, 1992; Gilroy, 1992; Hoggart, 1957; Williams, 1962).

Americanization typically refers to the influence of the U.S., and more specifically, of its values, ideology, economics, and culture, beyond that nation's borders. Rebhun and Waxman (2000) speak of an act or a process of conformity. Azaryahu (2000) claims, "It involves cultural importation and transplantation" (pp. 41–42). Aronoff (2000) points out, "The implication is that the diffusion of influence and values comes directly and exclusively from the United States" (p. 93).

Beyond whatever the local audience chooses to make of it, an import that has arrived via the U.S. has the additional cachet of having become a phenomenal success in "America." The image projected by the United States of America has connotations of prosperity, modernity, and the way of the future. "America" is a symbol that represents "the ideals of endless progress, self-creation, achievement, and success—the mythicized dream" (Campbell & Kean, 1997, p. 23). This dream is perpetuated in novels, film, television, the print media, and advertising. It is for many, far more real than anything else. As Vasey (1993) states:

> The popular media of the United States have had such an extraordinary influence upon
> the nation's image of itself, and upon the face it has presented to the rest of the world,
> that it has become virtually meaningless to attempt to distinguish between the creations
> of the media and "reality" in contemporary America. (p. 213)

Frith (1988) claims, "America, as experienced in film and music, has itself become the object of consumption, a symbol of pleasure" (p. 46). Likewise, Campbell and Kean (1997) discuss the impact of the mere symbol that the country has become, or the influence of "reflection on the very idea of America" (p. 265).

Admiration for things American is evident around the world—whether it is in China, where Budweiser beer is advertised using the slogan that it is "America's favorite beer" (Lee, 2000), or in South Africa, where one reporter wrote, "South Africans of all colors love American culture" (McNeil, 1997), or in Israel where an advertising executive stated, "The [mere] implication of America is very compelling for an Israeli" (Klein, 1996). Item after item, regardless of its actual country of origin, is marketed by claiming that it is the most popular in the United States. For example, a baby pacifier made in Austria is advertised as "the pacifier most sold in America" (Yehoshua TBWA, 1999), and the British Land Rover is marketed as having been "elected the best multi-purpose vehicle of the year in America" (Avraham & First, in press).

Certainly outside the U.S., "America" has an existence all on its own that has nothing to do with reality. When one of the authors visited the Philippines, someone asked if she had ever visited Marlboro country, a question based on cigarette ads. In her analysis of young people's reactions to Coca-Cola ads, Gillespie (1997) found that the preference for American advertisements comes from conflating the advertisement with the product.

A cross-cultural comparative study of children and youth in Europe has also highlighted the fact that, for older children and adolescents, who are the greatest consumers of cultural products that do not originate in their own nations, American products are associated with quality, innovation, and "coolness." They are perceived as being more technically advanced, more true to life, and better marketed (Lemish et al., 1998).

In a study on the perceptions of children outside the U.S., through their reception of the World Wrestling Federation (WWF) programs, Lemish (1999) found that "America" served as a metaphor for bigger, better, and richer. She found reactions of awe and admiration for the U.S., as well as perceptions of its being the strongest, most violent, and most dangerous country in the world. At the same time, the U.S. was considered to be the most creative country, with the best infrastructure for innovations, a place where the "American dream" is alive and well.

This perception of readiness for innovation and creativity may be partly attributed to the fact that the U.S. is essentially a society of immigrants. This implies a dynamic encountering of differences with a steady influx of new values, perspectives, and ideas.

American society has long been represented by the assimilationist metaphor of the melting pot, a term derived from Israel Zangwill's 1908 play about the immigration experience. The melting pot was a utopian vision of immigration, in which each individual would be entitled to realize the American dream, significantly bettering himself or herself financially, regardless of ethnic origin. More than this, it stressed decreasing differences among people while emphasizing the communal values that brought them together. Over the years, there has been increasing disillusionment with the idealistic portrayal of the mix of immigrant groups (Glazer & Moynihan, 1970) as a melting pot, or even a mosaic, or a salad bowl, or what presidential candidate Jesse Jackson referred to as a rainbow coalition (Cooper & Nothstine, 1992). King (1993) claims, "In fact it is not clear that there is—or ever has been—an American culture or national character … the plurality of American culture emerged with full force as an ideal after the 1960s" (p. 373). Although nationalism subsided, ethnicity arose in its place. As Ostendorf and Palmié (1993) explained: Despite the fact that, by the 1990s, everyday culture in the U.S. had become increasingly unified, the population had become more fragmented both ethnically and ideologically, and we would add, intellectually. Hughes (1975) discussed the migration of intellectual thought from Europe to the U.S.—including the philosophy of Ludwig Wittgenstein, intellectual critiques of fascism, the mass society by the Frankfurt school, and Freud's psychoanalysis—as well as the transformations and twists that unfolded in the process.

Campbell and Kean (1997) put forth the concept of *hybridity* to express the sociocultural makeup of the United States. They maintain that this term represents the ambiguity, the contrary needs, and the processive nature. Similarly, Gitlin (1998) says that today in the U.S., "One belongs by being slightly different, though in a similar way" (p. 172). Fender (1992) talks about the U.S. behaving as a sect that defines itself through difference, where the discourse of immigration and by immigrants plays a crucial role. In a later work, Fender (1993) claims that American models of national identity involve "becoming" (p. 2) in the sense of a process of renewal after a period of trial. Fender's (1993) description might be most comparable to the process that actually occurs when an individual seeks to acquire a new nationality, or what immigration officials term "naturalization." In most countries this entails a type of trial period or time of adaptation, followed by a new identity or rebirth. This rebirth as a new immigrant is played out in such popular films as *Kane and Abel, Moscow on the Hudson,* and *Green Card.* To cite Gitlin (1998), "one becomes 'American' now by taking pluralism to be the form of American commonality" (pp. 172–173). This is similar to what happens in the case of products undergoing the megaphone effect: Foreign imports become Americanized even when their foreign origins are widely known and recognized.

The Frontier and Sea Change Theses

Beyond the fact that the U.S. is an immigrant culture, an additional explanation of why the U.S. has successfully assumed the role of diffusing texts to the rest of the world, or *megaphoning,* is the American myth of the frontier. Turner's (1961, 1962) *Frontier Thesis,* which states that the ever-receding frontier has always conditioned the American character, was one of the most dominant influences on American historians (Billington, 1971). According to this, the differences between American and European civilizations might be attributed to the unique environment of the new world, whose most distinctive feature is the continuously advancing frontier of settlement. Based on this assumption, the U.S. had not become an imitation of the old world, but was radically altered by the 300 years of pioneering the frontier. Turner (1961) contended that this process resulted in the development of a unique people with the frontier as the most formative experience of the American culture. He also attributed personality traits and the characteristic of the American intellect to this: "coarseness and strength combined with acuteness and inquisitiveness," a "practical, inventive turn of mind, quick to find expedients," a "masterful grasp of material things," a "restless, nervous energy," a "dominant individualism," and a "buoyancy and exuberance which comes from freedom" (p. viii).

Although there is a certain amount of debate over Turner's theory (e.g., Ellis, 1969; Moen & Lervik, 1996) and the importance he assigns to the frontier, his thesis is worth considering with regard to the megaphone effect. Assuming that the concept of the frontier has indeed had an influence on the mindset of the American people, it could be argued that once they reached the west coast and claimed it as their own, what remained was the rest of the world, and finally outer space. In his acceptance speech for the Democratic nomination to the presidency on July 15, 1960, John F. Kennedy stated that the U.S. was "on the edge of a new frontier" (JFK Library, 2002). Following this, the notion of breaching new frontiers was often attached to his programs.

Himmelstein (1984) discusses how the great American dream and the good life come about in terms of the myth of eternal progress, or economic expansion of both the society as a whole and of personal rewards, and a desire for personal fulfillment beyond material possessions. Fender (1992) explains that the individual attains a higher level of understanding and knowledge through the act of transcending the frontiers of communal and individual culture.

If one subscribes to the idea, a frontier mentality may serve as an explanation for the American spirit that operates the megaphone. The prominence of the various American mass media and the fact that the entire communication industry is so highly evolved in the U.S.

attests that the nation has both a very loud megaphone, as well as a strong tendency to proclaim messages through it. Tunstall and Machin (1999) point out that "the United States is the only genuinely global exporter across a range of media and into most countries in the world" (p. 2).

A related theory is that of the *sea change*, originally concerning the unique relationship that has existed between the United Kingdom and the U.S. for the past 400 years. Since the time of the industrial revolution, many innovations have originated in the U.K., while the U.S. supplied the technology and market to develop and spread these concepts. This is a pattern that repeats itself in the history of the relationships between the two nations (Hughes, 1975; Abegglen, 1994).

By way of illustration, Tunstall and Machin (1999) note with regard to the mass media, the U.S. is so highly intertwined with the U.K. that:

> British films do not qualify as "foreign" films at the Academy Awards. Reuters, the London news agency, is often referred to as an American news agency; nor does the BBC seem really foreign to U.S. viewers of PBS and other up-market networks. (p. 262)

To further exploit our metaphor of the megaphone, we might say that frequently the U.K. serves as the *message* bearing with it the idea, the innovation itself, the essence of object, while the U.S. is the *medium*, representing the energy and force, the technology, and the marketing by which the voice is brought forth. In McLuhan's (1964) terms, if the U.S. is the medium, it is also the message, which could crowd the contributions of the U.K. (or any other country from which a cultural text originates) out of the picture so that in the final analysis, it is primarily the U.S. that seems to count.

Summary

Rather than seeing globalization as a lost battle against the mighty American economy and its culture, we propose that the local can and does influence the global. It does so by steering a course via the U.S. itself, thereby using that country's power to its own advantage and adhering to the prescription "if you can't beat 'em join 'em". This expression encapsulates a number of issues relevant to this work. Interestingly, its origins are uncertain. Intuitively it is American, seeming to capture the spirit of a country that offers endless possibilities, for when one route is unsuccessful, another choice can always be pursued. At the same time, the notion of compromise is reflected, together with a practical assessment of the distribution of power. In addition, the expression encourages taking advantage of the forces that exist even if one's needs are different from those of another group. Resistance is not always the only way to satisfy one's goals. Beyond this, these simple words express the possibility of combining forces with a more formidable group, thereby indicating that the larger group is both able and willing to accommodate difference. Perhaps most importantly, it advocates self-empowerment: Power is achieved, neither through passive co-optation into something, nor through aggressive domination by another group, but rather through the active, voluntary choice of joining.

Tomlinson (1999) is optimistic about the cosmopolitanism of a globalized world, exemplified by the visible presence of non-Western cultures in the Anglo American world. He claims that there is more openness to cultural pluralism in what he calls the cosmopolitanism of a globalized world. We would argue that this openness is the result of the megaphone effect because one aspect of globalization is an attempt to incorporate difference. The result of this is that as each new difference becomes incorporated into the fold, it becomes part of the established, recognized mainstream.

In other words, it is commonly accepted that texts are given a local interpretation and thus domesticated. We are claiming that the reverse is also true. Other items that do not come from the U.S. are accepted in other parts of the world after they have been given an American interpretation. To put this another way, the international popularity of many cultural items occurs precisely because they come to the world via the U.S., thereby obtaining a valued seal of approval. We contend that even elements not originally from the U.S. go through a process of being accepted in that country. It is only after they have been adopted by Americans that they become widely popular internationally.

We suggest that the process of Americanization has its roots in various cultures around the world, all of which contribute to sustaining it. Our view is optimistic: Whereas most of the literature on globalization concentrates on the influences the global has on the local, we are focusing on the influences the local has on the global. The megaphone effect provides a further refinement of the globalization argument by showing that it can be perceived, not in unidirectional terms, but rather as a dynamic, transactional process, where at least the opportunity for some measure of empowerment exists for less dominant groups.

Linda-Renée Bloch and Dafna Lemish, Excerpt from: "The Megaphone Effect: The International Diffusion of Cultural Media via the USA," *Communication Yearbook, vol. 27, ed. Pamela J. Kalbfleisch*, pp. 163–168. Copyright © 2003 by Taylor & Francis Group. Reprinted with permission.

Moving Forward

Our previous reading discussed the magnitude of the United States' cultural producing machine. In our next selection, we move towards understanding how popular media contributes in creating stereotypes. In fact, most stereotypes are propagated through popular culture. For example, what comes to mind when you hear the term nerd? Chances are your visualization of this term has been influenced at one point by a piece of popular media, and that piece has helped you shape your idea of what a nerd looks like.

As you move through this next reading, keep in mind the following questions: What is the difference between inflexible and flexible stereotyping? How does the media shape how we see other cultural or ethnic groups?

MEDIA IMAGES AND STEREOTYPING

Media images shape the way we view dissimilar others from different cultural/ethnic groups. As a result, we associate different stereotypes as "character types," or as specific ethnic groups who represent the associated images. For example, Elizabeth Bird (1999) observed that American Indian males seen in films and on television are often cast as "doomed warriors" who are strong and attractive. However, they are also often cast as either sidekicks to European American male actors or loved by strong, independent-spirited White women (e.g., *The Last of the Mohicans*). Another stereotype is the wise elder, how has the knowledge and is the source of ancient wisdom. Female American Indians are seen as maidens or princesses (e.g., Pocahontas), who are symbols of ancient wisdom and harmony with nature, more so in graphic art than on television and in movies (Bird, 1999). African Americans and Latino/as do not have it any easier. According to Orbe and Harris (2001), African American males are typically relegated to comedic roles, such as Sambo (lazy and content), Uncle Tom (quiet and respectful), and Buck (athletic and sexually powerful). African American women, however, are either sexually enticing or asexual and nurturing mammies. Latino/a Americans are limited to stereotypical roles associated with lower-status occupations.

It is inevitable that all individuals stereotype. The key to dealing with the issue is to learn to distinguish between inflexible stereotyping and flexible stereotyping. *Inflexible stereotyping* holds on to preconceived and negative stereotypes by operating on automatic pilot. We dismiss information and evidence that is more favorable to the outgroup, and we presume on member's behavior represents all members' behaviors and norms. In comparison with inflexible stereotypes, we need to address the characteristics of *flexible stereotyping* (see Table 7.1).

Essentially, to be more mentally flexible means to become aware that we can and will stereotype members of an entire group. However, refraining from typecasting an entire group on the basis of slim evidence, or no evidence, is a good first step. Using loose, descriptive categories rather than evaluative categories is another way to mindfully *flex* our stereotypes. Using a qualifying statement or a contextual statement to frame our interpretations allows an outgroup member to be an individual and *not* a representative of an entire group. This is a critical destereotyping step. Finally, being open to new information and evidence gives us an opportunity to get to know, in-depth, the most important membership identities of the individuals within the group.

Flexible stereotyping allows us to be more open-minded, but inflexible stereotyping makes us shortsighted. Flexible stereotyping reflects a willingness on our part to change our loosely held images based on diversified, direct face-to-face encounters. Interacting with individuals who are different from us can be uncomfortable at times. We may even feel nervous or anxious because of their strange behaviors or unfamiliar accents. By being aware of our own zone of discomfort and admitting that we are anxious or confused in terms of how to approach the cultural stranger, we may also be taking a solid step forward, moving from inflexible stereotyping to flexible relating and connecting. *Perceptions*, *ethnocentrism*, and *stereotypes* provide the contents of our filtering process.

Moving Forward

As we learned in our last reading, stereotyping is inevitable and can be an issue in intercultural communication. Stereotypes are often created by the media that we consume, and these perceptions can be both positive and negative. For example, a negative stereotype is illustrated in Jaguar's 2014 Superbowl commercial. The commercial featured British actors that each play a villain in a popular movie. After viewing this commercial, you may view all British people as being villains. Similarly, you may view all British people as fans of the science fiction series, Dr. Who. This is a positive stereotype as it causes no harm. Obviously, both these negative and positive stereotypes are not universally true of British people. The following reading discusses two viewpoints on stereotyping.

As you move through this reading, pay attention to the selection's argument about whether stereotyping, while frequently harmful and misguided, can be occasionally useful. With which viewpoint do you agree or disagree?

STEREOTYPING AND INTERCULTURAL COMMUNICATION

The *Compact Oxford Dictionary* defines stereotype as 'a preconceived and over-simplified idea of the characteristics which typify a person or thing'. A simple example might be 'Iranian businessmen put family loyalty before business'. The issue of cultural stereotypes is central to the business of intercultural understanding and also connects with a broader cultural politics within international English language education. I shall begin by setting out two basic arguments and then present my own analysis of the way forward. The first argument derives from concerns that cultural descriptions may be chauvinistic and encourage racism. The second is the more popular belief that stereotyping is normal and useful. I shall leave this until second because, against expectations, it is the more complex view and leads to the greatest part of the debate.

The Cultural Chauvinism Argument

This argument is that cultural stereotypes are in the main overgeneralizations which are based on the describer's imagination of an inferior Other rather than with objective information about what the people being described are actually like. In a browse through my own annotated bibliography almost every reference to stereotypes emphasizes this suspicion. For example, Homi Bhabha (1994: 94) asserts that the stereotype is 'the major discursive strategy' in establishing fixed notions of how people are, and that this can be used to justify the cultural improvement which was a stated aim of European colonization. Clark and Ivani č (1997: 168) associate stereotyping with the way in which writers impose 'a view of the world' on readers, and give the example of sexist or 'any language that presents powerless groups of people in a stereotyped and/or unfavourable light'. Kim M-S (2005: 105) tells us that 'empirical data have consistently shown the stereotypical model to be false' with 'massive variation' and 'overlap within and across cultures'. Even Hofstede (2001: 14, 17), who has been a major source of national cultural characterizations, warns us against the ethnocentrism of 'heterostereotypes' about others, such as 'all Dutch are tactless', and 'autostereotypes' about our own groups, such as 'we Dutch are honest'. Kumaravadivelu (2007: 65–9) maintains that cultural stereotypes which are believed to be egalitarian by their users are an influential underpinning of US notions of cultural assimilation which in turn impose ethnocentric cultural viewpoints.

The issue with cultural stereotypes has been linked with professional prejudices in English language teaching in which 'non-native speaker' teachers and students have been characterized as culturally deficient (e.g. Kubota 2002; Holliday 2008). Kumaravadivelu (2003: 715–5, 2007) locates chauvinistic stereotyping within what he considers to be an essentially racist Western society which generates binary 'us'–'them' categories. My own work (Holliday 2005, 2007b) relates this further to the way in which a modernist, technicalized 'native speaker' English language teaching methodology sets out on a missionary quest to correct the cultures of a non-Western Other through the imposition of prescribed learning behaviour. This cultural chauvinism argument is generally rooted in critical applied linguistics (e.g. Pennycook 1998; Canagarajah 1999), and Edward Said's (e.g. 1978, 1993) influential theory of Orientalism. Said argues that negative stereotypes of the non-Western Other (as dark, immoral, lascivious, despotic and so on) are constructed by Western art, literature and political institutions. Especially after September 11 we have seen a confirmation of Said's assertion in the form of Islamophobia, in which 'all Muslims' are characterized as 'terrorists'.

Stereotypical models of national and regional cultures have been used extensively in intercultural communication research and training. One such model, which was developed by Hofstede (op. cit.) in the 1960s and has sustained in popularity, distinguishes between two cultural types. On the one hand, individualist cultures, situated in North America, Western Europe and Australasia, are described as prioritizing self-determination. On the other hand, collectivist cultures in the rest of the world are described as prioritizing group conformity (Triandis 2004, 2006). Elsewhere (Holliday 2007a) I argue that this distinction, while pretending to be an objective measure based on empirical research, is in fact ideologically constructed along the lines described in the previous paragraph—so that individualism represents an idealized Western Self, and collectivism represents an imagined, deficient, non-Western Other. Kim (op. cit.: 108) also notes that Hofstede's model 'forced a single bipolar dimension of individualism and saw collectivism as an absence of individualism' that was derived from the need to negatively Other 'barbarians'.

The Practicality Argument

The cultural chauvinism argument thus suggests that stereotypes cannot be objective measures of what people are really like and are always going to be culturally chauvinistic. In contrast, the practicality argument suggests that cultural stereotypes are natural and useful mechanisms for aiding understanding of cultural difference, and that, although we know that they are over-generaliz ations, they are good as starting places. This view is the one that has been more established and supported by psychometric research such as that of Hofstede, and also fits better with popular belief. Waters (2007a, 2007b) sees stereotypes as almost always inevitable and ordinary starting points for perception, and feels that recognizing and accepting this will provide a firmer footing than attempting to outlaw them – thus working towards replacing negative stereotypes with more accurately positive ones. He describes such a process as follows:

> Step 1: I am working in a culture which is unfamiliar to me. I feel it might help if I got some basic information about it, in order to begin to get to know it better.
>
> Step 2: In the light of this knowledge, what can I do (i) to limit culturally inappropriate behaviour on my part, and (ii) improve my ability to understand/accept behaviour on the part of locals?
>
> Step 3: In the longer-term, how can I use this information to give me a basis for building up a better general picture of how expatriates and locals can live and work together as well as possible, and to help me perceive the individual person behind the cultural 'mask'?
>
> (2007a: 284)

He sees this as 'acquiring knowledge that will be used not as a static end in itself, but dynamically, as a means to gradually increasing understanding and contributing to the development of productive inter-cultural relations' (ibid.).

An extension of the practicality argument, which Waters (2007a, 2007b, 2007c) presents in some detail is that the cultural chauvinism argument amounts to an imposition of 'political correctness'. Citing the work of social theorist Browne (2006), he defines political correctness as a hegemonic force which has become dominant in English-speaking Western society and creates the impression that everyone is either an 'oppressor' or a 'victim' (Waters 2007b: 354). His response to the cultural chauvinism argument in English language teaching is that this imagined oppressor–victim relationship is portrayed indiscriminately as native speakers versus non-native speakers, teachers versus learners and '"global" versus local methodologies' (ibid.: 355).

Waters (2007a) cites a number of early theorists, such as Lippman (1922) and Allport (1954), to support the point that while there is an early acknowledgement that stereotypes are 'defensive, partial and rigid representations of the world, which obscure variety and particularity, and which the individual should resist', to deny the usefulness of stereotypes in 'economizing attention' would be to 'impoverish human life', and to deny the categorical nature of all human perceptions, and the possibility of working with their complexity and diversity to arrive at more valid truths. He therefore makes the following claim:

> Suspension or suppression of stereotypes is an impossibility, a vain attempt at 'thought control', and all perception can be seen, to a greater or lesser extent, as inevitably stereotyped, for both better or worse. Thus, rather than stereotyping all stereotyping as innately unhealthy or aberrant, because *some* forms of stereotyping from *some* points of view are seen to have negative consequences, the starting point needs to be one based on accepting the immanency of stereotyping, instead of attempting to deny its rationality and central role in the development of perceptions. Such a stance recognises that some stereotypes will offend, but why this is so and what might be done about it can then be approached from a very different perspective. (ibid.: 228, his emphasis)

Intercultural Communication Methodologies

Waters' warning against a knee-jerk demonizing of all stereotyping needs to be taken seriously. However, while it claims more realism than the cultural chauvinism position, his argument may also be naïve in its lack of belief about how easily the best intentioned people can be taken in, not by the hegemony of political correctness, but by the discoursal power of, in his words, the apparently innocent 'economized' explanations that stereotypes provide. Much can be learnt here from another branch of Applied Linguistics, that of Critical Discourse Analysis, which shows us how prejudices can easily be hidden in apparently neutral everyday talk, and in institutional, professional and political thinking (e.g. Fairclough 1995). Kumaravadivelu (2007: 52) puts this very well:

Even people with an egalitarian, non-prejudiced self-image can act prejudicially when interpretive norms guiding a situation are weak. In such a scenario, people easily justify their racially prejudiced acts and beliefs on the basis of some determinant other than race.

Kumaravadivelu's view of society, as an inherently racist system, is very different to that of Waters. Waters suggests that an initial, stereotyped understanding may subsequently be modified or abandoned in the light of experience. If we accept Kumaravadivelu's view, however, it is difficult to accept Waters' opinion. Once the easy repertoires of stereotypes are in place they provide basic structures of understanding that are very difficult to remove. In Western cultural history destructive narratives of an imagined uncultured East repeat themselves again and again. The cultural chauvinism and the practicality arguments each produce a methodology for intercultural communication which falls on either side of this tension.

Awareness Through Cultural Descriptions

The practicality argument encourages the established, dominant approach where people are introduced to a description of the new culture they are about to be introduced to—very much following Waters' steps. Taking the example of Iranian society, with which I am familiar, this methodology would very probably introduce the prospective visitor to aspects of Iran as a collectivist and a Muslim society. These two macro characterizations may deal with such detail as 'Iranian businessmen put family loyalty before business' (the example from the beginning of this chapter) or 'it is not appropriate to deal directly with women'. On arriving in Iran the visitor would hopefully begin to discover that there are many 'exceptions' to such rules; and, indeed, much current intercultural communication theory does warn against the danger of over-generalization (e.g. Gudykunst 2005; Samovar and Porter 2006).

Awareness Through Interrogating Issues of Self and Other

The cultural chauvinism argument is very cautious of the cultural description route. As argued above, macro characterizations such as collectivism are perceived to be ideologically motivated; and, especially in an era of Islamophobia, any form of characterization of Islam has to be treated extremely cautiously. The methodology emerging from the cultural chauvinism argument would therefore avoid imposing cultural descriptions. The focus would instead be on the structure of prejudice arising from the stereotyping process, and the development of disciplines for avoiding them. The prospective visitor to Iran would therefore be asked to interrogate her or his prejudices about Iran and to address inhibitions to understanding arising from them. Behaviour considered 'exceptions' to the stereotype in the cultural description methodology would be considered normal until found otherwise. The model of society would therefore be one of complexity rather than cultural unity, with an emphasis on looking for commonality rather than foreignness, given that many stereotypes are founded on a chauvinistic expectation of difference. Statements such as 'Iranian businessmen put family loyalty before business' or 'it is not appropriate to deal directly with women' would not therefore be taken as descriptions of how things are, but as 'easy answers' which need to be deconstructed in terms of a superior Western Self imagining a deficient non-Western Other. In other words, stereotypes are perceived as problems rather than solutions.

This sort of methodology can be found in Holliday et al. (2004: 48–49), and might involve disciplines for seeing such as: (a) excavate and put aside preconceptions and ready-made systems for understanding, (b) appreciate complexity, (c) avoid over-generalizing from individual instances, (d) submit to the unexpected and what emerges from experience, (e) seek a deeper understanding of how negative stereotypes are formed, and (f) accept that even innocent looking beliefs can have political and patronizing undertones. These disciplines have much in common with those of qualitative research, where the emphasis is on finding out the nature of culture without being influenced by preconceptions. Similarities may also be found in the work of Byram and colleagues (e.g. Byram and Feng 2006), who encourage foreign language students to carry out their own personal ethnographic research projects while visiting other people's countries—to find out for themselves the nature of other cultures. They are encouraged to begin by making sense of what is going on in its own terms, employing a 'willingness to seek out or take up opportunities to engage with otherness in a relationship' (Byram 1997: 57).

Loose Ends

In conclusion it needs to be emphasized that I have presented an over-tidy picture of the issues surrounding stereotypes—learning something from Waters in appreciating how easy it is to stereotype arguments about stereotypes. The question of stereotypes needs to be looked at within the context of complexity. Either because the world is changing, within a process of globalization, or because we are more tuned to appreciate it, the nature of culture is far from straightforward. Culture is something that flows and shifts between us. It both binds us and separates us, but in different ways at different times and in different circumstances. There are many aspects of our behaviour which are culturally different. We must, however, be wary not to use these differences to feed chauvinistic imaginations of what certain national or ethnic groups can or cannot do—as exotic, 'simple', 'traditional' Others to our 'complex', 'modern' selves. The foreign is not always distant, but often participant within our own societies; and the boundaries between us are blurred. Culture is therefore cosmopolitan, and as such resists close description.

What is clear, however, is the moral imperative which underpins issues in intercultural communication and problematizes stereotypes—to counter what Kumaravadivelu (2007) projects as a major activity of the twentieth and twenty-first centuries, one half of the world chauvinistically defining the other as culturally deficient.

SUMMARY

Popular culture is everywhere. We can choose to consume popular media or choose to reject it. Popular media enables us to visualize places we have never been, like Disney World, or the Eiffel Tower. However, popular culture can, and often does, reinforce stereotypes. The United States is the top distributor of popular culture. However, Americans do consume popular media from other countries.

In this chapter, we focused on the power of popular media and popular culture. Our first reading examined the megaphone effect and the power the United States exhibits as a popular culture industry machine. We learned about Americanization, and we have seen that many items sold overseas are popular simply because they are from the United States. As consumers, we have to choose to either consume popular culture or resist popular culture, and as the reading revealed, sometimes resisting is not always in our best interest.

Our second and third readings concerned stereotypes and perceptions of other cultures in popular media. The second selection revealed that stereotyping is inevitable and we must be aware of flexible and inflexible stereotyping; and our third reading expanded upon stereotyping, discussing positive and negative stereotyping and two different arguments pertaining to stereotyping. Continue on to the discussion questions and put your knowledge of popular culture to the test.

DISCUSSION QUESTIONS

1. Why has the United States taken the position of leader in the world of popular culture? How does this position of leadership affect the way people from other cultures look at the United States and communicate with Americans as we travel around the world?
2. What are some of the most obvious images of American popular culture that seem to dominate in the world? How have other countries introduced elements of their cultures onto the world stage? Is promotion of these other cultural elements by American popular culture essential to their acceptance?
3. Can anything be done to reduce the impact of cultural stereotyping resulting from the promotion of positive/negative characteristics of particular groups through the media?
4. Is cultural stereotyping inevitable in the world of popular culture? What communication strategies could be used to reduce the impact of this stereotyping?

DEVELOPING INTERCULTURAL RELATIONSHIPS

CHAPTER 8

STUDY OBJECTIVES

After completing this chapter, you will be able to:
- Identify and describe challenges that people in intercultural relationships may face.
- Describe how power plays a role in intercultural relationships.
- Explain why cultural sensitivity is needed in intercultural relationships.

INTRODUCTION

Reflect on your relationships: your close friendships, your family, your co-workers, your classmates, and any other relationships that we might have missed. How might these relationships differ from one another? We assume that your relationships have a variety of differences; differences such as, age, gender, religion, race, ethnicity, nationality, and so on.

Intercultural relationships are everywhere. Can you imagine how boring it would be if everyone with whom you had some social relationship reflected the same gender, age, ethnicity, religion, or other set of cultural elements as you? Intercultural relationships bring new experiences to those involved. They provide different opportunities and help break stereotypes, and those involved in the relationship learn from one another.

However, relationships can be difficult and intercultural relationships are presented with different challenges. In this chapter, three readings focus on different aspects of intercultural relationships. Our first reading focuses on intimate relationship development and examines how couples define and communicate their relationships to those outside of the relationship. Our second selection discusses inequality in power distribution and the tensions that inequality may bring to intercultural relationships. Finally, the last reading argues the need for cultural sensitivity in relationships. When introducing differing cultures into relationships, problems can arise unless both partners are culturally sensitive to one another. When cultural sensitivity exists in any relationship, satisfaction increases.

At the end of this chapter you will find a collection of discussion questions that will enable you to put your newly developed knowledge about intercultural relationships to the test. Make sure to contemplate and answer each question carefully before progressing to the next chapter.

Moving Forward

Our first reading concerns intimate relationship development. When an intimate relationship develops, a couple must define the relationship and communicate their "coupleness" to others. As a couple defines its relationship, the partners must choose to accept, reject, or negotiate society's norms. Often society offers expectations or stereotypes of what a relationship should look like. It is up to the couple if or how society's expectations will play a role in their relationship. As you move throughout this reading, consider the following questions. How can a couple signal their physical and psychological autonomy? How can society play a role in a couple's relationship? How might culture impact the development of a relationship and the communication of the relationship to others?

COUPLES AND CULTURE

COMMUNICATING AUTONOMY AND CONNECTION

The couple's resources for communicating their autonomy and their connection with society are associated with two major aspects of relating within a social context. The first involves developing a sense of the relationship, what it is and what it is not, the essential qualities that produce the partners' "coupleness." The second involves signaling these qualities of the relationship to others.

Developing a Sense of the Relationship

Two individuals must achieve a significant level of dyadic coordination in order to act together as a couple (Pearce & Cronen, 1980). While it may not be necessary for partners to think about or describe their relationship in exactly the same way, it is important that their actions fit together in a way that both find meaningful. Although couples can achieve this level of coordination in a variety of ways, two general trends predominate, each stressing a different pole of the autonomy/connection dialectic.

Adopting the Social Norm: A Vehicle for Connection

One way to achieve coordination as a couple is for partners to act as others act in similar relationships. In acting normatively, partners achieve a kind of coordination that emanates from the social order. Partners use the knowledge they have of various relationship types within their culture to inform them about their own relationship.

Assuming the existence of relationship prototypes suggests one way for understanding this process. Prototypes are conceptualizations people have of the typical features of different relationship types. A prototype represents the clearest example of a relationship category. For instance, recent research has drawn the basic outlines of people's conceptualizations of friendship and love relationships (Davis & Todd, 1985; Fehr, 1986). These two relationship types share such qualities as affection, trust, and companionship, but differ in terms of passion (fascination, exclusiveness, and sexual desire) and depth of caring (willingness to make sacrifices, being the champion of the partner's interests).

Davis and Roberts (1985) argue that people adopt such prototypical conceptualizations to different degrees, but they describe one type of couple, composed of "rote status assigners," who exist in a "prefab" world created entirely in the social order. The authors compare this kind of couple to chess players who play "only games that have already been written in the chess book—never inventing a new opening or a new pattern of moves" (p. 149). The relational negotiation for this kind of couple is uncomplicated, effortless, and smooth. Passionate conflict is minimal because both partners are following the same guidebook for how to relate. That guidebook contains the conventional rules, roles, and scripts of the existing social order. Considerable research effort has been directed to describing such social conventions in personal relationships (see review by Argyle, 1986; Fitzpatrick, 1988; Ginsburg, 1988).

Establishing a Relational Culture: A Vehicle for Autonomy

Couples also can define their coupleness in such a way as to assert their autonomy from society. Specifically, they can separate themselves from the larger social culture by establishing a culture of their own. Styles of relating can be worked out over time, with partners adapting to each other and their circumstances, negotiating their expectations about appropriate ways to act, to divide responsibilities, and to contribute time and material resources in support of the relationship (McCall, 1970). Partners also can develop unique interpretations of communicative events. Private message systems can emerge that often bear little resemblance to public language rules. These unique understandings and ways of relating make up what has been called a "private culture" (McCall, 1970) or a "relational culture" (Wood, 1982).

The more a couple establishes a unique relational culture, the more they assert their autonomy from society. A unique culture sets them apart from other couples and groups. It emphasizes the differences between what other people do, say, and think and what the couple does, says, and thinks.

Of interest here is what communication characteristics lead to the establishment of a relational culture. The simplest answer is the sheer amount of interaction between partners. That is, the more two people talk with each other, the more likely they are to develop a shared unique approach to the world and to each other. Such an explanation is suggested in a number of theories that link communication and relationship development (e.g., Berger & Bradac, 1982; Knapp, 1984; Miller & Steinberg, 1975).

There is no doubt merit to this conclusion in that it is definitionally impossible for couples to develop a relational culture without any communication. But the frequency of interaction alone is not sufficient to explain a uniquely shared worldview. This conclusion is supported by Stephen's (1986) investigation of geographically separated and nonseparated couples, which indicates that while all communication between partners contributes to defining the relationship, separated couples evidently concentrate and compress culture-building qualities into their more limited interactions.

Denzin (1970) suggests some qualities that count in building a relational culture:

> Each social relationship may be viewed as a peculiar moral order, or social world. … Contained within it are special views of self, unique vocabularies of meaning and motive, and, most important, symbol systems that have consensual meaning only to the participants involved. In relationships of long duration … rules of conduct are built … giving order, rationality, and predictability to the relationship, (p. 71)

More recent work elaborates on Denzin's ideas. In fact, the notion that relationship partners develop unique meanings for behaviors has received wide endorsement and support (Gottman, 1979; Montgomery, 1988; Watzlawick et al., 1967). An almost universal axiom in the study of interpersonal communication is that meanings are not brute facts; they are not indisputable assertions of what is and what is not represented by a particular symbolic behavior, Rather, meanings are a product of social negotiation. To be sure, this negotiation is usually subtle, implicit, and sometimes even unconscious. For the sake of communicative efficiency, we typically build current negotiations upon past ones, making use of established meaning systems, but relying on standardized meanings is not necessary or even desirable at times.

This is particularly so within the context of intimate relationships. Harris and Sadeghi (1987, p. 484) illustrate the potential of created meanings with the example of Sue and Fred, for whom such statements as "Your cooking smells" and "So does your breath" count as acts of affection. Baxter (1987) provides additional examples as she explicates the concept of relationship symbols, which typically take the form of interaction routines and games, special nicknames and idioms, and events, places, or objects that are imbued with relational significance.

Jointly enacted relationship symbols carry an overlaid message that the relationship is special, unique, and differentiated from other relationships. As Hopper, Knapp, and Scott (1981) suggest, symbols such as idioms

> promote relationship cohesiveness and identify relationship norms. Romantic pairs may use personal idioms as expressions of mutual commitment in the task of working out the integration of their behavioral styles.

Interviews with partners in intimate relationships substantiate these conclusions. Among other functions, couples report that relationship symbols represent the closeness, intimacy, and affection between partners, promote togetherness and sharing, and provide a sense of privacy or exclusivity from others (Baxter, 1987).

The notion of *relational schemata* may help to explain how partners develop and maintain such private meaning systems. Planalp (1985) defines relational schemata as "coherent frameworks of relational knowledge that are used to derive relational implications of messages and are modified in accord with ongoing experience with relationships" (p. 9). Relational schemata are pertinent to this discussion to the extent that they are particularized to a specific relationship, providing a reference frame of expectations, salient concepts, stored experiences, explanations, and rules useful for dealing with the partner. Morgan (1986) calls such specific schemata "shared knowledge structures"—a similarity between partners in the way that information is gained, organized, and interpreted that evolves from the couple's interaction.

Creative relational standards for good communication (Montgomery, 1988) are an example of a shared knowledge structure. Creative standards are a unique set of mutually held beliefs that partners develop about what constitutes competent interaction between them. They are distinguished by being decidedly different from more global, societal standards and by being the product of negotiation and agreement between partners. Thus partners are free to agree to count arguing as caring, lying as saving face for the partner, or put-downs as attentiveness. No matter the exact meaning system negotiated, it appears beneficial to relationships to have developed some unique standards (Sabatelli, Buck, & Dryer, 1980; Stephen, 1984).

In summary, communication can function to particularize the association between intimate partners. As with cultures in general, a relational culture arises when a couple develops a meaning system and evaluative norms that set them apart from other couples. These unique ways of engaging in, interpreting, and evaluating communication behavior represent and reinforce the unique identity of the couple in comparison with others. In other words, private meaning systems help intimate partners realize autonomy from the rest of society in the uniqueness and specialness of their relationship.

Summary

To enhance conceptual clarity, I have isolated the discussions of conventional and unique ways of defining relationships. Realistically, however, it is hard to imagine many couples living entirely within the confines of society's conventions or entirely outside of them in their own relational culture. Most couples likely define their relationships by incorporating aspects of both society's norms and uniquely negotiated patterns of relating. At minimum, society's stereotypical conceptions and expectations must inform the couple about their own relationship, either as an ideal to be sought in their relationship or as an initial reference point for creating their own relational culture.

Signaling Coupleness to Outsiders

Asserting autonomy and connection involves not only developing a sense of coupleness, but also communicating that coupleness to others. Couples regularly signal how dependent or independent they are with regard to the rest of society. They do this in two different spheres of social existence—the physical and the psychological.

Couples regulate their *physical accessibility* by controlling the amount and the kinds of exchanges they have with outsiders. A couple signals physical autonomy by separating themselves from others (Baxter, 1987) and by discouraging intrusion when they are in the presence of others (Scheflen, 1965). Conversely, couples can emphasize their physical connection with society by being available and accessible to interact with others. They can spend relatively long periods of time in public places and in close proximity with others. They can encourage interaction with outsiders with various nonverbal immediacy behaviors (Mehrabian, 1981). In so doing, the couple signals a physical connection with society.

Couples also regulate their *psychological accessibility,* stressing either separation from or integration with the meanings, beliefs, and values of society. Separation is communicated with the use of private meaning systems—idioms, games, rituals—in public (Baxter, 1987). Bell, Buerkel-Rothfuss, and Gore (1987) explain how the public use of private message systems enables outsiders to make attributions of intimacy in two different ways. First, outsiders are likely to conclude that two people have a special relationship when they appear to interpret messages differently from others who are present. Second, even when outsiders are not aware of idiosyncratic interpretations, they may be aware of highly coordinated behavior between the intimates that stems from idiom use. Partners' use of secret codes to coordinate leave-takings, requests, or out-of-bounds conversational topics, for example, produce highly synchronized interactions that outsiders are likely to notice. From outsiders' points of view, the use of these kinds of relationship symbols emphasizes the privileged, particularized quality of the couple's relationship and sets it apart from other relationships.

Mandelbaum's (1987) research on partners' joint storytelling activity illustrates another way that couples can signal psychological separation from society—by engaging *together* in an activity that is typically engaged in by *one* person. The unusually high level of interpersonal coordination required in *interactively* initiating, developing, and emphasizing an unfolding story signals not only that the partners shared in a past experience that can be turned into a narrative, but that they also share in the present experience of the telling as well. For the observer, the unusualness of the latter, particularly, is likely to foster a sense of separateness from the couple. Other examples of joint behavior include two partners shopping for clothing for one of them, or two guests bringing the same bottle of wine for the dinner host. Communication behaviors like these call the public's attention to the couple status of two people by setting them apart from others.

Psychological integration is asserted in opposite ways. Couples employ the traditional meaning system in the presence of others. Thus the sharing of meanings expands past the couple to include the community. Private stories and signals are avoided. Jokes are grounded in community knowledge, not intimate knowledge. The couple partakes in the cultural practices of the day, affirming in their actions the actions of the community.

Some writers have noted the particularly presentational quality that such psychological integration can take (Patterson, 1988; Rawlins, 1989a; Scheflen, 1974). That is, couples sometimes orchestrate their interaction so as to foster impressions about the kind of intimate relationship they would like others to think they have. For instance, Goffman (1959) discusses team presentations or performances that require the conspiratorial cooperation of team members to project and maintain a particular definition of the situation. In a similar vein, an intimate couple can manipulate communicative cues to encourage certain kinds of attributions about their relationship and discourage others. Patterson (1988) gives the example of a quarreling couple who, when they arrive at a party, conceal their argument by holding hands and smiling at each other.

Goffman (1971) has referred to such behavior as "tie-signs," behavioral evidence as to the type, relevant conditions, and stage of a relationship. He presents a detailed analysis of hand-holding as an illustration of how partners can signal the exclusiveness and sexual potential of their relationship to others. Goffman suggests that such tie-signs are often employed when mere proximity is not sufficient to signal the nature of a relationship and to ensure that the definition will be honored by others. Thus a couple arriving at a party where they will be mingling separately may, just before they part, smile warmly at each other or touch hands. Not only does such a display reinforce the intimacy they feel for each other, it also serves "to provide the gathering with initial evidence of the relationship and what it is that will have to be respected" (Goffman, 1971, p. 203).

Public celebrations and rituals are among the most visible of tie-signs that signal a couple's identity to others. A wedding ceremony, for instance, not only legally, socially, and emotionally binds partners together, it also broadcasts new limits on the relationships others may have with the spouses. These limits, set in the social order, are affirmed by the couple when they participate publicly in the marriage ceremony. In Western culture, for instance, a wedding marks the exclusivity of the partners, discouraging outsiders from engaging them in some kinds of interactions—romantic encounters, for instance—and encouraging other kinds of interactions—encounters with couples rather than individuals, for instance.

Thus communication functions to inform the public of the partners' bond and to contextualize that information with an assertion of connection with social norms or autonomy from them. This communication occurs more at the relational level than at the content level. The implicit message of autonomy overlays the joint telling of a story just as the message of connection overlays the couple's participation in social rituals.

Society as an Agency of Communication

Societies have a vested interest in the nature of their constituents' interpersonal associations. A society's ethical, political, and economic wellbeing is tied to its social well-being. In the cause of self-protection, then, society—the people in collective—attends to the ways its members relate to one another.

Understanding the nature of this attention is complicated by the need to take into account the collective nature of society. The members of any society form a great number of collectives, depending upon the criteria one chooses with which to divvy them up. A list of the collectives with immediate, vested interests in how personal relationships are conducted would have to include children, spouses, educators, lawyers, therapists, religious groups, social scientists—and the list goes on.

Further, sociologists tell us that each of these collectives is likely to have a *distinctive* interest with regard to how personal relationships are conducted (e.g., Bellah et al., 1985; McCall & Simmons, 1982). These interests, while distinctive, are not independent. Rather, they partially repeat, reformulate, and rebut one another. Complicating matters further, any collective usually has more than one set of interests, and these sets are often contradictory and sometimes mutually exclusive (Hall, 1988). This is the essence of the dialectical tension in social processes. Adolescents, for an example, want the protection and security that dependence on parents brings, but also want the feeling of self-determination that can come only with independence from parents. Their age-defining struggle, therefore, tends to be as much with their own conflicting interests as with members of other collectives (e.g., parents).

Given that society contains many collectives with varied and sometimes contradictory interests, the assertion that society is a communicative agency challenges one to specify what exactly constitutes the "agency" and the "communicative" message. Within the frame of relational theory, the agency and the message are metaphors for relational information contained in patterns of the collectives' behavior These patterns emerge from the ways members of collectives represent the world to one another; how they talk about it, act within it, and present it in classrooms, at family get-togethers, in churches and theaters, on television, and in scholarly texts. Bateson (1979, p. 138) suggests that these generated and enduring patterns of interaction emerge through a process of "practice." Interestingly, a similar notion is advanced within the cultural perspective, which uses the label "practices" to describe the patterns of interaction that carry the communicative force of social ideology (Althusser, 1971).

Relational theory assumes that these messages, or practices, are open to multiple and different interpretations, depending upon the circumstances of the particular communication events. Members of different collectives, with different histories and interests, are likely to interpret patterns differently. What ensues, then, is a process of intergroup negotiation in which collectives work out appropriate meanings for these messages.

This process of negotiation underscores the active, dynamic involvement in a communicative system of both the "readers" of a relational pattern and the "enactors" of a relational pattern. Neither enactor nor reader resigns indifferently in the face of the other's assertions. As in any communication system, each element is constantly informing, interpreting, and influencing the other. In this way a recursive system emerges in which members of society, in this case couples, both read and enact relationship practices. That is, couples actively participate in the reproduction and reconstitution of society's relational ideology.

The Logical Force of Society's Assertions

Assertions by a collective about the nature of things, including its relationship with particular couples, exist in a rhetorical context. That is, the assertions have a logical force. Different possibilities exist for understanding the nature of this force.

First, society's assertions may be *descriptive*. They may assert the way "things are," reflecting how couples actually relate in and to the larger social order. A few have argued that this is so, for instance, in the portrayal of relationships in novels (Alberts, 1986; Ragan & Hopper, 1984). Further, historical tracings regularly cite such literary sources as *The Iliad* or the Bible as evidence for how relationships were conducted in times gone by (see, e.g., Kirkpatrick, 1963). Strong voices, however, have argued that these kinds of social practices distort "reality." Ulrich (1986, pp. 146–148) cites an array of researchers who have found significant inconsistencies when comparing fictional novels, television series, and docudramas to real-life interpersonal experiences. Similar conclusions have been reached in studies of magazine ads (Brown, 1982) and informally communicated folk wisdom (e.g., "Love conquers all," "Women are romantics at heart"; see Walster & Walster, 1978). Parks (1982) examines another social practice in the form of scholarly portrayals of personal relationships in texts and journals and reports significant inconsistencies between the prevailing social scientific depictions and much "empirical" evidence.

A troubling aspect of this debate about whether or not practices reflect reality, however, is the assumption made by both camps that reality can be known apart from socially constructed practices. Only if the two are independent can either be used to validate the other. A growing number of scholars are arguing that this independence does not exist (Gergen, 1985; Harre, 1983; Livingstone, 1987; Shotter, 1984). For instance, Hall (1985) makes the point that "there is no experiencing *outside* of the categories of representation or ideology" (p. 105). Bateson (1979) contends that "all experience is subjective" (p. 31). If one accepts this tenet, then the question of descriptive representation becomes moot. There is no "reality" to be described by social assertions; there are only different forms and contents of social assertions.

With regard to personal relationships, rewards and punishments are often formally and explicitly offered as incentives to couples to act in certain ways. For instance, refusing to follow societal norms about incest results in execution in some cultures and imprisonment in others (Goody, 1968). In many societies marrying the appropriate mate, as defined by economic, social, or political criteria, brings riches in the form of dowries, legally sanctioned provisions for offspring, contractual economic alliances between family groups, and formally recognized (often via title) social position and status.

While such formal rewards and costs demand our attention because of their frequently dramatic and extreme nature, the system of informal reinforcements behind social assertions is much more ingrained in social organizations. These are the subtle social promises and threats that underlie personal beliefs, expectations, fantasies, and values. The folk belief that AIDS is a curse levied against those who defy social practices regarding who may properly mate is an example, as is the notion that those partners who "truly" love one another will live happily ever after.

In summarizing this discussion, the following observations are offered. Society is composed of multiple collectives representing special interests in social, political, and economic events. Collectives act as communication agencies with the enactment of various practices that carry implicit assertions about, among other things, the relative autonomy versus connection in the couple-society relationship. These assertions are rhetorically persuasive, in that they influence particular couples' actions. Society and couples actively exchange assertions, negotiating the nature of their relationship. This negotiation is ongoing and evolving. Positions, contexts, and negotiated outcomes continually change. With these stipulations in mind, we can consider some specific social practices relevant to the couple-culture interaction.

Moving Forward

Our next reading is a brief selection concerning the role that power can play in an intercultural relationship. Recent research taking a critical perspective of intercultural encounters typically will focus on power inequality. This critical perspective will often focus on individuals belonging to outgroups, or society's non-dominant groups. Power inequality creates tensions between groups where the imbalance exists. This next reading provides a glimpse into different power distributions. As you read the next few paragraphs, consider how power can play a role in intercultural relationships on a micro level and on a macro level. Can you think of any examples?

ROLE OF POWER IN INTERCULTURAL RELATIONSHIPS

Power Inequality in Intercultural Relations

Issues of power and intercultural interaction have gained prominence, spurred by recent works employing critical analysis to challenge some of the existing theories developed from the more traditional methodological perspectives of neopositivist, systems, and, to a lesser extent, interpretive approaches. Critical analysts have tended to question the legitimacy of some traditional theoretical accounts for their inherent "flaw" of reflecting and serving to reproduce the status quo of the dominant cultural ideology within and across cultures, ethnic/racial groups, and genders. In introducing an anthology of essays presented largely from a critical perspective, for example, Gonzalez, Houston, and Chen (1994) state their goal of presenting the perspectives of the authors' own cultural experiences "instead of writing to accommodate the voice that is culturally desirable by the mainstream Anglo standards" (p. xiv; see also Gonzalez & Tanno, 1997; Moon, 1998).

Critical analysts thus place a spotlight on the politics of identity and the subjective experiences of identity conflict and perpetual struggle on the part of nondominant group members as "victims." Collier and Bomman (1999), for instance, focus on the "dialectic tensions in group and individual identity orientations" in studying several historically dominant and non-dominant ethnic groups in South Africa. Likewise, based on interviews with a small group of Asian Indian immigrant women in the United States, Hedge (1998) characterizes immigrant adaptation experiences mainly in terms of "displacement," "struggle," and "contradictions" in the "world in which hegemonic structures systematically marginalize certain types of difference" (p. 36).

This depiction of adaptation stands in sharp contrast to the "stress-adaptation-growth" dynamic articulated in my own adaptation theory, described earlier. Other critical studies of intercultural communication similarly cast "traditionally muted groups" (Orbe, 1997) in the position of "victims" of power asymmetry rooted in the "oppressive" and "imperialistic" cultural practices of Western civilizations (e.g., Tsuda, 1986; Young, 1996).

Young Yun Kim, Excerpt from: "Mapping the Domain of Intercultural Communication: An Overview," *Communication Yearbook, vol. 24, ed. William B. Gudykunst*, pp. 146–147. Copyright © 2001 by Taylor & Francis Group. Reprinted with permission.

Moving Forward

Relationships can be challenging, regardless if they are romantic or platonic, or whether they are intercultural in nature. Our next reading acknowledges the difficulty that culture can bring to our relationships. This selection focuses on the need to become culturally sensitive in our relationships in order to understand and to be understood. Striving to be culturally competent communicators in our relationships can enhance our satisfaction with our relationships. As you move throughout this reading, consider how you might be able to adapt a relationship that you have with someone to accommodate for cultural differences and appreciation.

ENHANCING INTERCULTURAL RELATIONSHIP SATISFACTION

A meaningful life often entails deep relationship contacts with our families, close friends, and loved ones. However, with close contact often comes relationship disappointments and expectancy violations. If we already feel inept in handling different types of interpersonal relationships with people from our own cultural groups, imagine the challenges (plus, of course the rewards) of dealing with additional cultural factors in our intimate relationship development process. Interpersonal friction provides a sound testing ground for the resilience of our intimate relationships. According to expert researchers in interpersonal conflict (e.g., Cupach & Canary, 1997), it is not the *frequency* of conflict that determines whether we have a satisfying or dissatisfying intimate relationship. Rather, it is the *competencies* that we apply in managing our conflicts that will move the intercultural-intimate relationship onto a constructive or destructive path. Even if we do not venture out of our hometown, the places for people to meet, socialize, and to date are changing. For example, in Guam, the Kmart store, which opened in 1996, changed the social life of Guamanians. Kmart is "the island's social center, its unofficial town square, a place where you never fail to run into a neighbor, a friend, or a cousin" ("Shopper Flock ..." 1999). When locals want to shop, they come early in the morning. If locals want to hang out and meet people, they come at night before the store closes at midnight.

Another interesting phenomenon is online dating, both domestically and globally. In the past, dating was considered to be a private affair. Now, online dating services, chat rooms, and services allow people to meet on the basis of criteria they find important. Some people may disclose their ethnicities, and some people may not, in the early stage of courtship and flirting. Brooks (2003) reports that 40 million U.S. individuals date online! With match.com and various dating services, the supply is definitely in demand in this Hook-Up Age. With the dramatic rise of intercultural marriages and dating relationships in the United States, intimate relationships are a fertile ground for culture shock and clashes. According to U.S. census data for 2000, the nation has more than 1.3 million racially mixed marriages. California is reported as the top-ranked U.S. state with a biracial heritage population of 1.6 million, followed by New York and Texas. A recent Gallup Poll revealed that more than twice as many U.S. teenagers of all races reported a willingness to date interracially as did teenagers in a similar poll in 1980. Teenagers are often more receptive to developing close friendships and dating relationships across

All racial lines than their parents' or grandparents' generations. Intimate personal relationships often involve friction because we have such high hopes and expectations riding on these exclusive relationships. Understanding the possible external and internal obstacles that affect an intimate intercultural relationship can increase our acceptance of our intimate partners. Intercultural relationship conflict, when managed competently, can bring about positive changes in a relationship. It allows the conflict partners to use the conflict opportunity to reassess the state of the relationship. It opens doors for the conflict individuals to discuss in-depth their wants and needs in a relationship.

On the topic of intercultural relationship satisfaction, for many U.S. adoptive families, which countries do you think most foreign-born adopted children come from? Take a guess and check out Jeopardy Box 8.1. The U.S. Census Bureau's very first profile of adopted children reveals that 1.6 million adopted kids under age 18 are now living in U.S. households. Although foreign adoptions are increasing and getting the most headlines, the report shows that 87 percent of adoptees from diverse ethnic-racial backgrounds under 18 were born in the United States. As more U.S. families are becoming families of color, the challenge is to grapple with issues of race and ethnicity. For example, Matt Plut and his wife adopted a 4-year-old African American boy. He recalls, "We are white parents. We don't know what it is like to grow up black in America. Looking back, I know I was a sheltered white person

Jeopardy Box 8.1 Top-Ten Countries of Birth for Foreign-Born Adopted Children Under Age 18 in the United States

COUNTRY	TOTAL	PERCENTAGE
South Korea	47,555	24
China	21,053	11
Russia	19,631	10
Mexico	18,201	9
India	7,793	4
Guatemala	7,357	4
Columbia	7,054	4
Philippines	6,286	3
Romania	6,183	3
Vietnam	4,291	2

Source: U.S. Census Bureau Data (2000).

in a white community. I remember how my peers and everyone talked about race. It is not a comfortable feeling to know this is what you were taught" (as cited in MacGregor, 2002, p. E1). Other relevant and important issues include where to live and raise a biracial family, reaching out and making connections with those ethnically similar to the adopted child, and understanding the dilemmas and problems of a child's or adolescent's racial/ethnic identity development stages.

Culture-sensitive intercultural communication can increase relational and family closeness and deepen cultural self-awareness. The more that intercultural partners and family members get to know each other on a culturally responsive level, the more they can appreciate the differences and deep commonalities among them. The power of being understood on an authentic level can greatly enhance relationship quality, satisfaction, and personal insight.

Stella Ting-Toomey and Leeva C. Chung, *Understanding Intercultural Communication*, pp. 10–12. Copyright © 2007 by Oxford University Press. Reprinted with permission.

SUMMARY

Intercultural relationships surround us. They bring about new experiences, opportunities to share and learn with one another, and often break down stereotypes. However, they are not without their difficulties. Cultural differences can add strain to relationship development.

In this chapter we focused on intercultural relationships. Our first reading examined relationship development, particularly as couples define and communicate their relationships to those outside of the relationship. Often a couple must accept, reject, or negotiate societal norms in their relationship. The second reading briefly discussed inequality (power distribution) in intercultural relations. When an unequal power distribution exists, tensions are created within the relationship and are felt by both parties; this can become a challenge in developing intercultural relationships. Recently researchers have focused on power distribution in intercultural relationships from a critical perspective, framing non-dominant group members as victims of dominant society. Power certainly is an element to pay attention to when creating and maintaining relationships.

Our last reading focused on how common intercultural relationships have become in today's society, as compared to a few generations ago. This selection discussed the difficulty that culture can bring to relationships and called for the need to be culturally sensitive in our relationships. When we are culturally competent communicators in our relationships, we are able to understand the other partner in the relationship and are able to be understood ourselves. When both partners understand one another, chances are their satisfaction with the relationship increases. Continue on to the discussion questions to apply your knowledge about intercultural relationships.

DISCUSSION QUESTIONS

1. How are relationships among individuals who are of the same cultural background different from relationships between people who are of different cultural backgrounds? How does this affect the communication between them?

2. In what ways does intimacy affect communication? For example, what expectations do couples have about communication that is different than the expectations between friends or acquaintances?

3. How is power in a relationship influenced by the cultural backgrounds of the individuals within that relationship? Does power affect the way individuals in a relationship communication? What are some positive and negative aspects of communication where power is a factor?

CULTURAL IDENTITY

CHAPTER 9

STUDY OBJECTIVES

After completing this chapter, you will be able to:
- Define cultural identity.
- Describe and explain how identities are created.
- Identify and describe several theories used to study cultural identity.

INTRODUCTION

How do you identify yourself? Do you identify yourself as a student? As a son or daughter? American or Indian? Sister or brother? Baseball fan? Hockey fan? Runner? Singer? Piano player? There are many ways to identify yourself. In fact, if you were to list all the different ways you identify yourself on a piece of paper, we bet you would soon be needing the back of the paper or a second piece, maybe even a third. Certainly, you may identify yourself differently based on the situation you are in or you may identify yourself differently with different groups of people. For example, you may identify yourself primarily as a student when speaking with your instructor, but as a pianist when speaking with other musicians.

Identities are complex and multi-layered. They are negotiated and renegotiated throughout our entire lives. Identity, and particularly cultural identity are key factors in studying intercultural communication, and researchers use many theories to study identity. In this chapter, we explore identity through three readings. Our first reading provides us with an overview of cultural identity research and provides a brief glimpse into several approaches to studying cultural identity. Our second selection offers a contemporary view of identity, defining identity and revealing that identity is a negotiating process. Last, our final selection further explores identity creation and examines popular theories used in studying identity. At the end of the chapter, you will find discussion questions that will help you to apply your newfound knowledge about cultural identity.

Moving Forward

Our first reading introduces us to an overview of different approaches to studying cultural identity. This selection discusses the increased attention that researchers have given cultural identity in recent years. Researchers previously considered cultural identity as a *fixed* identity, but in more recent years they have begun to learn that cultural identity is dynamic and complex. This complexity is an example of the evolution of cultural identity research.

While this selection does not define cultural identity, it does provide you with an overview of some of the history of cultural identity research. As you read this brief selection, keep in mind that current research is always building on previous research. Consider how you might define and describe your cultural identity as you continue throughout the chapter.

APPROACHES TO STUDYING CONTEXT

Cultural Identity in Intercultural Contexts

Cultural identity (as well as such related concepts as national, ethnic, ethnolinguistic, racial, and group identity) has received increasing attention in recent years from intercultural communication researchers, coinciding with the rising interest in critical analysis of intercultural communication phenomena. By and large, investigators have conceived cultural identity to be integral to an individual's identity, offering a sense of historical connection and embeddedness and of a "larger" existence in the collectivity of a group. As such, cultural identity has been conceptualized as an essentially uniform and stable social category or a communal entity, with little attention to individual variations within a group and the dynamic, evolutionary nature of cultural identity as it is enacted in an individual's everyday life. Most researchers, from neopositivists (e.g., Ting-Toomey, 1993; Ting-Toomey & Kurogi, 1998) and interpretive investigators (e.g., Carbaugh, 1993; Wieder & Pratt, 1990) to critical analysts (e.g., Tsuda, 1986; Young, 1996), have treated an individual's cultural identity as if it were an ascription-based, monolithic entity or communally shared symbolic system exclusive to a particular group of people.

Given this prevailing conception, however, recent efforts have been directed toward stressing the complex nature of cultural identity. Collier, for example, has emphasized "identity negotiation" in theorizing about intercultural communication competence (see Collier & Bornman, 1999; Collier & Thomas, 1988). Ting-Toomey (1988, 1993, 1999; Ting-Toomey& Kurogi, 1998) makes a similar point; as noted previously, she places face negotiation at the core of intercultural communication activities. Moving beyond identity flexibility and complexity,

I have explained the dynamic and evolving nature of identity from a systems perspective (Kim, 1988, 1995a, 1995b; Kim & Ruben, 1988). As an aspect of my adaptation theory, I have explained that an individual's identity is not a fixed entity, but can be transformed by extensive and cumulative intercultural communication experiences. Accordingly, I have addressed the phenomenon of "achieved identity" (compared with ascribed identity) and have explained the evolution of an individual's identity into an intercultural identity as more than one set of cultural elements are incorporated. In this developmental process, two interrelated changes tend to occur in an individual's self-other orientation: "individualization" (ie., particularization of group categories) and "universalization" (i.e., transcendence of group boundaries). This systems conception is consistent with Casmir's (1999) model of "third-culture building" as a desirable goal for intercultural communicators. Empirical findings from a number of studies of immigrant and ethnic groups in the United States have provided data that suggest identity transformation, including the study of Asian Indian immigrants in the United States (Boekestijn, 1988; Dasgupta, 1983) and in England (Hutnik & Bhola, 1994), as well as of Cuban Americans (Szapocznik & Kurines, 1980).

Young Yun Kim, Excerpt from: "Mapping the Domain of Intercultural Communication: An Overview," *Communication Yearbook*, vol. 24, ed. *William B. Gudykunst*, pp. 145–146. Copyright © 2001 by Taylor & Francis Group. Reprinted with permission.

Moving Forward

Our next reading provides a more contemporary view of identity. The reading supports the idea that identity is not fixed, but rather complex and dynamic. Identity is something that an individual will negotiate and renegotiate throughout a lifetime.

Further, the reading reveals that individuals typically do not think about their culture or their cultural identity until they encounter someone from a differing culture. As you move throughout this next reading, recall a time when you were faced with identifying your own culture. How did you process your cultural identity? What prompted you identify your culture?

DEFINING IDENTITY

"Identity is about belonging, about what you have in common with some people and what differentiates you from others" (Weeks, 1990: 88). Identity is therefore recognition of cultural belonging, which is internal to the individual, while culture is external. Identity is no longer seen as a unitary or ever stable construct. As Norton (forthcoming) has noted, and as our contributors attest in their narratives,

> [e]very time we speak, we are negotiating and renegotiating our sense of self in relation to the larger social world, and reorganizing that relationship across time and space. Our

gender, race, class, ethnicity, sexual orientations, among other characteristics, are all implicated in this negotiation of identity. (p. 2)

Such negotiation is interwoven with power, politics, ideologies and "interlocutors' views of their own and others' identities" (Pavlenko & Blackledge, 2004:1).

The metamorphic nature of the construct has become ever more apparent with globalization and the emergence of a globalized citizenry. We are witnessing the emergence of a more dynamic type of identity formation that confronts people with hybridized or cosmopolitan identities in the twenty-first century. As Delanty (2003:133) states,

[s]trangeness has become more central to the self today, both in terms of a strangeness within the self and in the relationship between self and other. This experience of strangeness captures the essence of the postmodern sensibility, namely the feeling of insecurity, contingency and uncertainty both in the world and in the identity of the self.

In this current view of identity

the capacity for autonomy is no longer held in check by rigid structures, such as class, gender, nation, ethnicity. The self can be invented in many ways. The contemporary understanding of the self is that of a social self formed in relations of difference rather than of unity and coherence. (p. 135)

In the narratives that follow, you will see this theme being played out time and time again. Language is another construct that has resulted in hundreds, if not thousands of book-length treatments. (See for example, Nunan, 2007.) Kramsch argues that:

Language is only one of many semiotic systems with which learners make sense of the world expressed in a different language. The acquisition of another language is not an act of disembodied cognition, but is the situated, spatially and temporally anchored, coconstruction of meaning between teachers and learners who each carry with them their own history of experience with language and communication. Culture is not one worldview, shared by all the members of a national speech community; it is multifarious, changing, and, more often than not, conflictual. (Kramsch, 2004: 255)

Each of the contributions to this collection represents an exercise in reflexivity, reflexivity being "… the process of continually reflecting upon our interpretations of both our experience and the phenomena being studied so as to move beyond the partiality of our previous understandings and our investment in particular research outcomes" (Finlay, 2003:108). They also bear out Finlay's contention that

When we narrate our experience (be it in an interview or when providing a reflexive account) we offer one version—an interpretation—which seems to work for that moment. Like an external observer, we have to reflect on the evidence and recognise the indexicality and non-conclusive nature of any of our understandings. "All reflection is situational … always subject to revision." (McCleary cited in Finlay, 2003: 110)

The pieces in this collection weave together learning histories, personal narratives, and theory. The words "theory" and "theorizing" get tossed around rather loosely in the literature. The following statement from Julian Edge, one of our contributors, comes closest to capturing our sense of the term and reflects what our contributors have done in situating their narratives within the research genres that intersect with the concerns, issues, and perspectives that emerge from the narratives.

> … what I mean by theory is an articulation of the best understanding thus far available to investigators as to why things are the way they are. This kind of formulation can exist at the level of a Nobel Prize winner, and at the level of a novice teacher. One tries to make a statement that accounts for the data as one understands them. (Edge, 2008: 653)

As we attempted to define key constructs, we came to question their separability. In other words, we became reflexive about our own area of inquiry. To what extent is it possible to separate culture and identity, language and culture, language and identity? In many texts, one is defined in terms of the other. Our own stance is that culture is an "outside the individual" construct, while identity is an "inside the individual" construct. Culture, as we have said, has to do with the artifacts, ways of doing, etc. shared by a group of people. Identity is the acceptance and internalization of the artifacts and ways of doing by a member of that group.

While reading and reviewing the contributions to the volume, we also came face-to-face with the "identity paradox." We all have multiple identities, and these can weld us together into cultures and subcultures separated by existential chasms. However, if we look beyond these chasms, we are all part of the human race, with similar aspirations and ideals.

In casual conversations with friends, colleagues, and even strangers, we found that "culture" and "identity" are pervasive but invisible until they are pointed out. Just as a fish is unaware of water until it is pulled from the ocean, the river or the stream, so most people are unaware of their culture or identity until they are confronted with other cultures and identities.

Moving Forward

Our last selection in this chapter discusses the different layers that make up an individual's identity. This reading builds on our knowledge of identity and reveals that identity is influenced by several factors, particularly the way it is co-created with others through our communication. This reading explores the relationship between identity and communication and presents several popular theories that are used to study and research identity. As you move throughout this next reading, keep in mind the following questions: How is identity created? How does identity influence our communication behaviors? Can identity be objective and subjective?

THE ROLE OF IDENTITY IN INTERCULTURAL COMMUNICATION

Communication scholars have recognized the importance of identity in intercultural research (Collier & Thomas, 1988; Lustig & Koester, 2000) and have articulated it in several different ways. Among others, scholars have differentiated between racial identity, based largely on physical characteristics (Martin, 1997), and cultural identity, the extent to which individuals hold their larger culture to be important (Ting-Toomey et al., 2000). Ethnic identity has been described as "a set of ideas about one's own ethnic group membership, including self-identification and knowledge about ethnic culture (traditions, customs, values, and behaviors), and feelings about belonging to a particular ethnic group" (Martin & Nakayama, 1997, p. 74). Consistent with an "intergroup" approach (see Giles & Coupland, 1991), this latter definition is our preferred conceptual stance because we contend ethnic identity is likely to be salient, given that group distinctions are often evoked when engaging in intercultural communication. Little attention has been directed toward the processual nature of the relationship between identity and communication. Our goal is to explicate its transactional and intergroup characteristics.

Scholars have offered various perspectives on studying identity. The social psychological emphasizes that it is created, in part, by the self and, in part, by group membership and acknowledges "persistent sharing of some kind of essential character with others" (Erikson, 1959, p. 109). Social identity theory (SIT) proposes that an individual's self-concept is composed of both *social* and *personal* identities (Tajfel & Turner, 1986).

Personal identity refers to an individual's unique characteristics, irrespective of cultural or social group, and social identity is defined as one's knowledge of membership in certain social groups and the social meanings attached to the group. The central tenet of SIT is that the groups with which individuals identify (and there usually are a myriad of them) determine their social identities. Age, gender, profession, nationality, region, religion, and so forth all serve as different social identities and have their own cultural components of shared values, habits, and history. For example, many African Americans, who strongly identify with their ethnicity, will likely view themselves as "belonging" to "their" group.

Research, generally, conceptualizes identity as a multidimensional concept. For example, Kashima, Kashima, and Hardie (2000) distinguished two dimensions: self-typicality (perceived typicality of the self as an ingroup member) and group identification (the affective-evaluative response to ingroup membership). This distinction may be particularly important when considering ethnic identity, Phinney (1992) argues that the behavioral component of ethnic identity involves the degree to which individuals engage, and are competent, in the activities associated with their ethnic groups. These activities can include, but are not limited to, eating ethnic foods, engaging in ethnic behavioral patterns, speaking and writing the languages of the ethnic group, sharing networks with ethnic group members, and demonstrating common communication styles (Gudykunst, 2001; Gudy-kunst, Sodetani, & Sonoda, 1987). Although individuals may define themselves as a member of a certain ethnic group, they may not perceive themselves as being a "typical" member of it. Other individuals may both highly identify with their ethnic identity and perceive themselves as typical. Either way, these conceptions of identity may manifest themselves communicatively in differing ways.

For example, recent research suggests that one way ethnic identity is communicated is via conflict patterns. In their investigation of the impact of ethnic identity on conflict styles, Ting-Toomey et al. (2000) reveal individuals with a strong ethnic identity use integrating conflict styles (i.e., a high concern for both self and others during negotiation), whereas individuals with a weak ethnic identity use neglecting (tactfulness and consideration of others' feelings conveyed through the use of obligation and avoidance in conflict) and third-party (using a third party to deal with conflict issues) conflict styles. The authors argue that because the larger U.S. culture tends to engage in a low-context mode of conflict patterns, individuals who strongly identify with the larger U.S. culture will directly negotiate conflict. More specifically, they found that Asian Americans with a weak cultural identity use avoiding more than other ethnic groups, whereas Latino Americans with a weak cultural identity use neglecting more than other ethnic groups.

The Influence of Identity on Communication Behaviors

A communication perspective emphasizes that the self does not create identities alone instead, they are co-created through communication with others (Martin & Nakayama. 1997). The central tenet is that identities emerge when messages are exchanged between persons (see Table 9.1). in this way, Collier (1997) argues that ethnic identities are negotiated, reinforced, and challenged through communication, and she describes how the respective "properties" of ethnic identity are enacted and developed through communication. One of these, she argues, is that identities are enacted in interpersonal contexts through *avowal* or *ascription* processes. Avowal is the self an individual portrays (i.e., saying, "This is who I am"), whereas ascription is the process by which others attribute identities to an individual (e.g., through stereotypes). The avowal and ascription processes acknowledge that identity is shaped by our own and by others' communicated views of us. Identities are also expressed through *core symbols, norms,* and *labels* (Collier, 1997). The Mexican flag, the yarmulke, Kwanza, and the adjective Japanese American are examples of how ethnic pride is communicated via norms, symbols, and labels. The property of ethnic identities being dynamic and context related (Martin, 1997) underscores that they are emphasized depending on whom we are communicating with and the topic of conversation.

Although Collier (1997) intended that the properties of ethnic identities she articulated would help build models of ethnic identity and communication, theorists have been slow to articulate the symbiotic and transactional relationship. The processes whereby individuals construct and reconstruct their identity through communication is often absent in intercultural theorizing, despite prominent intercultural theories including, explicitly or implicitly, the roles of identity in intercultural communication (see Wiseman, 1995). Gudy-kunst (1995) argues that the management of anxiety and uncertainty is fundamental to effective communication, with identity influencing uncertainty and anxiety but not being directly related to effective communication. This is an assertion we would question given the growing body of evidence linking identity to particular communication styles.

Table 9.1 Identity as Communication

	CONVERGENCE DIVERGENCE

Nonverbal behavior	Ingroup rejection Assimilation	Positive allocation bias Smiling, gaze, gestures Time		Outgroup rejection Ethnophaulisms Negative allocation bias Symbols	Crowd behavior Conflict Physical boundaries
Language	Outgroup language with nativelike pronunciation Language acquisition	Outgroup language with features of ingroup pronunciation Topic choice Code switching Language intensity	Ingroup language with slow speech rate Conversation interruptions Conversation turn taking Sarcasm, hostility, disagreement	Ingroup language with normal speech rate Non-language acquisition Labels	Patronizing talk
Paralanguage	Accent, dialect, idioms, speech rate, pauses, utterance length, phonological variants can all be modified to signal convergence	Self-disclosure (quality and quantity) Language		Accent, dialect, idioms, speech rate, pauses, utterance length, phonological variants can all be modified to signal divergence	

NOTE: Please contact the chapter authors if interested in specific citations for exemplars in each cell.

Similarly, cross-cultural adaptation theory (Kim, 1995) describes the process and structure in which individuals adapt to a new and unfamiliar culture. Although the three primary assumptions underlying the theory discuss the complex and dynamic process of adaptation and highlight the importance communication plays in one's social environment, identity is ostensibly absent in the theory. Although one could argue it is "identity" that is undergoing transformation in adapting to new environments, the interplay of how it may be negotiated is neglected. Instead, Kim (1995) contends that an "intercultural identity" emerges as a result of the intercultural transformation.

Face-negotiation theory addresses how issues of face are negotiated in cross-cultural conflict. Ting-Toomey (1988) proposes that conflict is an identity-bound concept in which the *faces* or *situated identities* of the interactants are called into question, particularly with persons from individualistic and collectivistic cultures having different situated identities. In turn, these different face concerns will lead to different conflict styles. In her continual attention to intercultural theorizing, Ting-Toomey (1993) directly pursues the issue of identity and intercultural communication competence. According to her, effective identity negotiation refers to the "smooth coordination between interactants concerning salient identity issues, and the process of engaging in responsive identity confirmation and positive identity enhancement" (Ting-Toomey, 1993, p. 73) and, as such, requires an individual to draw on a wide range of cognitive, affective, and behavioral resources to deal with intercultural situations. Although communicative resourcefulness highlights the importance of identity in intercultural interactions, we might challenge the assumption of the theory. That is, in many intercultural interactions, individuals may not be overly concerned with having smooth interaction but rather may take bold measures to highlight their distinct ethnic identities. Communication, of course, is crucial in underscoring ethnic identity.

Identity management theory (IMT) also seeks to understand and explain communication competence in intercultural interactions. Cupach and Imahori (1993) argue that although intercultural interactions involve those with different social identities, the universal desire to maintain face (own and other's) will propel them to forge a more interpersonal relationship. In essence, intercultural interlocutors become interculturally competent as a new enmeshed relational identity emerges for them. Similar to communicative resourcefulness, IMT focuses on the achievement of effortless interaction. Most notably, it assumes that interactants eventually reach a point where identities can, in fact, be enmeshed—a stance we contend to be overly optimistic.

Intercultural theorizing has yielded important insight into intercultural dynamics. Even so, little understanding of the fundamental relationship between communication and identity has been offered. The same limitations of intercultural theory also plague models of identity development (Collier, 1997; Martin & Nakayama, 1997). Contrary to the view that one is simply born into an ethnic identity, most scholars endorse the notion that it develops over time and is created, in part, by the self becoming aware of its own ethnic group as well as through communication with other group members. Although identity development models acknowledge that ethnic identity is negotiated, most of these stage models culminate in some type of identity resolution or achievement that results in an uncharacteristically finite appraisal. Both intercultural theory and models of identity development neglect to address two important issues: the role communication plays in the formation of ethnic identity, and its nego-tiative character. Hence, identity is more peripheral to the theoretical boundaries of intercultural communication, and current positions treat it as a static input-output variable, not something dynamic that is constantly being reconstructed (Brewer, 1999; Deaux, 1996).

Although some theories discussed above feature *intergroup* communication, they attempt to understand intercultural interactions primarily as interpersonal encounters. Intergroup communication scholars argue that there is much to be gained by combining the social-psychological and communication perspectives and that such a synergy can better elucidate the transactional relationship between communication and identity.

In particular, communication accommodation theory (CAT) maintains that language and speech (as well as other communicative markers, such as dress, house, artifacts, tattoos, festivals, marches, etc.) are important elements of personal and social identity. CAT explains the process of how identity may influence communication behaviors in that individuals are motivated to accommodate (move toward or away from others) our use of language, nonverbal behavior, and paralanguage in different ways to achieve a desired level of social distance between the self and our interacting partners, The degree to which the communicator feels positive or negative about their identity may be manifested through communication behavior, and CAT theorists propose many types of accommodation, convergent and divergent strategies being the most fundamental. Convergence is a strategy whereby individuals adapt their communicative behavior to become more similar to their interlocutor, particularly those they identify with and admire (Giles & Noels, 1997). Divergence refers to the way in which speakers accentuate communicative differences between themselves and others.

Based on assumptions of SIT, CAT maintains that individuals categorize the social world according to groups and derive a part of their identity and self-esteem (social identity) from groups to which they belong. Assuming people are motivated to maintain self-esteem (see Aberson, Healy, & Romero, 2000), CAT proposes they will tend to communicatively differentiate their own group from other groups (providing they are content with their membership in that group), sometimes just on the basis of perceiving cues of the other's outgroup membership. In sum, the central premise of CAT is that individuals will assert their identity through their communication patterns. For example, individuals may wish to communicate identity solidarity with their partner by convergence or, conversely, by divergence in order to distinguish one's identity. Identity may be communicated (as continuous variables) several ways, with respect to subordinate and dominant groups, some of which are summarized in Table 9.1.

Thus far, we have articulated how identity is communicated, but less clear is what determines convergence or divergence. Intergroup encounters do not occur in a vacuum, and when interactants come together from different cultures there is often a history of relations that may include rivalry, conflict, social inequity, and prejudice (Hewstone & Brown, 1986). It stands to reason that majority and subordinate groups will communicate their identity in different ways. For example, when an encounter is defined (consciously or unconsciously) as "intergroup" by participants, the accommodative norm is for the subordinate group to converge toward the dominant group (rather than vice versa). We turn now to consider the reality that intergroup encounters are often characterized by social stratification based on demography, power, and status inequalities.

Identity is Subjective

Most conceptualizations of identity include some assignment to a socially derived category, which exists and accrues meaning only through opposition to other social categories with contrasting features (Giles, Bourhis, & Taylor, 1977); as those contrasting features change, so does one's identity. Given its contextual nature, social identity cannot be discussed meaningfully without contemplating social comparison processes. A review of identity theories (Leets, Giles, & Clément, 1996) demonstrates that conceptualizations of identity have become increasingly subjective and contextual, moving from identity as a result of group affiliation (e.g., SIT) to identity as situated in social relationships (symbolic interactionism) to identity as entirely context dependent (constructivism) to identity as entirely interactive. According to SIT (Tajfel Sc Turner, 1986), to assess social identity one engages in social comparison, but only with those groups whose relative positions in society provide diagnostic information. Put another way, identity guides social comparison at the same time that social comparison refines and reinforces one's self-concept. Identity, therefore, is both subjective and processual and seen as a dialectical interplay between objectivity and subjectivity. Therefore, discussions of identity reasonably situate the person within the individual's social-psychological world, accounting for such subjective assessments as the pride of group membership (ingroup identification), the extent to which the community is a viable group (vitality), and the group's ability to take on characteristics of a dominant group (social boundaries). Ethnolinguistic identity theory (ELIT; e.g., Giles & Johnson, 1981) was, arguably, among the first intergroup communication theories to acknowledge the importance of the sociopsychological climate in which intergroup relations occur. It predicts that if an individual perceives high ingroup identification, cognitive alternatives to ingroup status, strong group vitality, and hard, closed boundaries, intergroup differentiation will occur. It is within this framework that we discuss subjective perceptions of identity and offer propositions for intergroup encounters that could generate future research.

Members of socially derived groups exhibit varying levels of ingroup dependency and solidarity; both of these subjective assessments are not limited to intragroup qualities, however. Group members also make ingroup-outgroup distinctions according to such construals as the ratio of perceived ingroup-outgroup differences (Oakes, Haslam, & Turner, 1994), Indeed, current operationalizations of identity fall along both intra- and intergroup subjective dimensions—attraction to group, depersonalization, perceived self-group interdependency, and intergroup competition (Jackson, 1999). In a study of minority groups in a multigroup setting, it was found that social identity has quite different effects on intergroup bias depending on which subjective dimensions of identity are taken into account. An "open" social identity is composed of ingroup attraction, compatible intergroup goals, positive appraisals by other groups, satisfaction with status quo, and self-reliance and was found to be inversely related to ingroup bias. A "threatened" identity, however, composed of ingroup attraction, self-group interdependency, and intergroup competition, predicted higher levels of intergroup bias and perceived group interdependency (Jackson Sc Smith, 1999).

Regarding dominant groups, although research has shown that strong anti-outgroup views are often held by strongly identified whites, dominant group identity need not be inevitably divisive. Increasing the centrality of the group to one's identity can have a positive impact on intergroup relations. For example, white students who think a lot about being white, and about what they have in common with other white students, were found to demonstrate fewer negative views of conflict about, and report more positive interactions with, various groups of color and support multicultural policies. It is suspected that centrality prompted reflections on power and privilege in critical ways that transformed identities (Gurin, Peng, Lopez, & Nagda, 1999). These findings demonstrate that although much still needs to be learned about social identity for minority and majority group members, the very act of ingroup identification is subjective with varying implications for intergroup relations, as proposed in the following:

Proposition   *la.*

Individuals who are highly dependent on their group, consider it central to their being, feel high solidarity for it, and possess a threatened social identity are likely to perceive intergroup encounters in intergroup terms.

Proposition   *lb.*

Individuals who are not dependent on their group, do not consider it central to their being, feel little solidarity for it, and possess an open social identity are not likely to perceive intergroup encounters in intergroup terms.

As ELIT makes clear, broad, societal forces also impact the subjective experience of identity. The types of sociopsychological processes operating between groups in contact will differ according to whether the groups have high, medium, or low vitality. Vitality, composed of status, demography, and institutional support factors, is both an inherently objective and subjective concept (Harwood, Giles, & Bourhis, 1994). For example, the signing of a treaty is an objective occurrence that is open to subjective interpretations, which correspond to group memberships. As we shall see, those subjective, group-based interpretations may be as—or more—important to intergroup relations than objective differences. Explicitly or implicitly, researchers are using the subjective dimensions of vitality proposed by Giles and colleagues, demonstrating differences in intergroup bias as predicted by group status, size, and power. For example, Jackson (1999) found support for the phenomenon of "the few, the proud" in that participants expressed the most ingroup attraction when the group was small and of high status. In addition, Gurin et al. (1999) found a power differential in that dominant group identity is associated with negative intergroup perceptions, attitudes, and behaviors, and subordinate group identity is associated with positive perceptions of intergroup relations.

Language is another status component of vitality that is increasingly recognized for its subjective qualities and seen less as a static reflection of power than as an "active coplayer in the exercise of power" (Reid & Ng, 1999, p. 120). Although it is true that low-status speakers tend to use powerless forms of language, language can also *create* power as in the case of females who may use low-power language to gain a turn when among males only to establish conversational control. Perhaps it is this strategic use of language that best presents its subjective nature. Reid and Ng (1999) explain that Aborigines cast themselves as "original Australians" in an effort to highlight a need for reparations while also appealing to a superordinate mainstream identity. However, the government response implicitly categorized Aborigines as simply Australians, thereby rejecting their status as a legitimate special interest group. Meanwhile, a study by Tong, Hong, Lee, and Chiu (1999) demonstrated that evaluative reactions to bilingual code switching appear to be governed by norms regarding ingroup-outgroup behavior. When a Hong Kong speaker converged to the official language of the mainland, self-identifying "Hongkongers" evaluated the speaker less favorably than did those who claimed a genuine "Chinese" identity. In addition, the Chinese-identity respondents judged the Hong Kong speaker more favorably when he converged to the mainland language than when he maintained a Hong Kong dialect. Whether the goal is to depoliticize power, as in Australia, or to maintain distinctiveness via language evaluations, as in Hong Kong, language attitudes expressed by dominant and subordinate groups both reflect intergroup relations and shape them, thereby underscoring the dialectical qualities of identity components such as language.

Proposition 2a.

Groups high in vitality will be more likely to express ingroup attraction and negative intergroup perceptions, and they will be more likely to use language strategically to achieve or maintain a positive and distinct social identity.

Proposition 2b.

Groups low in vitality will be less likely to express ingroup attraction and negative intergroup perceptions, and they will be less likely to use language strategically to achieve or maintain a positive and distinct social identity.

It is also critical to assess groups' sociohistorical status, but here, too, perceptions of history are subject to group-based interpretations. In a study of the Maori (Polynesian origins) and Paheka (European origins) in New Zealand, both Maori and Paheka agreed that the Treaty of Waitangi was the most important event in New Zealand history, but only the Maori (the subordinate group) demonstrated ingroup favoritism in their judgments of the treaty (Liu, Wilson, McClure, & Higgins, 1999).

Inevitably, political climates change and research shows that identities change accordingly. For evidence of this, we turn to a variety of studies conducted in Hong Kong during the transition from British to Chinese rule. Brewer (1999) found that the change of sociopolitical context was less problematic for Hongkongers, who see themselves as possessing independent Hong Kong (regional) and Chinese (ethnic) identities, than for the "Hong Kong-Chinese," who see their ethnic identity as nested within their regional identity. Thus, a corresponding shift in self-labeling from Hong *Kong-Chinese* to either *Hongkonger* or *Chinese* is interpreted as an identity conflict for those who saw their regional and ethnic identities as intertwined in a context that now fosters distinctiveness between the two. Similarly, Fu, Lee, Chiu, and Hong (1999) found that the referential meaning of Hongkonger changed when the immediate sociopolitical context changed. When the context called for an essay regarding the Beijing government's policies, "primarily Hongkongers" and "primarily Chinese" demonstrated an intergroup orientation. However, that intergroup orientation was not evident when these same two groups were called on to write about protecting Chinese territory from an external aggressor. In other words, when that referential meaning is made salient, Hongkongers may differentiate from those from the mainland. However, *Hongkonger* may also refer to a subordinate identity nestled within a Chinese entity that, upon activation, may prompt differentiation from those not ethnic Chinese.

Therefore, when the immediate context changes, the frame of reference changes accordingly, and so will referential meanings of identity. Taken together, these findings tell us that not only are perceptions of history subject to group-based interpretations, but efforts at optimal distinctiveness are subject to a shifting political climate, with corresponding shifts in ethnic identity. All of which is further evidence of Liu et al.'s (1999) contention that history can be both a unifying and divisive mechanism for social identity and that the social context should not be treated like a "black box"—something largely outside the scope of intergroup theory.

Proposition   *3.*
Group-based efforts at vitality and positive distinctiveness will prompt interpretations of history and shifts in identity consistent with the sociohis-torical and sociopolitical context.

ELIT contends that another predictor of intergroup bias is the perception of hard, closed group boundaries. We return to Hong Kong to illustrate this process. Indeed, the very method by which individuals make social comparisons in a changing sociopolitical context appears linked to their implicit theories about human character, interpreted herein as subjective assessments of the boundaries of human nature. Hong, Chiu, Yeung, and Tong (1999) found that those who believe that character is a fixed attribute ("entity theorists") used trait-based dimensions in social comparison to achieve group distinctiveness. Such fixed-attribute thinking suggests that entity theorists perceive human nature as having hard and closed intergroup boundaries. In this framework, it makes sense that entity-Hongkongers relied more on economic wealth as a frame of reference than did entity-Chinese, because such a trait-based dimension provided Hongkongers with optimal distinctiveness in their social comparisons. By contrast, "incremental theorists," who subscribe to the view that human attributes and character are malleable, did not display a systematic relationship between their social identity and the weight given to trait-based comparisons. This finding may suggest that incremental theorists perceive human nature as having permeable boundaries. Given the fluid aspect of human nature, therefore, trait-based dimensions do not allow for optimal distinctiveness in social comparisons and, most important, do not mesh with incremental theorists' subjective views of human nature. Therefore:

> *Proposition* 4a.
> The perception of hard, closed boundaries contributes to trait-based intergroup distinctions consistent with cultural values and optimally suited for positive distinctiveness.

> *Proposition* 4b.
> The perception of permeable boundaries is not associated with trait-based intergroup distinctions that conflict with an implicit theory of human nature as malleable and thus are not optimally suited for positive distinctiveness.

This recent intergroup literature reiterates the value of SIT and ELIT in understanding intergroup behavior as well as the ongoing need to frame identity as a concept that is highly variable and subject to the active construction of the individual. In sum, these propositions tell us that because identity is neither fixed nor merely reflective of a given context but rather influenced *by* it, it is logical to surmise that identity is a vibrant phenomenon subject to societal, situational, and communicative forces; just as identity prompts communication, so too does communication create and alter identity.

The Influence of Communication on Identity

Recognizing that identity is not only objective but also subjective, we have stressed that rather than perceiving it as static, identity is continually negotiated. This final section is devoted to furthering our understanding of the transactional relationship between communication and identity. Although identity influences communication, the latter can be critical to identity construction. In their discussion of language, power, and intergroup relations, Reid and Ng (1999) demonstrate that identity is enacted via a communication process that is contextual. For instance, they found that it is the *ability* to take a conversational turn on the floor, not the very language style adopted, that leads to perceptions of higher influence. This suggests that the very root of identity can be found in the process of interaction and should be understood from a contextual perspective.

Given the influence of the immediate context, the relevant state of the individual's "power mosaic" is not so much the community at large but the *communication network* that defines the individual's interpersonal context and identity referents (Leets et al., 1996, p. 135). The empirical challenges of testing it notwithstanding, Hecht (e.g., Hecht & Baldwin, 1998) in his development of a "communication theory of identity" agrees that the individual's speech community serves to create, expand, preserve, validate, and perpetuate language and identity. However, that community must not be divorced from its own origins but instead must remain tied to ancestral, cultural, and linguistic roots. Ebonics and Spanglish, which emanate from and reinforce African and Hispanic cultural goals of linguistic collectivity and separatism, respectively, can be seen as supporting this notion.

The influence of communication on ethnic identity, however, is often overlooked given the focus on individual processing, which fails to address the creation of shared meanings among group members. Indeed, group consensus is either taken for granted or ignored. Only recently have models of social categorization recognized that consensus "is not simply an automatic outcome of intrapsychic processes, but rather results from processes of debate among group members—albeit framed by social cognitive factors" (Sani & Reicher, 1999, p. 280). Recognizing that people who share a salient self-categorization may debate core dimensions of their common social identity, Sani and Reicher (1999) examined the split in the Church of England that took place as a result of the ordination of women. They hypothesized that the anti-ordination group would perceive the inclusion of women clergy as contradicting the very essence of the group's identity, such that consensus with pro-ordination church members would be blocked and differences nonnegotiable. Indeed, debate between the "pros" and "antis" on an identity-relevant matter was significant enough that people perceived they could not be members of the same group, and a schism resulted. Communication created identity.

Communication, in the form of labels, also shapes identity, each in its own way (Tanno, 1994). Think of the various labels that represent a Hispanic identity. *Spanish* designates ancestral origin, *Mexican American* describes a dual cultural background, *Latina* represents historical connectedness to others of Spanish descent, and *Chicana* suggests a political perspective. Because no label exists outside of its relational meaning, these and other ethnic labels construct relational meaning within communication episodes. Just as we may communicate our identities to others, they are also very much tied to the way that others represent our interests, and when created identities are incongruent, they must be renegotiated (Martin & Nakayama, 1997).

In an explicit attempt to bring awareness to the experiences of older women, Paoletti (1998) examined the construction of older women's identities in Perugia, Italy, who took part in the European Older Women's Project. Her analysis shows how they resisted age-group memberships. Aware that the label *old* is value laden, rejection of it is particularly evident in the women's discussion of their group name. The moniker chosen, the Italian Association of Active/Older Women, is an indication that these elderly women wished to communicate a more positive identity.

We turn (and, in one case, return) to two theories that further our understanding of communication-identity linkages. Social dominance theory (SDT), a macro explanation of the human predisposition toward group-based social hierarchies, *implicitly* (albeit far from explicitly) places communication squarely in the middle of its framework in the form of legitimizing myths (Sidanius & Pratto, The theory begins with group status, sex/gender, socialization, and temperament, which are seen as contributing to a social dominance orientation. That orientation then leads to the communication of legitimizing myths, which have a reciprocal relationship with individual and institutional discrimination, behavior, and group-based social hierarchy. Therefore, group-based inequality is created and re-created through the language of legitimizing myths that provide moral and intellectual justification for social hierarchies. Hierarchy-enhancing myths include ideologies such as racism, manifest destiny, and internal attributions for being *poor*, and hierarchy-attenuating myths include ideologies such as feminism, liberation theology, and themes in the American Declaration of Independence. An assumption of SDT is that conflict between hierarchy-enhancing and hierarchy-attenuating forces yields a relatively stable social system that always entails some sort of group-based hierarchical arrangement. As much as legitimizing myths (e.g., the U.S. meritocracy) contribute to dominance and subordination, communication can be seen as creating social identities and the tension between opposing myths as maintaining them. SDT does not explicitly address how a social dominance orientation may be a product of communication, making only minimal references to socialization processes of education and stigmatization.

CAT affords insight, also perhaps implicitly, into the transactional relationship between communication and identity. In addition to demonstrating how identity influences communication, acts of convergence and divergence (see Table 9.2) communicate the strength of group identity in intergroup encounters (positive, moderate, and negative). Accordingly, divergence or convergence is largely driven by group identity, and these very social actions communicate how individuals feel about their group identities. In an effort to promote their distinctiveness, those whose groups have a positive social identity are more likely to diverge in intergroup encounters in an effort to demonstrate their distinctiveness.

Keeping in mind that communication may entail nonverbal, language, and paralanguage components, group members may use a myriad of communicative expressions. A most extreme form of groups communicating their positive, identity is crowd behavior (protesting, pushing, shouting). This act of divergent communication implies group members feel strongly about their group membership, such that they are willing to engage in physical confrontation (Drury & Reicher, 1999). Similarly, subordinate and dominant groups may use *etknophaulisms* (ethnic slurs) when referring to outgroups in an attempt to differentiate their group and communicate a positive social identity (Mullen, Rozell, & Johnson, 2000). Conversely, subordinate groups who have a negative social identity are likely to converge to the dominant group (Giles & Johnson, 1981). Positive allocation bias, discrimination against outgroups when the outcomes involve the allocation of positive resources (e.g., money or praise), is a form of ingroup bias that communicates negative group identity for the outgroup (Jackson, 1999).

Acquiring the outgroup's language can also communicate negative social identity. Moreover, ingroup members who attempt to maintain a positive group identity through language may have disdain for ingroup members who adopt the outgroup language. When Hogg, D'Agata, and Abrams (1989) investigated the perceptions of ingroup members speaking the dominant outgroup's language, they found that the more people identified with their cultural ingroup, the more likely they were to have negative feelings toward fellow ingroupers who spoke the dominant group's language. Adjustments in accent, dialect, idioms, and speech rate may function in the same fashion. Groups may accentuate their accent in order to positively distinguish their group membership, whereas outgroups who have a negative social identity may attenuate their accent or dialect in an effort to appear similar to the dominant group (Burt, 1998). These examples all lend support to the notion that accommodation is a primary form of identity expression.

Regardless of the actual communicative act, accommodation is fundamental to identity construction. However, consistent with our claim of identity being subjective, individuals' accommodation will vary as a function of ingroup identity and group vitality (Giles & Coupland, 1991). Even so, as group members (be they subordinate or dominant) accommodate their communication, they continue to influence, shape, create, and re-create their identity. The scope of accommodation, though, can be broadened to include a *rhetorical* element. That is,

Table 9.2 Communicating Identity

	NONVERBAL BEHAVIOR	LANGUAGE	PARALANGUAGE
Positive social identity	Crowd behavior Conflict Physical boundaries Outgroup rejection Ethnophaulisms Negative allocation bias Symbols	Patronizing speech Ingroup language with normal speech rate Non-language acquisition identity Labels	Accent, dialect, idioms, speech rate, pauses, utterance length, phonological variants can all be modified to signal positive social identity
Moderate social identity	Smiling, gaze, gestures Time	Ingroup language with slow speech rate Conversation interruptions Conversation turn taking Sarcasm, hostility, disagreement Code switching Language intensity Topic choice	Accent, dialect, idioms, speech rate, pauses, utterance length, phonological variants can all be modified to signal moderate social identity Laughter
Negative social identity	Ingroup rejection Positive allocation bias Assimilation	Outgroup language with native·like pronunciation Outgroup language with features of ingroup pronunciation Language acquisition	Information density Self-disclosure

literal dialogue, argument, and debate are also critical to identity. SIT theorists have placed heavy emphasis on socially shared perceptions among group members. Potential intragroup dynamics are often ignored or similarity among group members is taken for granted (see Oakes et al., 1994). Yet, as Sani and Reicher (1999) explain, "by excluding the rhetorical dimension, we exclude the possibility that group members may differ even on core issues such as whether a given stance supports, subverts, or is irrelevant to the essence of group identity" (p. 296). In their analysis of the split in the Church of England mentioned above, these authors highlight the significance of the rhetorical element in communicating identity. Clearly, members of the Church of England had different conceptions of church identity, including that which produced a schism between members. These findings highlight the serious attention that must be paid to the rhetorical process in which groups engage.

Conclusion

Our goal has been to introduce and detail the transactional relationship between communication and identity. To do so, we have drawn on the social-psychological and communication literatures. Moreover, our strong theoretical underpinning provides insights into both identity and communication. The theories reviewed provide an extensive view of different levels and dimensions of identity. Similarly, we were able to demonstrate a multitude of communicative expressions. Communication does not refer just to language. Instead, actions, rules, behavior, discrimination, and labels are all communicative. Above all, we encourage those who are interested in the relationship between communication and identity to not only include "objective" notions of identity in their own research and theorizing but also consider the "subjective" aspect of identity. All this cannot be understood without consideration of context, history, and status between the conversants. If we can stress anything (see Figure 12.1), it is that identity and communication are mutually reinforcing.

References

Aberson, C. L., Healy, M., Sc Romero, V. (2000). Ingroup bias and self-esteem: A meta-analysis. *Personality and Social Psychology Review, 4,* 157–173.

Brewer, M. (1999). Multiple identities and identity transition: Implications for Hong Kong. *International journal of Intercultural Relations, 23,* 187–197.

SUMMARY

Understanding your different identities, including your cultural identity, is a key factor in studying intercultural communication. Identity is co-created with others through communication and is a multi-layered concept. While you may identify as a specific identity with one group, your identity may change with another group. For example, at the beginning of the chapter we mentioned that you may identify as a student while speaking with your instructor but later identify as a pianist while speaking with other musicians.

In this chapter we explored both cultural identity and identity. Our first reading provided us with an overview of several different approaches to studying cultural identity and introduced us to cultural identity research. Our second reading expanded on our first reading by defining identity and explaining that identity is a process of negotiating and renegotiating. Finally, our last selection explored identity creation further by delving into some of the more popular theories used by cultural researchers to study identity and examining the contextual elements in identify formation. Continue on to the discussion questions to apply your knowledge about cultural identity.

DISCUSSION QUESTIONS

1. How is an individual's cultural identity established? Are there certain aspects of a cultural identity that are determined by forces outside the control of the individual? What communication challenges face an individual seeking to create a different cultural identity?
2. What are the characteristics of *in-groups* and *outsiders*? How and when is positive communication between these groups challenged? What strategies might be helpful in bridging the communication challenges between these groups?
3. What aspects of cultural identity are objective? What aspects are subjective? Which seem to be the most dominant? Why?

CONFLICT AND NEGOTIATION

CHAPTER 10

STUDY OBJECTIVES

After completing this chapter, you will be able to:
- Identify different intercultural conflicts.
- Describe and explain the differences between individualistic and collectivistic conflict styles.
- Demonstrate and display effective conflict management.

INTRODUCTION

onflict is everywhere. If you watch the news, read the newspaper, or go online to a news source, you can see many examples of conflict on a daily basis. Conflict isn't necessarily always a bad thing; conflict can be both positive and negative. In an ideal world, during a conflict, all parties would be heard and everyone would leave satisfied after the conflict resolution. However, that is rarely ever the case when it comes to conflict. As culture can play a large role in conflict, it is important to understand what types of intercultural conflict can occur and how to manage conflict effectively.

In this chapter, our readings focus on intercultural conflict and negotiating. The first section in this chapter highlights a few different types of intercultural conflict. The second reading in this chapter reveals role differences in conflict styles between opposing cultures. Here individualistic and collectivistic cultures' conflict interaction styles are examined to expose to differences. After you have finished with this section, the next reading provides best practices to achieve effective conflict management. Finally, we have included a reading from a research study examining both sides of an intercultural conflict between German and Moroccan businesses. At the end of the chapter you will find discussion questions to test and apply your knowledge about intercultural conflict.

Moving Forward

Conflict occurs when two opposing opinions, or sides, disagree about the best resolution for a given situation. Conflict is often problematic. There are many kinds of conflict, and although conflict can be healthy, when it comes to intercultural communication, we tend to have negative reactions to conflict. Our first reading examines different types of intercultural conflict that are difficult to resolve. As you move through this reading, think of time when you experienced each of the conflicts the authors mention. How were the conflicts resolved?

RESOLVING INTERCULTURAL CONFLICTS

Our review summarizes and integrates existing research on interpersonal conflicts that are difficult to resolve. Research indicates that interpersonal conflicts can adversely impact families, individual health, team functioning, and intercultural relations. Hence, we need to better understand protracted disputes. We focus on two research programs directly related to interpersonal conflict (serial arguments and perpetual problems) and a third area of research that takes a macro approach to studying intractable conflict. We combine elements of the three approaches into an integrative framework that suggests nine questions worthy of future research.

Significance of Review

Conflict arises from incompatible activity (Deutsch, 1973) and comprises a frequent form of human interaction. Researchers have studied it in a variety of contexts (see Oetzel & Ting-Toomey, 2006), focusing on units of analysis ranging from the individual to the culture (see Roloff, 1988). This review concentrates on research regarding interpersonal conflicts that are difficult to resolve. Although a great deal of research on interpersonal conflict has been conducted in the context of close relationships (see Roloff & Soule, 2002), as Roloff noted, it has also been explored in other contexts such as group, organizational, and intercultural settings. Consequently, this topic interests many scholars across varied research specializations. Furthermore, research demonstrates that interpersonal conflict can have serious effects. Although scholars have long argued that interpersonal conflict can be functional (e.g., Wilmot & Hocker, 2001), evidence suggests that participants often characterize interpersonal conflict as a negative event (e.g., McCorkle & Mills, 1992). Ongoing, irresolvable interpersonal disputes can be especially problematic. We will briefly illustrate the negative outcomes in the following contexts: families, health care, organizations, intercultural contacts, religion, and political and ethnonational conflicts.

Family conflict can negatively affect the entire family. Marital arguments can be stressful for spouses (see Kiecolt-Glaser & Newton, 2001) and for children who observe the arguments (see Davies & Cummings, 1998). Marital conflict can adversely impact parenting behaviors (Krishnakumar & Buehler, 2000) and everyday interactions with children (Almeida, Wethington, & Chandler, 1999). Sibling conflict commonly occurs, even into adulthood

(Bedford, 1998; Stewart, Verbrugge, & Beilfuss, 1998). Adolescent sibling conflict has been linked to increased risk of anxiety, depression, and delinquent behavior (Stocker, Burwell, & Briggs, 2002). Caughlin and Vangelisti (2006) and Sillars, Canary, and Tafoya (2004) provided recent reviews of conflict communication in dating and marital relationships, and Koerner and Fitzpatrick (2006) reviewed research on family conflict communication.

Health communication researchers are increasingly interested in the aversive health effects of arguing. Conflict poses negative implications for individuals' psychological (e.g., Bolger, DeLongis, Kessler, & Schilling, 1989; Finch & Zautra, 1992) and physical well-being (e.g., Kiecolt-Glaser et al., 1993). For example, conflict can result in decreased vitality, increased physical symptoms (Reis, Sheldon, Gable, Roscoe, & Ryan, 2000), and anxiety and depression (Abbey, Abramis, & Caplan, 1985). According to Kiecolt-Glaser et al., intense negative affect expressed during conflict has been directly connected to decreases in immune functioning as well as increases in blood pressure. More specifically, irresolvable conflicts can harm individuals' health. Malis and Roloff (2006b) found that individuals who tended to believe that an ongoing argument in their relationship was not likely to be solved more likely experienced negative health consequences.

Health communication scholars also have discussed the difficult conflicts that can occur over decisions about limiting or withholding life-sustaining treatments (e.g., Breen, Abernethy, Abbott, & Tulsky, 2001) and deciding appropriate treatment plans (e.g., Back & Arnold, 2005; Iecovich, 2000). For example, in Breen and colleagues' study, health care providers perceived conflict in 78% of decisions regarding life-sustaining treatments for critically ill patients. Iecovich argued that patients' families often disagree with the treatment and care that their elderly family members receive in health care settings.

Furthermore, these conflicts can be exacerbated by cultural differences. For example, in a study of Chinese immigrants in Canada with medically unexplained chronic fatigue and weakness, the majority of respondents reported that they did not want others to know about their experiences of chronic fatigue (Lee, Rodin, Devins, & Weiss, 2001). Participants referenced a cultural rule against disclosing failures to others. They feared being labeled as lazy as opposed to suffering from a medical condition. Respondents also reported that disclosure of their symptoms could result in difficulty finding mates and disgrace their entire families, especially if others defined their conditions as mental problems. According to Lee et al., this conflict intensified patients' distress levels and prevented them from utilizing some treatment options, such as mental health services.

Further, prior research has demonstrated negative outcomes of interpersonal conflict in work groups and management teams, especially those conflicts that are perceived as unresolved (Gayle & Preiss, 1998). For example, Jehn and Chatman (2000) discovered that relationship and process conflict within management teams negatively relate to commitment, cohesiveness, satisfaction, and individual performance. Relationship conflict centers on personal and social issues not tied to work. Process conflict focuses on issues such as task strategy and delegation of duties. Furthermore, a recent meta-analysis determined that task conflict arising from group consideration of alternative solutions to a problem also can impede group performance (De Dreu & Weingart, 2003). Additionally, lengthy disputes in work groups and management teams cost considerable time and effort because conflict impedes group members' abilities to gather, integrate, and adequately assess valuable information (Jehn, 1995). Poole and Garner

(2006), Nicotera and Dorsey (2006), and Lipsky and Seeber (2006) have offered reviews of organizational conflict and communication.

Intercultural conflicts can be particularly difficult to manage because "misunderstanding, and from this counterproductive pseudoconflict, arises when members of one culture are unable to understand culturally determined differences in communication practices, traditions, and thought processing" (Borisoff & Victor, 1998, p. 152). For example, in a comparative study of China, Germany, Japan, and the United States, Oetzel and Ting-Toomey (2003) found that the degree to which a culture is individualistic or collectivistic directly and indirectly influences the conflict management styles that cultures tend to favor. Face concerns accounted for much of the variance in conflict management styles. Meanings of particular styles of conflict management differ across cultures (Kozan, 1997), and such differences can lead to or exacerbate negative intergroup encounters resulting in negative stereotypes (e.g., Stephan, Diaz-Loving, & Duran, 2000). Oetzel, Arcos, Mabizela, Weinman, and Zhang (2006) and Ting-Toomey and Takai (2006) provided reviews of intercultural conflict communication.

Moving Forward

There are many different types of conflict. One of these types of conflict that was not mentioned in our first reading is intergroup conflict. The next selection is a brief reading focusing on intergroup conflicts. As you move throughout this reading, consider a time that you personally may have experienced intergroup conflict; whether in an organizational group or during a time you lived somewhere with a different cultural group for a period of time. During this conflict, did you experience any anxiety or nervousness like the authors mentioned?

INTERGROUP CONFLICT

What determines the nature of intergroup conflict? Intergroup threats are present when individuals experience anxiety about interacting with outgroups (Tajfel, 1981). Individuals tend to experience high levels of anxiety if there has been little prior contact with or knowledge about outgroup members. Conversely, anxiety also results from a history of intergroup hostility and competition, especially if one group has been in a minority or low-status position. This is evident in recent international conflicts (e.g., Bosnia, Middle East) as well as interracial relations in the United States. Anxiety about interaction also is related to ethnocentricity. Being able to only see your own country or groups' point of view is ethnocentrism. When people want to show solidarity with an ingroup, communication tends to converge and when differences between ingroups and outgroups are being expressed, communication tends to diverge

(Giles & Coupland, 1991). Research by Hecht et al. (2003) revealed that satisfaction in ingroup conversations depends on feeling you have some power or control over the conversation as well as the establishment of relational solidarity; satisfaction with outgroup conversations is contingent on establishing common ground through the communication of acceptance, shared world view, not stereotyping, and understanding.

Moving Forward

This next reading discusses how different cultures interact with each other during conflict. As you previously have observed throughout this book, culture is dynamic. When two differing cultures clash, it can be difficult for the conflict to have a resolution and end. The following reading examines how conflict differs for individualistic cultures and collectivistic cultures. As you move through this reading, identify how you respond and interact in a conflict.

CULTURAL CONFLICT STYLES

In a conflict situation, individualists typically rely heavily on direct requests, direct verbal justifications, and upfront clarifications to defend one's action or decision. In contrast, collectivists typically use qualifiers ("Perhaps we should meet this deadline together"), tag questions ("Don't you think we might not have enough time"), disclaimers ("I'm probably wrong but …"), tangential response ("Let's not worry about that now"), and indirect requests ("If it won't be too much trouble, let's try to finish this report together") to make a point in the subtle, conflict face-threatening situation. From the collectivistic orientation, it is up to the interpreter of the message to pick up the hidden meaning or intention of the message and to respond either indirectly or equivocally. In addition, in an intense conflict situation, many collectivists believe that verbal messages can often times compound the problem. However, by not using verbal means to explain or clarify a decision, collectivists are often viewed as "inscrutable."

Silence is viewed as demanding immense self-discipline in a collectivistic conflict situation. On the other hand, silence can be viewed as an admission of guilt or incompetence in an individualistic culture. In addition, while open emotional expression during a stressful conflict situation often times is viewed as a signal of caring in an individualistic culture, proper emotional composure and emotional self-restraint are viewed as signals of a mature, self-discipline person in most collectivistic, Asian cultures. In comparing verbal and nonverbal exchange processes in Japan and the United States, Okabe (1983) summarizes:

The digital is more characteristic of the [North] American mode of communication. …The Japanese language is more inclines toward the analogical; its use of ideographic characters…and its emphasis on the nonverbal aspect. The excessive dependence of the Japanese on the nonverbal aspect of communication means that Japanese culture tends to view the verbal as only a means of communication, and that the nonverbal and the extra-verbal at times assume greater importance than the verbal dimension of communication. This is in sharp contrast to the view of Western rhetoric and communication that the verbal, especially speech, is the dominant means of expression (p. 38).

In short, in the individualistic cultures, the conflict-management process relies heavily on verbal offense and defense to justify one's position, to clarify one's opinion, to build up one's credibility, to articulate one's emotions, and to raise objections if one disagrees with someone else's proposal. In collectivistic conflict situations, ambiguous, indirect verbal messages often are used with the intention of saving mutual face, saving group face, or protecting someone else's face. In addition, subtle nonverbal gestures or nonverbal silence is often used to signal a sense of cautionary restraint toward the conflict situation. The use of deep-level silence can also reflect a sense of resignation and acceptance of the fatalistic aspect of the conflict situation. The higher the person is in positional power in a collectivistic culture, the more likely she or he will use silence as a deliberate, cautionary conflict strategy.

In terms of the relationship between the norm of fairness and cross-cultural conflict interaction style, results from past research (Leung & Bond, 1984; Leung & Iwawaki. 1988) indicate that individualists typically prefer to use the equity norm (selfdeservingness norm) in dealing with reward allocation in group conflict interaction. In comparison, collectivists oftentimes prefer to use the equality norm (the equal distribution norm) to deal with ingroup members and thus avoid group disharmony. However, like their individualistic cohorts, collectivists prefer the application of the equity norm (the self-deservingness norm) when competing with members of outgroups, especially when the conflict involves competition for scarce resources in the system.

Findings in many past conflict studies also indicate that individuals do exhibit quite consistent cross-situational styles of conflict negotiation in different cultures. While dispositional, relationship, or conflict salient factors also play a critical part in conflict-management patterns, culture assumes the primary role of conflict-style socialization process. Based on the theoretical assumptions of the "I" identity and the "we" identity, and the concern of self-face maintenance versus mutual-face maintenance in the two contrastive cultural systems, findings across cultures (China, Japan, Korea, Taiwan, Mexico, and the United States) dearly indicate that individualists tend to use competitive control conflict styles in managing conflict., while collectivists tend to use integrative or compromising conflict styles in dealing with conflict. In addition, collectivists also tend to use more obliging and avoiding conflict styles in task-oriented conflict situations (Chua & Gudykunst, 1987; Leung. 1988; Ting-Toomey et al. 1991; Trubisky, Ting-Toomey, & Lin, 1991).

Different results have also been uncovered concerning ingroup and outgroup conflict in the collectivistic cultures. For example. Cole's (1989) study reveals thatJapanese students in the United States tend to use obliging strategies more with members of ingroups than with members of outgroups. They also tend to actually use more competitive strategies with outgroup members than ingroup members. In addition, the status of the ingroup person plays a critical role in the collectivistic conflict process.

Previous research (Ting-Toomey et at., 1991) suggests that status affects the conflict-management styles people use with members of their ingroup. For example. in a collectivistic culture, while a high-status person can challenge the position or opinion of a low-status person, it is a norm violation for a low-status person to directly rebut or question the position or the opinion of the high-status person, especially in the public arena. Again. the issue of face maintenance becomes critical in high-low-status conflict interaction. The low-status person should always learn to "give face" or protect the face of the high-status person in times of stressful situations or crises. In return, the high-status person will enact a reciprocal face-protection system that automatically takes care of the low-status person in different circumstances.

Overall. the preferences for a direct conflict style, for the use of the equity norm and for the direct settlement of disputes reflect the salience of the "I" identity in individualistic, HC cultures; while preferences for an indirect conflict style, for the use of the equality norm, and for the use of informal mediation procedures reflect the salience of the "we" identity in the collectivistic, HC cultures. In individualistic, LC cultures, a certain degree of conflict in a system is viewed as potentially functional and productive. In collectivistic, HC cultures in which group harmony and consultative decision-making are prized, overt expressions of interpersonal conflict are highly avoided and suppressed. Instead, nonverbal responsiveness, indirect verbal strategies, the use of informal intermediaries, and the use of cautionary silence are some of the typical collectivistic ways of dealing with interpersonal conflict.

Stella Ting-Toomey, *Intercultural Communication: A Reader, ed. Larry Samovar and Richard Porter,* pp. 366–368. Copyright © 1993 by Cengage Learning, Inc. Reprinted with permission.

Moving Forward

Our next reading presents best practices of effective conflict management for both individualistic and collectivistic cultures. As you know, culture can play a large role when it comes to conflict. Understanding how another culture may perceive and handle the conflict can be beneficial to all parties involved and may hasten the conflict's end. As you move through this next reading, consider how you can implement these best practices into your conflict-resolution style.

MANAGING CONFLICT

Effective Conflict Management

Effective conflict management requires us to communicate effectively, appropriately, and creatively in different conflict interactive situations. Effective conflict management requires us to be knowledgeable and respectful of different worldviews and ways of dealing with a conflict situation. It requires us to be sensitive to the differences and similarities between low-context and high-context communication patterns and to attune to the implicit negotiation rhythms of monochronic-based and poly-chronic-based individuals.

Effects conflict management also requires the awareness of the importance of both goal-oriented and process-oriented conflict negotiation pathways, and requires that we pay attention to the dose relationship between cultural variability and different conflict communication styles. For both individualists and collectivises, the concept of "mindfulness" can serve as the first effective step in raising our awareness of the differences and similarities in cross-cultural conflict-negotiation processes. Langer's (1989) concept of mindfulness helps individuals to tune-in conscientiously to their habituated mental scripts and expectations. According to Langer, if mindlessness is the "rigid reliance on old categories, mindfulness means the continual creation of new ones. Categorization and recategorization, labeling and relabeling as one masters the world are processes natural to children" (p. 63). To engage in a mindfulness state, an individual needs to learn to (a) create new categories, (b) be open to new information, and (c) be aware that multiple perspectives typically exist in viewing a basic event (Langer, 1989, p, 62).

Creating new categories means that one should not be boxed in by one's rigid stereotypic label concerning cultural strangers. One has to learn to draw out commonalities between self and cultural strangers and also learn to appreciate the multi-faceted aspects of the individuals to whom the stereotypic label is applied. In order to create new categories, one has to be open to new information. New information relies strongly on responsible sharing and responsive listening behavior.

Some specific suggestions can be made based on differences in individualistic and collectivistic styles of conflict management. These suggestions, however, are not listed in order of importance. *To deal with conflict effectively in the collectivistic culture, individualists need to:*

1. Be mindful of the face-maintenance assumptions of conflict situations that take place in this culture. Conflict competence resides in the strategic skills of managing the delicate interaction balance of humiliation and pride, and shame and honor. The face moves of one-up and one-down in a conflict episode, the use of same status negotiators, and the proprieties and decorum of gracious "face fighting" have to be strategically staged with the larger group audience in mind.

2. Be proactive in dealing with low-grade conflict situations (such as by using informal consultation or the "go between" method) before they escalate into runaway, irrevocable mutual face-loss episodes. Individualists should try to realize that by helping their opponent to save face, they may also enhance their own face. Face is, intrinsically, a bilateral concept in the group-based, collectivistic culture.

3. "Give face" and try not to push their opponent's bade against the wall with no room for maneuvering face loss or face recovery. Learn to let their opponent find a gracious way out of the conflict situation if at all possible, without violating the basic spirit of fundamental human rights. They should also learn self-restraint and try not to humiliate their opponent in the public arena or slight her or his public reputation. For colleaivists, the concept of "giving face" typically operates on a long-range, reciprocal interaction system. Bilateral face-giving and face-saving ensures a continuous, interdependent networking process of favor-giving and favor concessions—especially along a long-term, historical time sense.

4. Be sensitive to the importance of quiet, mindful observation. Individualists need to be mindful of the historical past that bears relevance to the present conflict situation. Restrain from asking too many "why" questions. Since collectivistic, LC cultures typically focus on the nonverbal "how" process, individualists need to learn to experience and manage the conflict process on the implicit, nonverbal pacing level Use deep-level silence, deliberate pauses, and patient conversational turn-taking in conflict interaction processes with collectivists.

5. Practice attentive listening skills and feel the copresence of the other person. In Chinese characters, hearing or *wun* (問) means "opening the door to the ears," while the word *listening* or ting (聽) means attending to the other person with your "ears, eyes, and heart Listening means, in the Chinese character, attending to the sounds, movements, and feelings of the other person. Patient and deliberate listening indicates that one person is attending to the other person's needs even if it is an antagonistic conflict situation.

6. Discard the Western-based model of effective communication skills in dealing with conflict situations in the collectivistic, HC cultures. Individualists should learn to use qualifiers, disclaimers, tag questions, and tentative statements to convey their point of view. In refusing a request, learn not to use a blunt "no" as a response because the word "no" is typically perceived as carrying high face-threat value in the collectivistic culture. Use situational or self-effacing accounts ("Perhaps someone else is more qualified than I am in working on this project"), counterquestions ("Don't you feel someone else is more competent to work on this project …"), or conditional statements ("Yes, but …") to convey the implicit sense of refusal.

7. Let go of a conflict situation if the conflict party does not want to deal with it directly. A cooling period sometimes may help to mend a broken relationship and the substantive issue may be diluted over a period of time. Individualists should remember that avoidance is part of the integral, conflict style that is commonly used in the collectivistic, LC cultures. Avoidance does not necessarily mean that collectivists do not care to resolve the conflict In all likelihood, the use of avoidance is strategically used to avoid face-threatening interaction and is meant to maintain face harmony and mutual face dignity.

In sum, individualists need to learn to respect the HC, collectivistic ways of approaching and handling conflicts. They need to continuously monitor their ethnocentric biases on the cognitive, affective, and behavioral reactive levels, and learn to listen attentively, and observe mindfully and reflectively.

Some specific suggestions also can be made for collectivists in handling conflict with individualists. *When encountering a conflict situation in an individualistic, LC culture, collectivists need to:*

1. Be mindful of the problem-solving assumptions. The ability to separate the relationship from the conflict problem is critical to effective conflict negotiation in an individualistic, LC culture. Collectivists need to learn to compartmentalize the task dimension and the socioemotional dimension of conflict.

2. Focus on resolving the substantive issues of the conflict, and learn to openly express opinions or points of view. Collectivists should try not to cake the conflict issues to the personal level, and learn to maintain distance between the person and the conflict

problem. In addition, try not to be offended by the upfront, individualistic style of managing conflict. Learn to emphasize tangible outcomes and develop concrete actions plans in implementing the conflict-decision proposal.

3. Engage in an assertive, leveling style of conflict behavior. Assertive style emphasizes the rights of both individuals to speak up in a conflict situation and to respect each other's right to defend her or his position. Collectivists need to learn to open a conflict dialogue with an upfront thesis statement, and then develop the key point systematically, with examples, evidence, figures, or a well-planned proposal. In addition, collectivists need to be ready to accept criticisms, counterproposals, and suggestions for modification as part of the ongoing, group dialogue.

4. Own individual responsibility for the conflict decision-making process. Owning responsibility and using "I" statements to describe feelings in an ongoing conflict situation constitute part of effective conflict-management skills in an individualistic, LC culture. Collectivists need to learn to verbally explain a situation more fully and learn not to expect others to infer their points of view: Assume a sender-based approach to resolving conflict; ask more "why" questions and probe for explanations and details.

5. Provide verbal feedback and engage in active listening skills. Active listening skills, in the individualistic, LC culture, means collectivists have to engage in active verbal perception checking and to ensure that the other person is interpreting their points accurately. Collectivists need to use verbal paraphrases, summary statements, and interpretive messages to acknowledge and verify the storyline of the conflict situation. Learn to occasionally self-disclose feelings and emotions; they cannot rely solely on nonverbal, intuitive understanding to "intuit" and evaluate a situation.

6. Use direct, integrative verbal messages that clearly convey their concern over both the relational and substantive issues of a conflict situation. Collectivists should also not wait patiently for clear turn-taking pauses in the conflict interaction, as individualistic conversation typically allows overlap talks, simultaneous messages, and floor-grabbing behavior. Collectivists also may not want to engage in too many deliberate silent moments as individualists will infer that as incompetence or inefficient use of time.

7. Commit to working out the conflict situation with die conflict party Collectivists should learn to use task-oriented integrative strategies and try to work out a collaborative, mutual goal dialogue with the conflict party. Work on managing individual defensiveness and learn to build up trust on the one-to-one level of interaction. Finally, confirm the conflict person through explicit relationship reminders and metacommunication talks, while simultaneously working on resolving the conflict substantive issues, responsibly and constructively.

In sum, collectivists need to work on their ethnocentric biases as much as the individualists need to work out their sense of egocentric superiority. Collectivists need to untangle their historical sense of cultural superiority—especially in thinking that their way is the only "civilized" way to appropriately deal with conflict. Both individualists and collectivists need to be mindful of their cognitive, affective, and behavioral blinders that they bring into a conflict-mediation situation. They need to continuously learn new and novel ideas in dealing with the past, present, and the future for the purpose of building a peaceful community that is inclusive in all ethnic and cultural groups.

In being mindful of the potential differences between individualistic, LC and collectivistic, HC conflict styles, the intercultural peacemaking process can begin by affirming and valuing such differences as diverse human options in resolving some fundamental, human communication phenomenon. While it is not necessary that one should completely switch one's basic conflict style in order to adapt to the other person's behavior, mutual attuning and responsive behavior in signalling the willingness to learn about each other's cultural norms and rules may be a first major step toward a peaceful resolution process. In addition, conflicting parties from diverse ethnic or cultural backgrounds can learn to work on collaborative task projects and strive toward reaching a larger-than-self, community goal.

To be a peacemaker in the intercultural arena, one has to be first at peace with one's self and one's style. Thus, die artificial switching of one's style may only bring artificial results. Creative peacemakers must learn first to affirm and respect the diverse values that exist as part of the rich spectrum of the basic human experience. They may then choose to modify their behavior to adapt to the situation at hand. Finally, they may integrate diverse sets of values and behaviors, and be able to move in and out of different relational and cultural conflict boundaries. Creative peacemakers can be at ease and at home with the marginal stranger in their search toward common human peace. *Peace* means, on a universal level, a condition or a state of tranquility—with an absence of oppressed thoughts, feelings, and actions, from one heart to another, and from one nation state to another nation state.

———————————

Stella Ting-Toomey, *Intercultural Communication: A Reader*, ed. *Larry Samovar and Richard Porter*, pp. 368–371. Copyright © 1993 by Cengage Learning, Inc. Reprinted with permission.

Moving Forward

Our last reading for this chapter is from research reporting on conflicts that occurred between German and Moroccan businesses. You will read about the source of conflict for both German and Moroccan businesses and about how they resolved the conflicts. The conflicts experienced in the following reading are real, and the quotations that you read are from real individuals. Knowing what you know about conflict, what sort of suggestions would you give to both the German and Moroccan businesses?

CONFLICTS BETWEEN GERMAN AND MOROCCAN BUSINESSES

In order to explore the relationships between Moroccan and German businesses, a series of interviews was conducted between July 2000 and January 2002 (see Scherle 2004, 2006). A qualitative approach is especially well suited to sensitive and thorough analysis of culturally oriented research problems (Wiseman and Koester 1993; Kopp 2003). Qualitative methods are increasingly emerging as popular and powerful methods for exploring business practices in the tourism sector (Watkins and Bell 2002; Davies 2003; Bastakis *et al.* 2004). In total over 60 interviews were completed and during these interviews business attribute data were collected alongside information on their bipartite business relations with partners in Germany and Morocco respectively. In both samples, over 50 per cent were established businesses that had been operating for over ten years, over 60 per cent had less than 50 employees, and there were similarities in the levels of professional training (Table 10.1). Few had direct training in inter-cultural business management. Nevertheless, all but one German business had been co-operating for over a year, there was a relatively even spread of the durations of inter-cultural co-operations among firms in the two samples, and approximately 60 per cent of the individual German and Moroccan respondents had experience of intercultural business relations. Not indicated on this table, though, was that the primary mechanism for co-operation among the participating tour operators was a non-contractual arrangement, a collaboration form that allowed its actors an optimum of flexibility.

On the basis of the writings on inter-cultural management strategies and cultural conflict resolution outlined above, two broad sets of issues emerged as significant which are reported in more depth below: the sources of conflicts for the German and Moroccan interviewees in their collaborations with their Moroccan and German counterparts respectively, and the methods of conflict resolution.

Sources of Conflict for German businesses

For the German respondents, the most frequently mentioned sources of conflict were adherence to time agreements for meetings and the way in which Moroccan businesses dealt with disputes (Table 10.2). For 20 per cent of German respondents, there were problems associated with how business was conducted on the Moroccan side in terms of attitudes to and style of invoicing, employee motivation and the general conduct of business transactions.

German business persons perceived conflicts in how their Moroccan partners connected their organisational behaviours to their religious and cultural practices. Ramadan, the month of fasting, and its implications for co-operation, was a particular and frequent source of contention. Moroccan working practices were comparatively rigid, a feature which becomes more significant around major religious festivals and events. As the manageress of a small incentive operator observed, Ramadan impacts not only on the potential to conduct 'everyday business', it is perceived to have a direct impact on person-to-person interactions:

Table 10.1 A comparison of the main attributes of the German and Moroccan respondents

ATTRIBUTES	GERMAN RESPONDENTS NO. (%)		MOROCCAN RESPONDENTS NO. (%)	
Average age of business (years)				
< 1	—		—	
1–5	2	(6.7)	5	(16.7)
5–10	5	(16.7%)	7	(20.0)
> 10	23	(76.7)	19	(63.3)
Size of business (employees)				
< 5	10	(33.3)	3	(10.0)
6 – 50	9	(30.0)	19	(63.3)
51–100	5	(16.7)	4	(13.3)
101–500	2	(6.7)	4	(13.3)
> 500	4	(13.3)	—	
Business involvement in inter-cultural co-operation (years)				
< 1	1	(3.3)	—	
1–5	10	(33.3)	9	(30.0)
5–10	9	(30.0)	12	(40.0)
> 10	10	(33.3)	9	(30.0)
Respondent's professional training				
apprenticeship	8	(26.7)	7	(23.3)
university	17	(56.7)	18	(60.0)
other	1	(3.3)	—	
no response	4	(13.3)	5	(16.7)
% of respondents with inter-cultural experience	19	(63.3)	18	(60.0)
% of respondents with intercultural training	3	(10.3)	1	(3.3)

Sources: Scherle (2004, 2006).

Table 10.2 Frequencies by which typical sources of conflict were mentioned by German and Moroccan businesses

SOURCE OF CONFLICT	GERMAN BUSINESSES	MOROCCAN BUSINESSES
Adherence to time agreements/punctuality	13	5
Dealing with conflicts	9	5
Decision-making	4	0
Delegation of tasks	5	1
Employee motivation	6	1
Information exchange	5	6
Investments	3	1
Invoicing	6	2
Marketing/public relations	1	2
Performance	2	5
Programme development	2	5
Style of working	6	4
Total number of businesses	30	30

Sources: Scherle (2004, 2006).

> I have experienced little willingness to compromise, to adapt to Western culture; Ramadan being of course a good example … . This fasting has a tremendous impact. You notice an irritability, and the whole tempo is of course slowed down … . It affects our direct partners, who I'm talking about, who on their part are also dependent on their partners, i.e. the hoteliers, the people who rent out four-wheel-drive vehicles, the restaurants and so on, so that this slowing down practically multiplies … . And it is a really big problem that the German tour operators who should know about it also don't understand. They just come and say 'We need an answer tomorrow!', and when they [the Moroccans] say 'that is not possible, you know that', then they [the German tour operators] say 'that's your problem!'

Three features are revealed by this response: first, how easily and explicitly German interviewees' intercultural ignorance was exposed; second, the degree to which they were intolerant of differences, although many had inter-cultural experiences; and third, the magnitude of their concerns over the commercial difficulties presented to their businesses. These responses are clearly problematic in terms of racial stereotyping and show little attempt on the part of interviewees to respond positively or sensitively to cultural difference. Many other interviewees articulated the consequences of Ramadan for incoming tourists, such as restrictions in service which, in turn, lead to customer complaints and strained co-operations. Perhaps more concerning is that German business persons wanted a liberalisation of trade from the perceived constraints exerted by religious doctrine (Nienhaus 1996). However, they misjudged how difficult change would be. For instance, the Tunisian government's attempts to alter business practice during Ramadan, because of its far-reaching economic and social consequences, failed largely because of bitter resistance on the part of religious leaders (Dülfer 1997).

Personal relations played a central role in Morocco to a level that frequently troubled the German respondents. Friends and relations were frequently employed in the Moroccan businesses. Moroccan interviewees stressed that such interpersonal contacts are established and cultivated in Arab countries not only at business meetings but also in private settings. The intention is to create a network of trust which fulfils a crucial function giving security in countries that are traditionally associated with corruption (Heine 1996; Kuran 2004). Despite a basic awareness of these linkages, German respondents underestimated the role and outcomes of employing relatives. Within the (larger) German tour operators with pronounced horizontal and vertical business structures, such personalised business structures were judged as disconcerting. They had a propensity to induce acute conflicts in the day-to-day negotiation of business. A product manager of a leading German company summed up the frustrations of many German interviewees:

> One Moroccan firm we work with is closely linked to family. You'll hardly find a firm where people not belonging to the family occupy key positions … .Qualifications aren't important at all! That means, from the very beginning you have to expect great weaknesses in personnel because there are always positions, important positions, which are occupied in this firm by people who don't have the capacity, the know-how.

The product manager added that he could understand practically no personnel decision made on the Moroccan side in the last few years. While this may have been melodramatic, the consequences of 'familial' business structures for practical co-operation remained tangible such that German partners assumed the lead in their dealings with Moroccan partners:

> Over the years we have learned to take on more and more responsibility. That is, when they weren't pure agency tasks such as bus planning or day trip planning, tour leaders, local guides, then we took everything over ... so that we relied less and less on the partner's agreement, especially in fundamental decisions, such as personnel decisions.

The cultural dimension also caused complications in the conception and implementation phases of a co-operation as the following makes clear:

> A lot of Moroccan partners present themselves at [trade] fairs in an excellent light—what they have, what they can do, and whom they know—under the motto: 'In each hotel there's a relative of mine'. As a circumstance, this is of course not bad at all, but in the end it's often just a promise, which is not compatible with reality. Clearly a lot of things are being described, but in the end there's nothing behind then. You really have to filter .... I mean, of course I can't look into anyone's head or into the enterprise if I am not familiar with how they work there. But generally it is of course always rather difficult, because everybody promises everything and then you face again that issue of 'Inshallah' [If Allah (God) wants it].

Set against this backdrop, it is hardly surprising that ever more German tour operators prefer to co-operate with an incoming agency that offers a bicultural background/management. For instance, there is evidence of an increasing number of agencies being conducted by Moroccan–German couples, where the German partner is seen as a mediator (bridging the gap) between the cultures (Scherle 2006).

The gendered social relations of tourism production were identified by several interviewees as sources of irritation. Despite all attempts at modernisation in recent years, many North African women are still bound to a religious and patriarchal value system oriented around the Koran (Moser-Weithmann 1999). In a male-oriented tourism industry such in Moroccon, the presence of a high proportion of women in senior positions among their German counterparts created friction. Overall, this issue was not as problematic as either working practices or familial structure but it resulted in several poignant, troubling experiences for the female interviewees concerned. One product manager of a medium-sized German tour operator observed that in her experience,

Not every Muslim, Arab or Moroccan is open-minded enough to let a woman give him orders. I noticed that when I started to work in Morocco. The first three months were very hard, because they just tried to say: 'You woman, you European, you can't tell us anything.' Until one day the penny dropped, the tune changed, and after about three months I noticed, ah, they're accepting me as a woman, they're accepting what I say and they see that the work I do is good and gets results.

Sources of Conflict for Moroccan businesses

In their collaborations with their German partners, Moroccan interviewees identified economic sources of conflict, although this strength of feeling is not really adequately registered in Table 10.2. The apparent profitability of German businesses, asymmetrical flows of information and capital, and the perception that the viability of Moroccan companies was irrelevant to their German partners were frequent, strongly articulated complaints. One product manager of a medium-sized incoming agency from Casablanca epitomised this view: 'The negative aspects in cooperation are reflected most especially in the fact that continually less is paid and more quality is expected. Our outgoings are too high in relation to the price paid.' Relatively frequently Moroccan interviewees bemoaned financial arrangements in bilateral co-operation. For example, the manager of a small agency from Tangiers articulated the view that German mismanagement and bankruptcy induces problems for the (seemingly) powerless Moroccans:

> In Germany there are at the moment many firms which go bankrupt. Many of these agencies have no finances! That is a risk and we have been affected twice: once by an Austrian agency with 120,000 Schillings [outstanding debt] and a second time with a German agency with 16,000 Marks. You know that that is a lot of money for us. When we lose 16,000 Marks that corresponds to the profit from 15 groups [of visitors] .... We cannot cope with such a loss. That is difficult for us.

Clearly, Moroccan interviewees were aggrieved at being expected to trust the good name of the German partners without the same status being afforded them in return. In fact, because of disadvantageous experiences with their German partners over finance, 'trust' had been divorced from its purely moral meaning. Instead, as the ironic comments below make clear, trust had assumed a more calculative meaning as an outcome, not the foundation of a transaction:

> There is one important thing: for us, trust is synonymous with money. Personally, if I don't know you—even if I find you congenial—you would not be allowed to send me your group before we have checked the billing. That's trust! ... That's the reason why trust is synonymous for us with money. Pay me in time, I trust you. We could allow some days of delay, but it should not last too long.

Some Moroccan tour operators repeatedly referred to financial problems which stemmed from rationalisation in the German tourism sector through takeovers and insolvencies (Vorlaufer 1993, 1998; Freyer 2000; Bastakis *et al.* 2004). This had increased competition, especially among small Moroccan agencies, for collaborations with the diminishing number of German players in the market. The transnational activities of the larger overseas operators were viewed as threatening smaller-scale indigenous enterprises in Morocco. Whether rational or not, fear of globalisation was followed by the view that the takeover of local businesses would then put further pressure on other types of businesses elsewhere in the tourism value chains in a destination:

Globalization is a problem for many incoming-agencies. In three or four years the huge tour-operators will take over all the small agencies. That's not good at all for small destinations like Agadir. Our firm is not so much affected, because we co-operate with solid and independent enterprises. But of course that cannot rule out the possibility that one day we also might be taken over by a huge tour-operator. That's really bad for a destination like Agadir.

Many small operators had to forge alliances with one or more of the best-known (larger) German tour operators. While this broadened their product range, they had hoped to obtain further insurance against market conditions and fluctuating demand. Moroccan interviewees felt this had served to empower the German partners because there were fewer of them, they were being chased by broadly the same number of potential Moroccan partners, and they felt they could establish better terms from their potential partners. The situation conspired to make the smaller Moroccan businesses feel more vulnerable still: many forms of co-operation were not based on contractual agreements, with the result that German tour operators could switch partners and operating conditions relatively easily. For some Moroccan interviewees, these 'partnerships' with German businesses were 'unfair' practices. One agency manager in the incentives sector noted:

Difficulties and misunderstandings arise in the course of co-operation because the partner is looking for a new product every time although Morocco remains unchanged. We cannot always create a new product for him. Also, our partner doesn't like our way of working. We are always supposed to change our methods because of this and follow theirs. Moreover, we once went to court, because a German customer gave us a cheque that bounced. In such difficult situations we try to find a compromise. But if we are in a weak position we sometimes have to give up.

In practice, changing demand conditions induced further dilemmas. Product portfolio diversification remains a central dimension of Moroccan tourism policy, and it was welcomed by the German partners. However, the Moroccan businesses were worried about product development costs and the ephemerality of tourist demand. Their concern was that just as the new product would be introduced, demand would be diverted elsewhere. This perspective may be read from a Western perspective as representing a 'lack of initiative and entrepreneurial spirit', but it is not without some justification because Gray (2002) reports that Morocco suffers from a lack of repeat visitors. Interculturalists might argue that this relates to the so-called 'fatalism hypothesis', which has its origins in the view of Islamic theologians that human lives are largely preordained (Dülfer 1997; Kutschker and Schmid 2002). Whatever interpretation is placed on this situation the Moroccan respondents clearly felt the pressure to diversify reflected the asymmetrical power relations with their German business partners.

Conflict resolution: intercultural perspectives

Given the tensions stemming from cultural differences and market pressures, especially to diversify, it is no surprise that respondents highlighted conflicts that arose. When conflict occurred three principal approaches to resolution were identified as overwhelmingly popular and highly successful for both German and Moroccan interviewees: 'open discussions when needed' (>90 per cent of respondents); 'employee discussions' (>50 per cent); and 'regular team meetings' (>32 per cent). In each case less than 7 per cent of the businesses that employed these tactics reported poor success. 'Legal resolution' and 'management consultants' were used as conflict resolution by less than 5 per cent and 2 per cent of businesses respectively and each had poor success. Fewer than 17 per cent of businesses attempted to solve conflicts by 'pressure and compulsion', 'arbitration', 'intercultural training', and 'reputation' alone, and these were viewed by less than 7 per cent as successful (see Scherle 2006 for a fuller discussion).

Thus, the most frequently applied and successful methods were those that had a clearly personalised and discursive nature. The small and medium-sized nature of the businesses interviewed, combined with the often long-term nature of their bilateral relationships, meant that many had great volumes of social capital invested with their partners. Rather than recourse to the law or investment in more expensive solutions such as management consultants or inter-cultural training programmes, the businesses could fall back on their close personal contacts in order to fashion a solution through dialogue. Moreover, such solutions were often characterised by remarkable pragmatism on both sides. As one manager of a German tour operator wryly observed:

> I always say that there is a legal and a business solution . . . and we are always for the business solution, although I am a lawyer. This sector is much too small for legal solutions. In the 30 or 20 years I have been working, I have only twice gone for the legal solution and every other time the business solution. You keep running into people! And you cannot work in the future with someone you are at legal loggerheads with. . . . Everybody turns up again, our sector is much too small for that.

A senior employee of a Moroccan incoming agency in Agadir noted in a similarly realistic manner, albeit with a slight tone of despair, that 'we compromise so as not to lose our partner and to have work all year round'. This sentiment was repeated frequently, and it encapsulated a common anxiety among Moroccan partners: not only could they be the victims of commercial exploitation by their overseas partner, but also that they were too vulnerable to failure as a result of the increasing globalisation of tourism production and consumption. Increased concentration among German tour operators and the disappearance of previous partners provoked many small and medium-sized Moroccan operators to sense themselves as more open to exploitation because of the greater difficulties in establishing beneficial collaborations. As the managing director of an incoming agency in Agadir opined:

> It is becoming more and more difficult to find business partners, as globalisation is made for those who are already strong and who become even stronger with globalisation. When you talk about globalisation you have to automatically think of the three large groups in the Moroccan market: TUI, Neckermann [now Thomas Cook] and LTU. These are the biggest, who will benefit, and for us everything will get harder.

There were also complaints that the purchasing power of the large groups is growing, and that local tourism businesses may be further marginalised, especially in the centres of mass tourism (primarily Agadir) where the global players are established and dominant in all types of tourism. Interviewees noted variations in outlook for co-operations in different markets. Moroccan agencies specialising in narrow market segments (such as desert and trekking tourism, thalassic therapy) reported better prospects. They looked back on long years of often exclusive cooperation with small and medium-sized niche operators in Germany, whose customer numbers have remained relatively constant. Given the diversification of tourism production pursued by the Moroccan government especially in peripheral areas, incoming agencies in established co-operations, and who are able to respond flexibly to market conditions, considered they would have an advantage in deflecting some of the competitive pressures from larger operators. However, this would be reliant on a highly personalised style of co-operation, sometimes even based on genuine friendships. Both would facilitate the solution of potential conflicts in an uncomplicated manner, but ironically both were the sort of personal relationships that troubled many German businesses.

Discussion: Reconciling Intercultural Positions

When the empirical material is mapped against the conceptual framework (Tables 10.1–10.6), significant juxtapositions begin to emerge. German businesses mainly subscribed to a 'culture-free' approach with their Moroccan partners (Tables 10.5–10.6). They were, by and large, above all concerned with the effective and optimal operation of commercial partnerships. Profit and efficiency were motive forces whereas cultural aspects were mainly seen as a burden not as a resource. German respondents' relationships with Moroccan partners were on the whole positive, although their behaviour was characterised by relatively low levels of intercultural competence and a propensity to revert to stereotypical views of Moroccan business, culture and society. Cultural barriers to effective business such as time management, conflict resolution and gender-specific experiences proved more irksome than business-related differences. Strict adherence to religious doctrine as well as the frequent use of family and relatives in the Moroccan labour force were disconcerting.

The 'culture-free' approach of the German businesses is further evident in their strategies and tactics for dealing with their Moroccan partners. Their initial strategies have strong resonances with Lukes's second and third dimensions of power. German businesses attempted to keep culture off the commercial agenda through their individual business practices. Furthermore, they attempted to establish what was in their Moroccan counterparts' 'real' interests: namely, to adopt a much more systematic approach to business operations, reminiscent of German (i.e. Western) methods and best practices in which business is for business's sake. Rather than an asset, the entwining of family and culture in operations presented a threat to the 'legitimate' and expert power plays in their culture-free approach (Table 10.2). Knowledge, remunerative power and, where necessary, coercive power were the bases of power while in their structural position, expertise and opportunity were the sources of power (Table 10.3). Tactics of rational persuasion, exchange and pressure were used as basic starting points in their commercial dealings with Moroccan partners (Table 10.4).

The German businesses' preference for non-contractual arrangements might be seen as hypocritical in this context, but it reflects their relative empowerment. Where German businesses perceived themselves in control of a commercial relationship, they felt suitably empowered to work with non-contractual arrangements. Although they were prepared to tolerate what they saw as the negative aspects of working with Moroccan partners, ultimately they perceived control because they felt their commercial lessons were being received and they held the ultimate sanction: they could terminate the relationship at any time to lessen their exposure to risk. Nonpayment was also used as a punitive measure to reinforce control. German businesses felt that Moroccan entrepreneurs needed a commercial arrangement with them more than they needed one with the Moroccans. Although Moroccan partners were demanding better terms and conditions, they were chasing relationships with a declining number of German operators, businesses on whom they relied to deliver large numbers of visitors, and businesses who understood their dependency through the Moroccan policy context that promoted diversification.

Culture and business were on the whole closely integrated for Moroccan enterprises. They did not isolate obvious differences in cultural traits with their German colleagues as principal sources of conflict, nor did they revert to stereotypes of German culture as explanations of business tensions. Major complaints surrounded unequal power relations, commercial demands and flows of information which favoured German businesses, who were perceived to value their own profitability at the expense of their Moroccan partners. Importantly, economic considerations were not separated from cultural ones. To Moroccan enterprises, the unfamiliar business practices and allegedly unfair position their partners had assumed were read as synonymous with globalising Western culture, values and social practices; that is, the 'German business model' was read by the Moroccans not as culture free, not detached from culture, but as bound to Western culture.

Moroccan businesses used overt strategies more reminiscent of Lukes's first dimension of power. For them, there were certain fundamental issues that they overtly sought to get on the agenda in their dealings with their German partners. These included consideration of basic terms such as payment and cash flow, as well as (quality) standards of service and the nature of routine operations. Knowledge and remunerative power were the bases of power (Table 10.3) while expertise and opportunity typically formed the sources of power. Upward appeals, ingratiation, persuasion and inspirational appeals were the tactics initially used in their dealings with German partners (Table 10.4). Moroccan enterprises had bases of expert power and informational power (Table 10.2) given their knowledge of local culture, markets and service opportunities, but their reward and hence coercive power through their ability to frustrate service relations was latent power because of the way the German enterprises controlled the agenda. The Moroccan respondents had more modest expectations from their relationships with German partners. As lifestyle enterprises, empowerment was manifest in their being able to enter commercial arrangements with overseas partners, retain them and to grow the relationship; to extract even modestly better terms and conditions was even more desirable given the marginal nature of many of the businesses and the substantial benefits the German businesses could deliver. Moroccan businesses felt disempowered partly because government policy made them more vulnerable through the need to develop new products and markets. It was the Moroccan businesses, not the German partners, who had to carry the costs and risks of product development.

On this basis, one may have expected the German and Moroccan businesses to adopt different conflict resolution strategies. This was not the case. Both were loathe to seek redress in the law or costly commercial solutions. Instead, both often reverted to the long-term social capital they had developed with their co-operators as the basis for reconciliation. Once conflict precipitated, German businesses, like their Moroccan partners, participated in solutions which at first glance subscribed to the culturally bound approach. Personal relationships, discussions and meetings were primarily used to resolve differences and to reinforce the commercial relationships. When unpacked further, it is clear that some elements of the individualistic culture approach to conflict management were present: namely, conflicts occur and have to be solved; they are rooted in 'fact'; and they are open and direct. Similarly, several characteristics of a collective 'industry' culture were evident such as the perception of conflicts as negative and destructive, closely associated with individuals and status, and intuitively played out.

Among the German respondents, disagreements heralded a change in tactics. Prior to conflict, German businesses adopted more sophisticated, subtle power tactics based on what to exclude from the agenda and how to manipulate the Moroccans' real interests. Once disagreement emerged, they retreated back to positions of domination, authority, control of the agenda and coercion through the threat of sanctions, were they unable to find a solution. However, it was precisely in such circumstances when the apparently powerless could deploy their control strategies and where the Moroccans were further empowered. Disagreement cut through layers of pretence and dependency. There was then a more open discussion of cost-benefits to the respective parties. German businesses and their officers were independently responsible to investors and shareholders (cf. Watkins and Bell 2002: 15): for reasons of the balance sheet and corporate accountability, could they really afford either to enter a potentially costly legal case at home or overseas, or to deny themselves turnover and margin because they no longer wished to sell their erstwhile partners' products? In a game of brinkmanship, the Moroccans effectively implied that the German position also had an element of bluff about it: the German businesses and their employees, like the Moroccans, were vulnerable to market conditions, albeit in a different manner. Thus, it was often in disputes that the Moroccans were further empowered and where they were able to exert the extra leverage over their German partners to improve their situation significantly. This situation partly reflects the initial asymmetrical power relations but also reveals the contradictory nature of the operation of power; that is, during disputes, when it might be expected that those with greater resources might assert themselves, it is in fact the seemingly weaker partners who through the use of particular tactics have greater opportunity to enhance their position and power.

SUMMARY

Conflict occurs when two opposing views are brought together; and conflict can be both positive and negative. It can create an opportunity for all parties involved to discuss their differences. Understanding how culture affects conflict can help mitigate and resolve the conflict, while helping you to become a more culturally competent communicator.

In this chapter, we learned about different types of intercultural conflict and examined the role culture plays in conflict. Our first reading examined a number of difficult types of intercultural conflict. The second and third readings in this chapter explored the differences between individualistic and collectivistic cultures' conflict styles and provided best practices in effectively managing conflict. In the last section of the chapter, we explored a real intercultural conflict between German and Moroccan businesses. Continue on to the discussion questions where you will be able to apply your knowledge about conflict.

DISCUSSION QUESTIONS

1. Think of a conflict you recently had with a friend, co-worker, classmate, or person in your community. What was the basis for the conflict? What aspects of communication contributed to the conflict? In what ways did cultural perspectives affect the nature of communication?
2. How can personal relationships be used to mitigate conflict between individuals from different cultures?
3. Are there certain contexts where intercultural conflict is beneficial? How can communication be used to negotiate such conflicts?
4. Is it possible to have a conflict that is *culture-free*? Why or why not?

INTERCULTURAL COMMUNICATION AND BUSINESS

CHAPTER 11

STUDY OBJECTIVES

After completing this chapter, you will be able to:
- Identify and explain why intercultural communication is needed in business.
- Understand and describe the role culture plays in intercultural business transactions.
- Suggest ways to incorporate intercultural communication into business contexts.

INTRODUCTION

We live in a connected world where business is no longer confined to a specific time of the day or to a geographical location. Because of this, our world creates the need for intercultural communication competence in business. Intercultural communication is important both domestically and internationally. Domestically, the United States is experiencing a rapid growth of diversity, which, as you may recall, we discussed in chapter two. A changing domestic landscape connects different cultures to one another in common areas such as work place environments. Internationally, expanding global markets create the opportunity for companies to partner with other companies around the world and create new locations in new cultural settings.

As we have learned earlier that culture is dynamic and complex. When two or more cultures interact in a business scenario, the situation is ripe for cultural misunderstandings. Intercultural communication is important, as a cultural misunderstanding could cost the business money, clients, or worse.

From what you already learned about culture in chapter six, you know that there are many dimensions of culture. Think about what you have learned so far and apply that knowledge to a business environment. There are a lot of challenges when two or more cultures work together, challenges such as differences in language, communication styles, and business etiquette. Recall what you know about individualist and collectivistic cultures; what happens when individuals from both these types of cultures work together? An individual from the individualistic culture may primarily value the accomplishment of assigned tasks whereas an individual from the collectivistic culture may value their relationships over their tasks. This is an example of the challenges that occur in business and why intercultural communication is key for businesses.

In this chapter we explore intercultural communication in the world of business. Our first reading focuses on the changing cultural landscape of business and why it is important to be a competent intercultural communicator. After we explore this area, we move to our second reading focusing on the differences between how Americans and Japanese conduct business and providing insight into negotiating between individualistic and collectivistic cultures. Our last reading provides an interesting case study, examining both sides of view from individuals experiencing an intercultural work experience. Finally, you will find an opportunity to apply your knowledge via the discussion questions at the end of the chapter.

Moving Forward

The first selection in this chapter provides some background about the changing cultural landscape of the business world and highlights the skills an individual needs to be a competent communicator in this context. As you read through this section, are there any skills that you would include that maybe the authors did not mention?

THE CHANGING LANDSCAPE OF BUSINESS

Evidence abounds of an increasing escalation of business globalization (Bartlett, 1989; Nadesan, 2001; Prince, 2001; Sands, 2001). Increasing competitive pressure is being placed on international firms to develop worldwide communication networks within their own firms, as well as with their suppliers, customers and their external constituencies such as government agencies and special interest groups (Babcock and Babcock, 2001; Fisher *et al.*, 2001b). This phenomenon is compounded by the constant development in technologies that allow a rapidly expanding number of messages to be exchanged within a short span of time and across large geographical distances. Communication skills that bridge cultural boundaries are therefore critical to both employee and organizational effectiveness.

These trends mean that today's organizations must find effective ways to manage the increasing heterogeneity in their workforces and consumer bases (Ashkanasy *et al.*, 2002a). Research indicates environments where diversity creates *productive* conflict result in organizational effectiveness such as greater innovativeness (Jackson *et al.*, 1992), improved problem solving and decision making, and higher levels of creativity (Härtel and Fujimoto, 1999). On the other hand, failing to equip employees with the skill to deal with diversity runs the risk of promoting *destructive* conflict in the organization (Watson *et al.*, 1993; Ayoko *et al.*, in press), which results in reductions in team performance and increased turnover and absenteeism (Hambrick, 1994), as well as negative effects on individuals' emotional well-being (Fujimoto and Härtel, in press).

The organizational implications of diversity mean that individuals who come from different cultures and possess different language competence levels will require specific strategies that can help them achieve effective communication during business interactions. This is because it is anticipated that their roles as producers and customers will add value to interrelated global business networks (Porter, 1985). This is, however, no easy task. The diversity literature paints conflicting pictures of the effects of cross-cultural (compared to mono-cultural) interaction (for example Milliken and Martins, 1996; Chatman *et al.*, 1998; Härtel and Fujimoto, 1999). Specifically, studies show that, in comparison to homogeneous workgroups, diverse workgroups suffer from:

greater conflict

more turnover

higher stress

more absenteeism

greater communication problems (O'Reilly *et al.*, 1989; Zenger and Lawrence, 1989; Alder, 1991; Tsui *et al.*, 1992)

less trust

lower job satisfaction

low cohesion

poor social integration (Hambrick 1994).

While the greater likelihood of these difficulties occurring in diverse workgroups is well established, research in this area has offered organizations little information upon which management practices for interactions for culturally diverse workforces and customer bases can be formulated (cf. Pelled *et al.*, 1999).

The Relationship Between Culture and Communication

The communication literature has documented the interdependent relationship between culture and communication well (Gudykunst, 1997). *Culture*, as defined earlier, provides the structure of the communication process (Birdwhistell, 1970) whereas *communication* involves the verbal and non verbal transmission of information (Keesing, 1974, in Gudykunst, 1997). Therefore, the relationship between culture and communication has been described as a point between the two extremes of these constructs, that is, between culture and communication itself (Keesing, 1974, in Gudykunst, 1997). In other words, the way in which people communicate is influenced by their culture and, in turn, their culture is influenced by the way they communicate. As such, academics and scholars alike must be aware that culture plays an important role in the communication process. (See Gudykunst, 1997 for more extensive discussion.)

Skills Needed to Communicate Cross-Culturally

There are a myriad of skills and competencies that facilitate cross-cultural communication (Lloyd and Härtel, 2003). A communicatively competent individual has both the knowledge of the appropriate communication patterns for a situation and the ability to apply that knowledge (Cooley and Roach, 1984: 25). Researchers have also used a rule-based approach to conceptualizing communication competence (Harris and Cronen, 1979), identifying both *strategic* and *tactical* communication competence (Jablin *et al.*, 1994) as vital components in the process. Strategic communication deals with knowledge of organizational realities, what things mean in the organizational context and how they differ between organizations. Tactical communication competence, in contrast, is defined as an individual's ability to follow and manipulate regulative rules. Tactical communication competence, therefore, includes communication skills and performance capability to achieve personal, group, and organizational goals.

Based on theories of social cognition (Sypher 1984, Sypher and Zorn, 1986), tactical communication competencies, as opposed to strategic communication competencies, are viewed from a skill/performance perspective (cf. DiSalvo, 1980; DiSalvo and Larsen, 1987). Such skills include advising, persuading, instructing, interviewing, exchanging information, public speaking, leading discussions, delegating, problem solving, and listening (cf. DiSalvo, 1980; DiSalvo and Larsen, 1987). Underlying these skills are communication skills and knowledge communication. While these dimensions are generally germane across cultures, the specific characteristics of each dimension are likely to vary from culture to culture. Thus, cultural variability may be a major factor for which members from different national cultures develop their understandings of the strategic communication knowledge and tactical skills needed for communication competence.

Business communication is a dynamic, two-way, multiple influenced, and transformational translation process (Sherblom, 1998). The complexity and variety of the translation process is intricate given that individuals send and receive messages via multiple languages and cultures in varying business and social environments. Skills that enable individuals to be open to differences in interaction preferences are therefore critical to achieving positive outcomes in cross-cultural business interactions (Härtel and Fujimoto, 2000). This set of skills is what we call business communication competence (BCC) across cultures.

Moving Forward

Now that you have become more familiar with some of the skills that are required in order to become a more culturally competent communicator in business, we move to our second reading. This reading focuses on some of the differences that American and Japanese have when conducting business. As you recall from our chapter six, the United States is an individualist culture and Japan is a collectivist culture. What are some of the differences that come to mind when you compare these types of cultures to each other? The following reading provides insight into negotiation between an individualist and a collectivist culture.

DIFFERENCES BETWEEN JAPANESE AND AMERICAN BUSINESS PRACTICES

U.S. corporations lose money each year when their managers or negotiators are unable to deal with cultural issues overseas (Tung, 1991). It has been suggested that the cultures of countries such as Japan and China are so vastly different from U.S. culture that negotiators must understand the differences or suffer frustration and failure (Acuff, 1990; Blaker, 1977a, 1977b; Corne, 1992; Graham & Sano, 1989). If Westerners are not savvy in negotiating with Asian countries, their economic base will suffer (Pye, 1992). Thus the primary focus of literature in this quadrant is to provide practical knowledge that U.S. negotiators can use to assess unusual or unexpected behaviors and adjust their own behaviors and attitudes when encountering negotiators from other cultures (Hall, 1960). These works recommend that American business executives adopt native behaviors and values when negotiating outside the United States, assuming that "doing as the Romans do" will ensure success by increasing perceived similarity and understanding (Cahn, 1983).

The majority of descriptive/prescriptive literature focuses on the Pacific Rim, with particular emphasis on Japan and China (e.g., Acuff, 1990; Chen, 1993; Chu, 1991; Corne, 1992; Davidson, 1987; De Mente, 1981, 1987; DePauw, 1981; Downing, 1992; Eiteman, 1990; Goldman, 1994; Graham & Sano, 1989; Hu & Grove, 1991; Huang, 1990; Lee & Lo, 1988; Macleod, 1988; March, 1985, 1988; Pye, 1982, 1992; Scott & Renault, 1995; Shenkar & Ronen, 1987; Solomon, 1985, 1987; Stewart & Keown, 1989; Tung, 1982, 1984a, 1984b, 1991; Van Zandt, 1970; Walters, 1991; Wilhelm, 1994; Zhang & Kuroda, 1989). Only a handful of remaining articles and books provide descriptions of negotiation in other specific cultures (Soviet Union—Beliaev, Mullen, & Punnett, 1985; Rajan & Graham, 1991; Islamic markets—Wright, 1981) or across a variety of cultures (Acuff, 1993; Burt, 1984; Frank, 1992a, 1992b; Harris & Moran, 1991; Kennedy, 1985a, 1985b; Moran & Stripp, 1991).

This literature takes one of two approaches. First, the descriptive approach implies that knowing common behaviors provides negotiators with an appropriate model for achieving negotiation goals. For example, Frank (1992a, 1992b) recommends that when negotiating in Germany, Austria, and Switzerland, Americans should be prompt and efficient, but when negotiating in Mexico, Americans should "grant concessions that support the ego of the decision maker" (p. 66) and handle problems in a personal rather than a business manner. Building trust and friendship is important when negotiating with Scandinavians. Similar kinds of specific suggestions are made for negotiating with the British (Burt, 1984), in Chinese and Korean cultures (Acuff, 1990; Tung, 1991), and with Russians (Rajan & Graham, 1991).

Second, the prescriptive approach suggests that by understanding cultural values, negotiators may plan proactively. That is, the negotiator can predict likely cultural behaviors and thus plan appropriate, effective responses for negotiating. For example, some key values of Japanese culture include the maintenance of social harmony, protection of "face," enactment of social status within the organization, and the pursuit of long-term relationships.

To illustrate these two perspectives toward cultural behaviors across the descriptive and prescriptive literature, we examine more closely some works that describe negotiating with the Japanese.

Descriptions of Japanese Behavior

Several Japanese cultural behaviors are frequently cited. Japanese negotiators have very specific prenegotiation rituals in which business cards are exchanged and prenegotiation relationships are developed (Corne, 1992; Kennedy, 1985b; Moran & Stripp, 1991; Walters, 1991). Japanese dislike saying no and dislike confrontation and open conflict because of their concern with "saving face" (Corne, 1992; Tung, 1984b; Van Zandt, 1970). Japanese negotiators prepare thoroughly, proceed cautiously, and are known for attention to detail and persistence (Corne, 1992). They maintain high concern for long-term relationships (Corne, 1992; Graham & Sano, 1989; Kennedy, 1985b; Van Zandt, 1970). They are more aware of and bound by hierarchies—both within their own organizations and toward opposing sides' agent(s)—than are Westerners, noting the status of foreign negotiators within their organizations. Attention to hierarchy means that Japanese teams make decisions by consensus and take longer to make decisions than Americans are accustomed to (Corne, 1992; Graham & Sano, 1989; Tung, 1984a, 1984b; Van Zandt, 1970). More than one author has noted that Japanese are said to feign language difficulties as a tactic for their own benefit against their foreign counterparts (Corne, 1992; Walters, 1991). The frequent use of silence and apparent lack of emotion among Japanese negotiators may be disconcerting for visitors (Graham & Sano, 1989; Moran & Stripp, 1991).

Predicting Japanese Behavior

In contrast, several works tie negotiation behaviors to specific values underlying Japanese culture, showing how knowledge of the Japanese value system allows visitors to predict and understand ensuing behaviors. For instance, the emphasis on harmony (*wa*) means that Japanese companies desire not only a profitable agreement, but a business relationship that encompasses both moral and practical obligations. Thus the Japanese possess a different understanding of contracts and the commitments inherent in them (Chen, 1993; Corne, 1992; Graham & Sano, 1989; March, 1985; Zhang & Kuroda, 1989). Similarly, Hofstede (1980) points out that Japanese values toward collectivism make the "we" more important than the "I" (Acuff, 1990). As a result, the corporation is seen as a "paternalistic, cooperative effort of many employees for the collective good" (Zhang & Kuroda, 1989, p. 109) and conducts business differently from corporations in the individualistically oriented United States.

The value of "order" also drives Japanese behavior (March, 1985; Moran & Stripp, 1991; Van Zandt, 1970; Zhang & Kuroda, 1989). This need for order results in attention to hierarchies (*ringi-sho*) that affects negotiation rituals and results in rigid decision-making processes that must progress up through the ranks of the organization. Individual negotiators have no autonomy in making decisions.

Overall, differences in the ways Japanese and Americans view the world in general, and thus the specific problems and issues they are negotiating, result in vastly different ways of approaching negotiation. As March (1985) points out, awareness of cultural differences between Japan and the United States "should alert you to the fact that many of the Japanese you face do not think about problems in the way you do" (p. 26).

There are several behaviors recommended for Americans when encountering Japanese. For instance, some authors recommend that Americans should consider hiring cultural experts or interpreters to facilitate negotiations (Burt, 1984; Corne, 1992; Van Zandt, 1970; Zhang & Kuroda, 1989); should make extra effort to be prepared, giving special attention to learning as much as possible about Japanese customs and business practices (Chen, 1993; Corne, 1992; Tung, 1984a, 1984b; Van Zandt, 1970; Walters, 1991); should expect negotiations with Japanese to take longer than might be expected in the United States (Burt, 1984; Chen, 1993; Kennedy, 1985b; Walters, 1991); should not expect immediate responses to proposals (Corne, 1992); and should be careful to avoid confrontation and any show of anger (Acuff, 1990; Burt, 1984; Chen, 1993; Corne, 1992; Walters, 1991). In addition, Americans need to be aware of their own cultural assumptions about nonverbal behaviors and not allow superficial interpretations of Japanese silence, gestures and expressions, and indirect verbal communication to mislead them (Corne, 1992; Walters, 1991).

Summary

A common theme in Quadrant I is that cultural awareness will lead to more effective negotiating and higher likelihood of success. This assumption is valuable for guiding research. However, the descriptive approach . . . suffers the same limitations as most exploratory investigation. The observations are not systematic and not generalizable to intercultural contexts. Nonetheless, although aimed at the practical and applied level, these works give researchers valuable fodder for investigation because they lay out a host of assumptions about cultural behaviors and how the values of those cultures are likely to be enacted at the negotiation table.

Thus cultural assumptions, underlying values, expectations, and supposed appropriate responses on the part of visiting negotiators are phenomena that can be examined more closely in future research. Empirical investigation of the effectiveness of adaptation is particularly important given the emerging evidence that too much adaptation, or "acting the part" of a host culture member when one is merely a visitor, may be detrimental to effectiveness (Francis, 1991). Hammer (in press) asserts that a visitor is likely to be forgiven for cultural taboos because he or she is not expected, as an outsider, to be familiar with all practices in the host culture. This argument is validated in Marriott's (1995) analysis of linguistic deviations in Japanese-Australian negotiation. Although negative evaluation of linguistic deviations was expected, two of three deviation types were evaluated neutrally, indicating that in intercultural interaction, the participants may relax their expectations about communicative interaction.

Quadrant II: Guiding Principles

In direct contrast to the works in Quadrant I, those in Quadrant II avoid culture-specific analyses and advice. Instead, these works highlight issues of general concern for international negotiators. The basis for this approach is summarized by Salacuse (1988), who argues that books and articles that stress different negotiating styles across cultures promote cultural stereotypes. Rubin and Sander (1991) echo this concern about stereotyping, and propose that cultural stereotypes create self-fulfilling prophecies in intercultural negotiation, so that "what passes for [cultural/national] differences may well be the result of expectations and perceptions" (p. 252). Griffin and Daggart (1990) maintain that "what is needed is a skill and not an exhaustive compilation of generalizations. Indeed, generalizations … reinforce and exacerbate a negotiator's tendency to make false assumptions" (p. 3). Therefore, the literature in Quadrant II approaches the problem of negotiating across cultures in two ways: (a) by explaining negotiation factors on which cultures may vary, and (b) by proposing a "toolbox" of global attitudes and abilities for successful international negotiators.

Global Variations

Salacuse (1991) urges traveling negotiators to ask the right questions before taking action at the negotiation table. These "right" questions have to do with culture, political systems, and the negotiating environment. The effective negotiator must determine the consequences of his or her behavior after assessing such factors as home advantage, time delays, language and interpreters, bureaucracy, and political ideologies. Salacuse argues that culture affects business negotiations in 10 ways: through the negotiating goal, the negotiating attitude, the negotiator's personal style, the directness of communication, the negotiators' sensitivity to time, emotionalism, the expected form of agreements, how agreements are built (bottom-up or top-down), the organization of negotiating teams, and risk taking. Similarly, Weiss (1994a) and Moran and Stripp (1991) provide lists of cultural characteristics that can affect negotiations. These and other aspects of culture likely to affect the negotiation are echoed by various authors who take a global view of intercultural negotiation (for a summary of these characteristics, see Table 11.1).

Global Attitudes and Abilities

Schwartz (1993) defines an "international mind-set" as aji "open-minded, empathic attitude toward conducting business in countries and cultures different from our own" (p. 1282). To develop this empathic and open-minded attitude, researchers have identified numerous skills, such as building rapport and trust (Le Poole, 1989; Reardon & Spekman, 1994), planning for and anticipating the other's goals and expectations, coordinating alliances (Reardon & Spekman, 1994), and managing power within a negotiator's own party and with the other party's negotiators (Elgström, 1990; Reardon & Spekman, 1994). An international mind-set includes flexibility, open-mindedness, patience, and a long-term perspective, as well as knowledge of and appreciation for one's host culture (Casse & Deol, 1985; Donohue, 1992; Elgström, 1990; Le Poole, 1989; Moran & Stripp, 1991; Salacuse, 1988, 1991; Schwartz, 1993).

TABLE 11.1 Areas of Cultural Variation Relevant to Intercultural Negotiation

• Understanding of what *negotiation* means and accomplishes
• Importance of relationship
• View of "profit"
• Understanding of *individual, individual rights,* and *group*
• Perspectives toward time
• How trust is established and maintained
• Customs and norms, including importance of protocol and etiquette
• Makeup of the negotiation team
• View of hierarchies
• Use of interpreter and/or go-between
• Levels of risk
• Values, perceptions, and philosophies underlying the language—not just vocabulary
• Differences in interpreting nonverbal communication
• Manner of communicating information and proposals
• Decision-making processes and styles
• Use of emotions
• Need to save face
• Differences in thinking processes, logic, and reasoning
• Communication styles, including persuasive and conflict styles, use of small talk
• View of what "contract" represents and form of final agreement

Summary

Salacuse (1988) argues that the knowledge, skills, and attitudes necessary for international business negotiation are not those generally found in U.S. executives. It is wrong to assume that to be successful interculturally, negotiators must do *outside* as they do *within* the United States. However, one weakness in the guiding principles literature is that although the authors assert that certain skills are necessary for contract procurement, none describes exactly how negotiators should enact these skills. Exactly how will a negotiator who has adopted efficient principles for international negotiating communicate, verbally and nonverbally, with his or her counterpart? For example, Schwartz (1993) argues, "When in Rome, Tokyo, Moscow, Cairo, Rio, etc., one should do as the natives do. This does not mean that we should try to become them. Rather, for Americans it is important to remain in character, to be 'authentic'" (p. 1285). Communicatively, how to balance "doing as the natives do" and "remaining authentic" remains vague (Frank, 1992b), however compelling this idea may be intuitively. One notable exception is McCall and Warrington's (1984) explication of communication strategies for establishing intercultural understanding. For example, "flagging" is accomplished by forecasting one's behaviors, as in, "May I ask a question?" or "May I make a suggestion?"

It is our primary argument in this chapter that communication provides the vital link between culture and negotiation (Elgström, 1990). This is reflected in our perspective that interpersonal communication at the negotiation table determines success because it exhibits, or fails to exhibit, these attitudes and principles. Therefore, despite its shortcomings, this body of work is a rich resource for further research because its assumptions can be transformed into hypotheses about (a) the essential elements of effective negotiation that are grounded in communication, such as attitudes, and (b) how cultures vary along negotiation-relevant dimensions, such as "view of profit."

Moving Forward

The next reading concerns two cross-cultural business situations between Germans and Americans. In the first study, we meet Jim. Jim is sent to Germany to work with his company's partner company to help prepare for a product launch on the European market. He details his experience and struggles with working on a German team. Afterwards, a German co-worker offers his perspective of working with Jim. Here, we have the unique opportunity of having access to both sides' perspectives of what goes on during the time Jim is in Germany.

Similarly, in the second case study, we meet Klaus. Klaus is sent to the United States to work on the same product launch. He details his experience and troubles with working on an American team. In the same manner, afterwards, an American co-worker provides a perspective of working with Klaus. Once again, we have the opportunity to see both sides view reflect on working with each other. For further background information, make sure to read the case studies' introduction before diving into each case.

As you approach both of these case studies, keep in mind what you have just learned from the previous reading. As you examine this scenario from both the American and German perspective, think about what you know and have learned about culture in your readings. Knowing what you know about intercultural communication, consider the following questions: What advice would you give to Klaus about working on the team of Americans? What advice would you give the American team working with Klaus? What advice would you give to Jim working on the team of Germans? What advice would you give the German team working with Jim?

COMPARING INTERCULTURAL WORK TEAMS

This comprehensive case covers essential aspects and facets of cross-cultural cooperation and communication. These are illustrated through the fictitious depiction of a project carried out between Americans and Germans. More specifically, two situations will be presented: An American working on a team which is dominated by Germans (and their way of cooperating and communicating) and, the other way around, a German working on a team dominated by Americans. The difficulties, problems and misunderstandings both sides are facing are particularly stressed. For both situations, first the 'outsider' expresses his astonishment and irritation about the unfamiliar behavioral patterns and subsequently someone from the 'majority culture' explains and defends the rationale behind their way of doing things. It is believed that only through a better understanding of the respective 'other' party can the performance in cross-cultural cooperation and communication be significantly improved.

1. Situation: "The Project is Dominated by Germans"

The American Perspective

Introduction

Two months ago I was sent by my company from our Philadelphia headquarters to Stuttgart in order to prepare the launch of a new product on the European market. The product, a laser for eye surgery, was developed by a joint venture between us and our German partner. Even though the joint venture belongs in equal shares to both companies it was agreed that our German partner would take the lead in introducing the product on the European market and that we would have the say for launching the product in North America. For all other regions both partners agreed to work in tandem.

So I was selected to represent our company on what was otherwise a German team. Even though I had never worked in Germany before, I was considered to be the natural candidate for the assignment: I speak fluent German as my wife is German. In addition, I thought I was also culturally quite well prepared for the job. Next to speaking the language and having gotten used to putting up with my wife's tick for over-punctuality, I also regularly travel to Germany to visit my wife's family. Also, I have had frequent e-mail exchanges and telephone conversations with our German partners. But now, after two months working around the clock with my German team colleagues, I realize how difficult it has been for me to cooperate and communicate effectively with them. Our project of preparing the launch of our new laser is finished now and in the end we did a good job, but it was very tough and certainly not without frictions. Now I am happy and relieved to be returning to the States.

Planning Phase

The problems already started with our first meeting. We were supposed to define our key objectives, our main challenges and our overall strategy. I was expecting something like a brainstorming session, in order to develop some general ideas and solutions, select the best ones, develop a plan and delegate specific tasks to the project team members. I anticipated this meeting to last for one morning or so. Instead, we sat there for three full days. All details were discussed at great length, but no concrete decisions were taken, no real plan was developed and no clear-cut objectives were formulated. The Germans love to see themselves as "Volk der Dichter und Denker" (people of poets and thinkers), but we don't have to endlessly dispute everything and act like a bunch of little Immanuel Kants in order to get a laser on the market! In the beginning, I patiently sat there, joined the discussion and thought it best to just go with the flow. On the second day, however, I became increasingly impatient and suggested several times to focus on what we should do now and then start working. But I was only looked at with amazement and was told that this was still much too early for any specific plan and so our philosophy seminar continued. Much of the third day of the debate I hardly bothered to pay attention anymore.

At the end of day three we finally came up with a decision of where to go from there, but I still was not content. We had wasted a lot of time to achieve so little. This was all very inefficient. How would we ever get the project finished if we continued like this? And moreover, I still did not have a precise idea of what I was supposed to do now. My German team members had discussed all issues at great length and from every possible perspective and developed a fantastic picture of the overall problem, but spent little time on spelling out our next activities. Many details which were relevant to our tasks were mentioned in our lengthy discussions but were never systematically summarized on a chart or so. How should I remember everything which was said during a three day long discussion? Furthermore, we came up with overall objectives to achieve, but never specified any broken down targets. How can we effectively work without having specific targets by which we can measure our progress and our performance along the way? An overall objective is just not providing enough guidance. To summarize, the Germans are obsessed with their focus on the problem, whereas we Americans focus more on solutions.

Working Under The Team Leader

I would have expected my German team leader to be much more decisive. He was the boss, so he should have called the shots. But no, in particular during the planning phase he consistently asked his team members what they were thinking, was patiently listening to everyone and acted more like just another team member. For a while I would have listened to everyone's opinion, but then I would just have made my mind up, announced my decision, delegated the tasks and controlled the outcome.

I also got particularly annoyed that the team leader frequently interfered in my work. He kept insisting that I had to double-check every little detail before I pass it on to other team members. I don't like to be controlled all the time, I know what I am doing. At the end of the assignment I am happy to get evaluated on my performance, but until then I prefer to be left alone, so that I can do my job. My team leader also constantly reminded me to observe certain procedural rules of which the company seemed to have an endless amount. It seemed to me that they followed their internal procedural rules for the sake of it. It is like the red traffic lights. No German pedestrian crosses the street on red, even if no car is in sight for miles.

Another thing, I thought our team leader was a poor motivator. Instead of pushing people, making them excited about the job and provide them with encouraging feedback, our team leader was always very reserved, formal and fact oriented. No emotions ever came across. Sometimes a pat on the shoulder wouldn't do any harm.

Working With The Team Members

Not only had I no clear understanding of what I was supposed to do when we started our assignments, I also didn't have a good understanding of what my German colleagues were working on. And there was little exchange of information among us. I am used to working sequentially on a clear set of well broken down targets and at every step of the way getting the information I need from my colleagues. However, whenever I went over to my team members and asked them a specific question, they did answer me politely, but I had the impression they felt disturbed by me asking them questions. Everyone just worked on his or her own.

Furthermore, I was deliberately brought in to share my specific know-how with the Germans. But when we started working on our assignments no one came to see me and asked me for advice. They probably thought they knew everything better and didn't need my expertise. But then why did they want an expert from the States on their team?

I was also puzzled by how badly my German counterparts reacted when I suggested some changes in our strategy. Whenever we hit a problem, it seemed natural for me to adapt our strategy, after all one cannot foresee everything at first and one needs to keep an open mind and remain flexible. It is through trial and error that objectives are reached. But no, we had to stick to our grand master-plan, because so much time was invested in reaching it in the first place.

The German Perspective

Introduction

For two months we had Jim, a marketing expert from our joint venture partner in the States, here in Stuttgart. His job was to help us in preparing the launch of our new laser on the European market. He was certainly well qualified for the job and also a really nice guy. He even spoke fluent German. That facilitated our job greatly. Otherwise it would have been quite odd, on a team with 16 Germans and one American, to speak English all the time. It's not so much of a problem during a formal meeting, when everyone listens to what the one speaking has to say. But what about a more informal setting, over lunch for example? If the American is listening, it's fine to talk in English, but if he directs his attention to someone else, should I then continue talking in English with my other German colleagues, as he might want to enter our conversation again? It is completely awkward to talk among Germans in English, searching for words for what you could otherwise express so easily in your own language. Also, to adapt to the Anglo-Saxon style and not look overly formal, we use first names when speaking in English. But it is very embarrassing to call my boss "Hans" when talking in English and then switch right away to "Herr Doktor Fischer" when speaking German again. In the end, with English entering our company communication more and more, we even tend to avoid addressing by name colleagues we have known for years, out of pure confusion over what to say. Therefore, we were really relieved when we heard that our American colleague was speaking German, it saved us from a lot of potentially embarrassing situations. But, as we found out, mastering the language is one thing, being able to truly communicate is a completely different story. I think Jim had no clue of how we do things here and he was little willing to adapt, always thinking that the American way is the only one which makes sense.

Planning Phase

First, all members of a newly established team gather all relevant information and discuss them intensively. The objective is to reach a holistic understanding of the problems to be solved. During this phase team leader and team members cooperate on quite equal terms. The team leader is more the moderator of this thought process. Our deliberations are rather complex and abstract, with the intention to establish an overall conceptual foundation that covers all possible eventualities, assumptions and ramifications which lead to a set of logical conclusions. In this process we focus on the underlying principles but already include all potentially relevant details to get to the bottom of our problem. From the multitude of information and ideas we subsequently generate the solution to our problem. By doing so we frequently recur to theories and scholarly methods. Subsequently, the group decides which tasks need to be tackled in order to reach the overall objective. It is expected that every team member brings his or her expertise and thoughts into this discussion process. The decisions to be reached should be based on a general consensus, be supported by everyone and be regarded as final. The decisions taken at this meeting will direct all ensuing activities. This process might take some time in the beginning, but in the end it might well save us time as we don't need to go back to the drawing board anymore.

Unfortunately, Jim didn't understand this concept at all. We tried to encourage him to share with us his perspective on our project. In fact, we specifically asked for an American expert who could share with us the experiences won on the American market, but he just didn't come forward with his knowledge. We found this particularly unhelpful. Instead, he always tried to push us prematurely to break up the work into individual assignments, but at this initial phase we barely started to grasp the problem we were facing. How are we supposed to break our work down into assignments if we collectively still don't fully understand what we are trying to achieve? After some time he even stopped paying full attention to our deliberations. But once we fully understood the problem, developed our strategy and subsequently started working we noticed that Jim just had not grasped the concept which was the basis of our work. Typical American: no willingness to invest time in the beginning to thoroughly understand a problem, just focusing on setting some superficial targets and then seeing later on how one gets along and muddling your way through. We prefer to do things a lot more methodically.

Working Under The Team Leader

Once we reached an agreement about what to do, all the team members started working on their assignments. They had a good understanding of our overall objective and how we wanted to achieve this. We had discussed all eventualities during the planning phase, so everyone had all the information which was needed and was now ready to focus fully on working individually on his or her job. That is everyone except Jim. As he hadn't paid attention when we had discussed our overall strategy, he was subsequently unable to understand what was expected from him. Instead, he felt confused by not having targets nicely broken down for him, so that he didn't have to think about the overall picture but could sequentially tick off one job after the other. This is what I call intellectual laziness.

I also thought Jim had completely different expectations from me as his team leader. He expected me to show more authority and be less participatory while we planned our project. I tried to explain to him my more "democratic" understanding of my role as team leader, that I perceived myself more as a "primus inter pares". As team leader I have probably the best technical know-how about our project and all its details, and this is also what my team members expect from me. However, this does not mean that I tell my team what they have to do, I moderate more the decision making process, keep the group together, promote consensus and control the outcome. It is only in the case of conflict that I will enforce a decision. But I think he considered this leadership concept just as a weakness. Also, during the implementation phase he wanted more guidance from me, as he continuously asked me what exactly he should be doing and the exact target against which his performance would be measured. I think our German team members are much more independent in the way they do their job.

Jim also seemed quite annoyed when I tried to align his work to our way of operating and insisted he knew best how to do his job. I should judge his results, not his methods, he said. However, we have certain procedures here and everyone is expected to follow them. I understand that while we have all worked here for at least 10 years and know our company procedures very well, all this was unknown to Jim. But he should have at least shown some respect for our methods and should have tried to follow them, instead of insisting on doing things in his own way. Furthermore, it only makes sense to check on someone regularly and not just evaluate the final result, because by then it can be already too late to adjust things.

Working with The Team Members

While all team members were concentrating on their jobs, Jim bothered them all the time with specific questions. If he had paid more attention in the first place, this would have been completely unnecessary. During the implementation phase we prefer to work individually in a focused way on our own and don't need much communication with other members of the team. At that stage group meetings only take place if another exchange of information is considered necessary. The incentive to such meetings can come from anybody in the group. And if we come together, we tend to have again a holistic discussion of the entire project, but this time based on a more advanced degree of understanding. What we certainly don't like is to make some little changes here and there, because it might be momentarily more convenient. We try to come up with fundamental solutions to fundamental problems and some quick fixes will only endanger the overall applicability of these solutions. We therefore expect that everybody sticks to what was initially agreed upon and solves their tasks in a way they will be in harmony to our overall plan. If we have to correct any mistakes then we will do this in a very systematic and thorough way and try to understand all possible effects a change in plan will have. Consequently, we were not too pleased that whenever a problem occurred Jim was willing to throw overboard everything we had carefully elaborated on and just try out something different. Changing direction without prior intensive reflection is a sign of sloppiness. Good solutions should last a long time and we try to work here for the long-term.

When we had the final meeting in which he presented us the results of his work, we noticed that he had actually done quite a good job. However, a little more modesty about his work would have been appropriate. He was also somewhat playing out too much his certainly well established presentation skills. I would have preferred a little more substance in his presentation and less of a show. For example, instead of just telling us his conclusions of what we should be doing and elaborating on that, he should first have explained more about the way he developed his proposals.

To sum up, I had thought the Americans were such great managers. But now, having had the experience of working with Jim, I honestly believe that our way of doing business makes more sense.

Situation: The Project is Dominated by Americans

The German Perspective

Introduction

While our company was responsible for the launch of the new laser in Europe, our American partners called the shots for the North American market. Still, I was sent over from our headquarters in Stuttgart to share with our American partners the experiences we gained in Germany and to make sure that our interests were also sufficiently considered on the American turf. In principle, the task wasn't that difficult, as we hardly had any genuine conflicts of interest. It was just a matter of getting it right. But, as it turned out, working with the Americans was not so easy. I always thought they were so professional, however I wasn't overly impressed by how the project was managed. But in the end we did alright and I am glad to return home now.

Planning Phase

Problems had already started in the planning phase. I am an expert in my field and could have contributed more thoroughly to the definition of our overall strategy. Instead, I was given right away specific targets and was expected to reach them in a very short period of time. But were these really the best targets I could have been given? I would have preferred to give more of my input during the all important planning phase. I was actually not overly convinced about the underlying assumptions on which our strategy was based. But for the sake of speed a thorough collection of information and discussion did not take place. How should one do quality work on this basis?

Working Under The Team Leader

Right from the word go, I was put under so much time pressure that there was no way that I could deliver something with real substance. And yet to my surprise what I did was good enough for my American team leader. Well, it wasn't for me. And indeed later on I had to substantially modify my original suggestions once more information became available. All these subsequent improvements here and there annoyed me greatly. These are indications of sloppy work and in the end cost more time and energy than if we had invested a little more thought in the first place. Moreover, these "quick and dirty" solutions and quick fixes are not exactly testament to the upholding of high quality standards. There was no sense of perfection.

I was always astonished to see how quickly my American team leader reached a decision. He briefly thought about a problem, announced his decision and that was it. Never any doubts about possibly being wrong. Also the other team members just accepted his decisions without ever questioning them. They were even expecting our team leader to make specific decisions all the time, so that they knew exactly what to do. Despite the casual tone in the company, my American colleagues were much more hierarchy oriented compared to what I am used to in Germany. Even though we are much more formal in Germany, I thought in the American company the atmosphere was in the end more authoritarian. This actually came as quite a surprise to me, as I wasn't expecting this.

The head of the department insisted that everybody addressed him by first name, but at the same time he wouldn't have the slightest problem firing someone as soon as he detected some underperformance. By contrast, in Germany we would never call our boss by first name (and neither would he address us by first name) even though we have known each other for more than ten years. But he would also never fire someone who works loyally for the company, after all we are a team, care for each other and the company has a social responsibility.

I was also put off by the speeches our team leader gave us all the time. I guess they were supposed to motivate us, but for me that was just cheap pep talk, probably copied from these motivation seminars the Americans are so fond off. However, what I really appreciated was the feed-back our team leader gave us, particularly as it always focused on the positive. I think that is something I'd also like to see in Germany.

Working With The Team Members

While working on our assignments, frequent adaptations had to be made. If we all had followed more precise procedures this could have been entirely avoided. Moreover, as long as we met our individual targets my American team colleagues didn't even care if the overall result made any sense or not. No team member except the leader has any holistic concern for the entire project and feels responsible for the greater picture. I found it somewhat of a paradox that the Americans, the archetype of capitalists, were almost as obsessed with reaching specific targets as the communists were under the centrally planned economy.

At one instance, I was criticized, because my work didn't fit with what the others were doing. But this was exactly my point. If we don't bother to make a detailed picture for ourselves in the first place, how should I know what to do? But I was only told I should have checked with my team members.

I always had problems with these informalities. I don't mind enjoying a drink after work, but during work we should refrain from joking around. As we say in German: "Work is work and schnaps is schnaps." I also noticed that women in the company don't like to be treated with special courtesy. Whenever I held a door open for a woman or, after a working lunch, helped a woman with her coat, I was looked at as if I was doing something bad.

And when we discussed our final results, I felt my American colleagues were all highlighting their individual inputs by far too much. We are all team members and there is no reason to brag about one's own achievements. All my American team members at first appeared to be so collegial but in the end everyone was fighting for his or her own. Everyone pretends to be good buddy with the others, but at the same time I have never seen so much open and almost aggressive competition among team members. In this company they always talk about their team spirit, but I think that is all corporate propaganda.

The American Perspective

Introduction

For two months we had Klaus working with us in order to prepare the presentation of our new laser system on the North American market. Klaus had been sent over by our German joint venture partner. He was certainly very competent and in addition a really nice guy, once one got to know him a little better. Nevertheless, working with him proved to be quite difficult, he just drove us nuts with his complete inflexibility. What can you say, a real German.

Planning Phase

Klaus just couldn't focus on specific targets and solutions. When we had our first meeting in order to decide who does what, Klaus wanted to drag us into a long discussion about fundamental issues which we just perceived as either irrelevant or something to think about at a later stage. He wanted to plan everything down to the last detail. But you just can't foresee everything and therefore you have to adapt and be flexible along the way. But Klaus just misunderstood our flexibility and openmindedness for superficiality which of course is nonsense. A first planning meeting should be solution driven. What exactly do we want to achieve? Once we understand this, we identify the specific steps we need to take in order to get there. The main task of the team leader in the planning phase is to assign specific team members to clearly defined tasks and develop a time plan, specifying what and when should be achieved. With the delegation of responsibilities the planning process is finished and off you go.

Working Under The Team Leader

Klaus was always quite nervous about the fact that as team leader I expected him to be fully responsible for his assignment. When I told him his evaluation would be primarily based on his results he got quite anxious about it, always saying that the final result could depend on many things some of which could well be beyond his control. But as a manager you have to stand up for your own performance. No excuses.

In our company it is the team leader who defines the overall objective and specific targets, who structures the assignments, and delegates responsibilities. Subsequently, during the implementation phase, the team leader is always available for questions, provides constant feed-back, supports the information exchange, keeps the morale of the team up, controls whether the various tasks are achieved on time and evaluates the team members according to their individual performance. Overall, the team leader has a strong position, he pushes the project forward.

In the end, Klaus came up with some good results, but in the final presentation he was completely underselling himself. How should people see whether you are a high performer if you can't even show how good you are? Also, instead of telling us his proposal right away he started out explaining at great lengths the specific assumptions on which his proposal was based, the various alternative solutions he formulated, what his selection criteria were etc. etc. When we all thought he would never come to the point, he finally told us what his proposal was. That was quite a clumsy way of doing a presentation.

Working With The Team Members

Once Klaus got his assignment he complained that he didn't have enough information to do his job. But that is what a manager is about: to make decisions under uncertainty. And if you don't have the information you need, well, then get it. First he complained that we hadn't discussed the problem enough, but then he just never really communicated with his team members or participated in the ongoing exchange of information. While we continuously popped into each others' offices to clarify things, Klaus just sat in his office and worked by himself.

When we get our tasks from our team leader we are expected to clearly structure our working schedule and solve each single task, one after the other. The trial-and-error principle is an important and often used mechanism. In this phase we use our own knowledge but also frequently ask our colleagues for advice. This implementation phase is usually characterized by an intense information exchange. We see constant feed-back from both team leader and team members as essential to achieving our individual tasks. This information exchange takes place in a very informal way, through e-mails, telephone calls, dropping by at others' offices or just a quick chat on the corridor. Everyone is available at every point in time for a short discussion. We frequently circulate written documentation to update each other on the various working steps. If we feel that we can improve the final solution by modifying our plan we do so at every stage in the process. If one solution doesn't work we try the next one. To quickly come up with a solution is important, but to be prepared to quickly drop a decision if a better one is found is equally important. This way we constantly improve the final outcome. For all this, good time management is important so that we can stick to the initial time plan. But I think Klaus had little understanding for all that.

Overall, I think Klaus should loosen up a bit. He can actually be quite a humorous guy and when we went to a bar after work we often had a good laugh. But the next day at work he was dead serious again, never made a joke and came across as rather unfriendly and cold. In particular, the secretaries didn't like him much, as he never spoke a private word with them, only focused on the job. Also female colleagues felt at times rather uncomfortable with his manners. They thought of the special attention and courtesy he paid them as rather sexist. I don't think he meant it in that way, but female managers in this country prefer to be treated as fully equal to men and that includes no preferential treatment.

Anyway, Klaus will be going back to Germany now. It was interesting to see how differently people from other countries act and behave. And I am relieved to say that our way of doing things clearly appears to me to make most sense.

_____

Markus Pudelko, "Cooperating and Communicating across Cultures: Americans and Germans Working on a Project in a Team," pp. 2–11. Copyright © 2006 by The Case Centre. Reprinted with permission.

SUMMARY

Cultures differ from one another and are dynamic. In the business world, when two or more cultures interact, trouble can occur if there is not proper communication. In this chapter, we focused on the importance of intercultural communication in the business world. Our first reading highlighted the skills needed for an individual to become a culturally competent communicator in business. Our second reading explored the role of negotiating between individualistic and collectivistic cultures, and we discovered that negotiating requires both cultures to compromise in order to achieve their goal. Finally, our last reading involved two case studies that enabled us to view of how both parties perceived their intercultural work encounter. This reinforced that cultural competence is essential in business encounters. Continue onward to the discussion questions for an opportunity to apply your knowledge about intercultural communication and business.

DISCUSSION QUESTIONS

1. How has your life been impacted by the global marketplace? Is globalization the future for the business community? How does communication contribute to the expansion of the globalization?
2. Why is competent intercultural communication essential in the workplace?
3. What are the differences between intercultural and cross-cultural communication in the workplace? Why are both kinds of communication essential in maintaining harmony?
4. How does consideration of the *other* person's cultural perspective contribute to the resolution of differences in the work environment?

INTERCULTURAL COMMUNICATION AND TOURISM

CHAPTER 12

STUDY OBJECTIVES

After completing this chapter, you will be able to:
- Define tourist and sojourner and explain the differences between the two.
- Define and explain what happens when someone experiences culture shock.
- Identify and provide suggestions on how to reduce culture shock.

INTRODUCTION

Travel and tourism is one of the world's largest industries. There are books, magazines, television channels, shows, blogs, and websites devoted to traveling. Chances are you have been a tourist at one point in your life, or will be one soon. Becoming a tourist does not require that you fly to another country, you can certainly be a tourist in your own country and even your own state. No matter where you may travel, being a tourist enables you to experience intercultural happenstances; especially if you choose to become a sojourner and study abroad.

In this chapter, there are two readings that explore intercultural communication and tourism. Our first reading explores the differences between tourists and sojourners. In this reading, we learn about culture shock and how to reduce culture shock as much as possible. Our second reading examines tourism through a business perspective, looking at how power plays an important role in intercultural tourism exchanges. Further, this reading takes us on a journey to the country of Morocco and discusses how citizens of this country experience intercultural communication regularly through the country's expanding tourism market. At the end of the chapter, you will find a number of discussion questions to put your knowledge concerning tourism and intercultural communication to the test.

Moving Forward

Our first reading focuses on culture shock and how individuals adjust to a new and different culture. Culture shock can happen when first experiencing a new culture and can happen regardless if an individual is a tourist or a sojourner. Everyone experiences some level of culture shock when traveling. As you move throughout this reading, pay attention to the tables, suggestions on how to manage culture shock, and explanations of the differences between a sojourner and a tourist. Can you recall a time where you or someone you know experienced culture shock? Would the following suggestions on how to diffuse culture shock have helped you?

TOURISM AND CULTURE SHOCK

The fundamental need for newcomers in an unfamiliar culture is addressing the sense of emotional insecurity and vulnerability. The more competent newcomers are at managing their identity threat level, the more they are able to induce effective adaptation outcomes.

New arrivals can defuse their perceived threats and, hence, anxiety level by (1) increasing their motivations to learn about the new culture; (2) keeping their expectations realistic and increasing their familiarity concerning the diverse facets of the new culture (e.g., conducting culture-specific research through readings and diverse accurate sources, including talking with people who have spent some time in that culture); (3) increasing their linguistic fluency and learning why, how, and under what situations certain phrases or gestures are appropriate, plus understanding the core cultural values linked to specific behaviors; (4) working on their tolerance for ambiguity and other flexible personal attributes; (5) developing strong ties (close friends) and weak ties (acquaintanceships) to manage identity stress and loneliness; and (6) being mindful of their interpersonal behaviors and suspending ethnocentric evaluations of the host culture.

Intercultural Adjustment: Developmental Patterns

The term **intercultural adjustment** has been used to refer to the short-term and medium-term adaptive process of sojourners in their overseas assignments. Tourists are different from sojourners in that tourists are visitors whose length of stay exceeds 24 hours in a location away from home and who have traveled for voluntary, recreational holiday-enjoyment purposes. Sojourners, on the other hand, are temporary residents who voluntarily go abroad for a set period of time that is usually related to task-based or instrumental purposes. Both tourists and sojourners can, of course, experience culture shock—especially when the country they visit is very different from their own. In fact, do you know which are the top worldwide tourist destinations? Take a guess and then check out Table 12.1. Where do you think most tourists to the United States come from (i.e., their countries of origin)? What do you think are the top-three tourism cities in the United States? Take a quick guess and check out Table 12.2 and 12.3. A tourist, while visiting another country, can be a welcome guest, a nuisance, or a downright intruder in a sacred land. Tourists, their hosts, and businesses/service providers all weave together interdependently to form impressions, to trade, and to share some memorable moments through brief encounters and amusing contacts.

Sojourners, however, are typically individuals who commit to a temporary residential stay in a new culture as they strive to achieve both their instrumental and socio-emotional goals. *Instrumental goals* refer to task-based goals that sojourners would like to accomplish during their stay in a foreign country. *Socio-emotional goals* refer to relational, recreational, and personal development goals during their sojourning experience. Thus, a Peace Corps volunteer might take an overseas assignment for a year or two for both task and personal enrichment purposes. A business person might accept an international posting for between three and five years. A missionary might go for a longer period, and military personnel are often posted overseas for shorter "tours of duty." Each year, for example, over 1.3 million students worldwide choose to study outside their countries. There are approximately 586,000 international students right now, studying in different U.S. colleges with the explicit aim of getting their college degrees here. They also bring $12 billion into the U.S. economy via out-of-state tuition and living expenses. In fact, do you know where most of the international students come from? Take a guess and check out Table 12.4. Do you know what are the top-pick countries for U.S. student-abroad programs? Take a guess and check out Table 12.5.

Table 12.1 Top Ten Worldwide Tourist Destinations, 2013

COUNTRY	
1. France	6. Turkey
2 United States	7. Germany
3. Spain	8. United Kingdom
4. China	9. Russian Federation
5. Italy	10. Thailand

Source: World Tourism Organization (UNWTO)
http://dtxtq4w60xqpw.cloudfront.net/sites/all/files/pdf/unwto_highlights14_en.pdf

Table 12.2 Top Ten Countries of Origin of Visitors to the United States, 2013

COUNTRY	
1. Canada	6. Germany
2 Mexico	7. China
3. United Kingdom	8. France
4. Japan	9. Korea
5. Brazil	10. Australia

Source: U.S. Office of Travel and Tourism Industries
http://travel.trade.gov/view/f-2000-99-001/forecast/Forecast-Countries.pdf

Table 12.3 Top Ten Tourism Cities in the United States, 2012

COUNTRY	
1. New York City	6. Orlando
2 Los Angeles	7. Washington, DC
3. Miami	8. Honolulu
4. San Francisco	9. Boston
5. Lad Vegas	10. Chicago

Source: U.S. Office of Travel and Tourism Industries
http://travel.trade.gov/outreachpages/download_data_table/2011_States_and_Cities.pdf

Table 12.4 Top Ten Countries of Origin of International Students to the United States, 2013

COUNTRY	
1. China	6. Taiwan
2 India	7. Japan
3. South Korea	8. Mexico
4. Saudi Arabia	9. Vietnam
5. Canada	10. Turkey

Source: Institute of International Education
http://www.iie.org/Research-and-Publications/Open-Doors/Data/InternationalStudents/Infographic

Table 12.5 Top Ten Countries of Origin of International Students to the United States, 2013

COUNTRY	
1. United Kingdom	6. Ireland
2 Italy	7. Costa Rica
3. Spain	8. Germany
4. France	9. Australia
5. China	10. Japan

Source: Institute of International Education
http://www.iie.org/Research-and-Publications/Open-Doors/Data/US-Study-Abroad

Indeed, most of the international students come from communal-oriented cultures, such as India, China, South Korea, Japan, and Taiwan. There are also approximately 11 percent or 154,168 U.S. students nationwide who embark on a one-year study abroad program. The favorite study abroad destinations of U.S. college students are the United Kingdom, Italy, Spain, France, and Mexico. These students cited personal growth, new perspectives on world affairs, and career enhancement as some of the reasons for why they opt to go abroad to study. Beyond instrumental goals, international exchange sojourners also pursue socio-emotional goals or fun activities, such as developing new friendships with the local students and hosts, visiting local marketplaces and museums, and learning about local histories, sports, and folk crafts.

Moving Forward

Our next reading focuses on tourism and the need for effective intercultural communication using a business perspective. Tourism involves the need for intercultural communication as members and organizations of the host country are exposed to individuals from another culture. Similarly, tourists are exposed to the host country's culture. As tourism increases within an area, the host country is forced to adapt to the culture of the visitors in order to accommodate for the tourism increase.

The following reading examines the country of Morocco and its experience with increasing tourism. As tourism continues to flourish in Morocco, a greater need for intercultural business exchange will develop. As you continue through this reading, keep in mind the following questions: How does power play a role in intercultural business interactions in tourism? Can you think of what a host country may need to do to promote intercultural communication in tourism?

TOURISM, INTER-CULTURAL CONTACT AND COMMUNICATION

As Jack and Phipps (2005: 6) argue, tourism as an 'inter-cultural activity, constructed within and through language, has been largely ignored in tourism research until very recently'; simply put, what limited attention there has been has focused primarily on host–guest encounters (Reisinger and Turner 2003; Hunter 2001) rather than business-to-business relations (cf. Scherle 2004, 2006). In contrast, inter-cultural communication has become a major focus for management studies. Mainly driven by Hofstede's work (1982, 1999), studies of inter-cultural communication have courted controversy (Moosmüller 1997; Thomas 2003). There are several reasons for this, but one of the more important is that there is a propensity to reduce culture to a mere factor, practically an ingredient that has to be present in successful international business (Johnson and Turner 2003; Rugman and Hodgetts 2003; Gesteland 2005). Inter-cultural communication is, however, a far more complex affair. Partners from different cultures have to cope with cultural differences which otherwise impede communication and, in the worst case, result in a culture shock and breakdown in social relations (Casmir and Asuncion-Lande 1989; Ward et al. 2001; Pütz 2003).

Inter-cultural communication depends heavily on the notion of inter-cultural competence. With its roots in linguistics, inter-cultural competence is the mutual avowal of the interactants' cultural identities where both interactants engage in behaviour perceived to be appropriate and effective in advancing both cultural identities (Collier 1989). Kühlmann and Stahl (1998) identify seven characteristics to facilitate inter-cultural competence: tolerance of ambiguity, behavioural flexibility, target orientation, sociability, empathy, polycentrism and meta-communicative competence. While each of these facets operates differentially, all should be present in competent and effective inter-cultural engagements, and abstract tolerance alone is rarely effective (Moosmüller 1997).

Two schools of thought have emerged concerning the relevance of culture in international business (Table 12.6). 'Culturalists' advocate that management techniques are intricately and mutually implicated with culture, or international business is 'culture-bound'. Businesses have to be more culturally competent, sensitive to the needs and operations of their partners in other cultural settings, thereby adjusting and gearing their own operations accordingly. For instance, prior to EU enlargement, *The Economist* (2003) reported that officials from the European Commission had described Polish officials as the most difficult among the 15 new member states. A series of 'golden rules' had been devised to facilitate their induction into the EU culture of doing business.

The 'culturalist' position is challenged by the 'universalists'. For them, management techniques are universal and therefore independent of culture-specific influences; business is 'culture free', low levels of inter-cultural competence are required, and operations need minimal, if any, adjustment to cater for bilateral business co-operations. Closely linked to these two postions are the concepts of convergence and divergence. The latter holds that culture is a central construct of organisational and management behaviour and hence should be more deeply appreciated. Differing values and behaviours, differing stages of development and the uneven distribution of resources will ensure diversity and inequality that must be embraced in business. Convergence theory holds that technology, structure and a global orientation by many firms render inter-cultural management unnecessary (Warner and Joynt 2002).

Table 12.6 Approaches to Business Management in Inter-Cultural Situations

POSITION	UNIVERSALISM	CULTURALISM
Cultural doctrine:	Society has a culture	Society is a culture
Management assumption:	'One best way'	'Several good ways'
Management paradigm:	Culture-free management	Culture-bound management
Typical business concepts:	— Planning instruments	— Management style
	— Investment analysis	— Motivation
	— Budget planning	— Flexible working
	— Production control	— Closer working relationships in all levels of organisation

Source: abridged from Kutschker (2001).

The culture-free and -bound positions have been contested (see Osterloh 1994; Bosch 1997; Hofstede 1999; Kutschker and Schmid 2002). While it may be tempting to use broad cultural designations, cultures are constantly evolving and highly differentiated into micro-cultural sub-systems. Such fissures and cleavages hint at how tensions form; they help to explain divergence and exceptional behaviours in bilateral co-operations (Moosmüller 1997); and significantly they expose the use of stereotypes in inter-cultural management. Some writers have argued that cultural stereotypes are used to simplify heterogeneity within complex cultural groups (Lippmann 1965) although racism and discrimination are perhaps equally valid explanations. The use of stereotypes may manifest the level of inter-cultural competence, but they may also be a demonstration of, and used as, a particular tactic to impose power by ordering other cultures and establishing a degree of authority. Inter-cultural business relations rely not just on the interpretation of who is *present* in the other, foreign culture, but more who is *perceived* to be present (Roth 1996).

In the context of inter-cultural business communications in tourism, the preceding discussion raises two important points. The first concerns the paradox that power is central to the mediation of these inter-cultural business relations, but power discourse has not been wired into studies of inter-cultural business communications. This is a notable omission because, even where inter-cultural competence is high, conflicts cannot be eliminated (Bruck 1994; Stüdlein 1997; Gilbert 1998). In fact, they are relatively common occurrences and the types of 'competitive tactical encounters' involving power are routine in cross-cultural business relations. Questions arise therefore of how the individual protagonists perceive their positions over power, what power strategies and tactics they are prepared to use in conflict situations, and how their approaches to power map against their other organisational characteristics.

Conflicts frequently have a cultural background (Moran *et al.* 1993; Steinmann and Olbrich 1994) and they occur with the interaction of interdependent people who perceive incompatible goals and interference from each other in achieving those goals (Hocker and Wilmot 1995). Kopper (1992) identifies two principal, idealised approaches to conflict management (Table 10.6). Individualistic cultures deal with conflicts in a more dispassionate, matter-of-fact way. They are designed to get beyond the implications for particular individuals and instead work towards the future of the organisation. They are based—in theory at least—on a rational and objective assessment of the circumstances. When mapped against inter-cultural management approaches (Table 12.6), there are obvious overlaps with the culture-free approach. In collectivist cultures, conflict management is more culturally bound. Conflicts are viewed negatively, as more destructive forces; they are constructed and resolved in more emotive, subjective and ambiguous ways; and they are associated with individuals and groups whose status is questioned during the conflict.

Of course, individual and collectivist organisations may use any or all of the tactics outlined in Table 12.4 depending on the precise circumstances of the conflict. However, when read against tables 12.6 and 12.7, there is a suggestion that individualist, culture-free organisations may be more predisposed towards rational persuasion, exchange and rewards tactics given their devotion to the one best way. In contrast, collectivist organisations where culture and business are intricately and messily bound, inspirational appeals, coalition tactics and consultation tactics may be more prevalent. This concern for tactics should not mask the importance of conflict management as a source of power. For conflicts to be resolved, especially where the protagonists originate from individualistic and collectivist cultures, there has to be a mutual recognition of each other's approach. Joint dialogue may advance creative solutions to improve future co-operations and it improves the actors' insights into, and understandings of, their counterparts' behavioural patterns (Bergemann and Volkema 1989; De Dreu 1997; Schneider and Barsoux 1999).

The second important issue in the consideration of inter-cultural business interactions in tourism is that the injection of power discourse requires us to rethink the structure and outcomes of international business relations. Cross-border activities may generate important economic outputs, but they are rarely straightforward and the economic gains for their protagonists are culturally preconditioned (Stüdlein 1997). Until now, readings of power in transnational business relations have consistently implied that there must be 'winners' and 'losers' in the process whereby one party's gain is the other's loss of power (cf. Bastakis *et al.* 2004: 153–154). Such views are rooted in Weberian notions of power, domination and authority and they suggest strongly that power is a finite capacity such that struggles over it are always set in a 'zero-sum game'. As Parsons (1963) has observed, power does not necessarily have to have a finite capacity. Empowerment is a culturally constructed and hence differentially understood term. Perceptions of whether (economic) empowerment has taken place and the relative shifts in empowerment vary depending on who makes them and their background. Significantly, this introduces the possibility that both parties may perceive themselves to be empowered through their unfolding inter-cultural commercial relations, or there is at least a perceived 'win–win', positive-sum outcome.

Table 12.7 Inter-Cultural Differences in the Context of Conflict Management

ASPECTS	INDIVIDUALIST CULTURES	COLLECTIVISTIC CULTURES
Conflicts are seen as:	positive and productive	negative and destructive
Optimum approach:	conflict solution	conflict prevention
Conflicts are:	handled and solved	avoided and oppressed
Conflicts and persons are:	mostly separated	closely connected
The conflict parties orient to:	proceedings and solutions	people and 'face'
The conflict style is:	rational and factually oriented	intuitive and emotional
The procedure in the context of solving conflicts is:	open and direct	ambiguous and indirect

Source: adapted from Kopper (1992: 239).

In the next section, we turn to consider the development of tourism and the emerging policy context in Morocco. Businesses from Morocco and Germany, with their contrasting and complex cultures which in part reflect very different colonial and migratory histories (cf. Bourdieu 1989), provide an opportunity to explore the processes and outcomes of inter-cultural interactions in a situation where the state has promoted tourism as a source of empowerment for indigenous entrepreneurs.

Key Issues in Recent Tourism Development in Morocco

According to Gray (2002), Morocco has been more successful than other North African states in harnessing the economic potentials of tourism. A systematic approach to tourism development was first evident in the 1960s with the creation of a five-year followed by a three-year plan to encourage modernisation (Kagermeier 1999). These plans extolled the advantages of international tourism. Package holidays, in particular, stimulated hard currency receipts, new employment opportunities, infrastructural improvements in local economies as well as domestic tourism (Müller-Hohenstein and Popp 1990). In the last forty years, there has been steady growth in tourism albeit the performance of the sector has fluctuated (cf. Barbier 1999; Sebbar 1999; Berriane and Popp 1999; Gray 2002; Kester 2003). In 1996, there were 2.7 million arrivals in Morocco and receipts were US$1.278 billion (Gray 2002: 398). In 2001, Morocco attracted an estimated 40 per cent of North African international tourist arrivals (second only to Tunisia) and 58.9 per cent of international tourism receipts (leading the market) (Kester 2003: 211). Its primary markets are mass package tourism based on the beach resorts and towns of Casablanca, Fez and Marrakech, independent travellers, and increasingly adventure tourists taking advantage of desert and mountain in the interior (Gray 2002: 399).

Recent tourism policy has been influenced by two critical issues. First, the Moroccan government has recognised the great contribution of tourism to the economy, and that the economy has frequently fallen victim to demand fluctuations (Gray 2002; Kester 2003). To support viable, sustained, long-term growth there is neither sufficient bedspace capacity of the quality and quantity required, nor a suitably diversified product portfolio. Second, since 2000 King Mohammed VI has directed the government to introduce a comprehensive programme of economic and social reform, with tourism as a key driver (Loverseed 2002). Early in 2001, the government in co-operation with the Central Association of Moroccan Business (CGEM) established a series of strategic guidelines and policy aims to harness more fully the economic potential of tourism.

This policy context has fostered, and will continue to demand, inter-cultural business exchanges. Tourism enterprises are encouraged to become more independent from the state to reap greater rewards from tourism and to spread the benefits through the country (Gray 2002). Not only does this desired process of empowerment compel them to seek out new markets and segments, but also it requires them to seek greater value from their transactions with tourists and their intermediaries from their existing (core) markets. This may be through increased visitor numbers, greater consumption of tours, excursions and peripheral offers, and/or the extraction of more favourable terms with their strategic partners. Rather than empower local businesses, such a policy has the potential to achieve the opposite by enhancing the power of overseas operators to act as information brokers and 'gatekeepers' to bedspaces (Ioannides 1998; Bastakis *et al.* 2004). Greater overseas visitor numbers and spend may be desired but, crucially, guests have to be 'delivered' from foreign markets. Moroccan destination marketing organisations overseas comprise one dimension of the infrastructure of supply (Loverseed 2002). 'Local' travel agents and tour operators in overseas markets function as important conduits of information about Morocco as well as retailers of Moroccan vacations especially in new niche markets such as golf tourism, meetings and incentives, desert safari tourism, skiing, mountaineering and trekking. Diversification of this type has created opportunities for, and requires the involvement of, Moroccan SMTEs. While these businesses are for the Moroccan government most welcome sector participants, they are also some of the most economically marginal; most sensitive to market fluctuations and the power of other businesses; and in need of assistance, co-operation and collaboration from Moroccan and overseas businesses and non-governmental organisations (Scherle 2006).

While Morocco retains strong links with France as the former colonial power, Moroccan tourism policy targets Germany, its businesses and NGOs because German tourists are already favourably predisposed towards North Africa as a destination, and there is a belief that visitors may be attracted away from Morocco's principal competitor, Tunisia (Scherle 2006). Thus, the success of current tourism policy and the prospects for long-term empowerment of Moroccan businesses depends in no small measure on the nature of cross-cultural communications and the way in which power relations are played out between indigenous enterprises and their strategic partners from countries like Germany.

SUMMARY

Travel and tourism is one of the world's largest industries. Individuals representing different cultures travel to new places where practices and customs differ from those they have experienced within their own culture. In tourism, there is a need for culturally competent communication; as tourists, sojourners, and individuals from the destination countries are interacting with cultures that are not their own.

This chapter focused on tourism with two readings. Our first reading introduced culture shock and provided some tips for managing culture shock. In this reading, we also learned the difference between a tourist and a sojourner and discovered some of the top tourist destinations and the top countries from which tourists were visiting the United States. Our second reading introduced us to tourism in Morocco through a business perspective. This reading examined how power plays an important role in intercultural tourism exchanges and discussed the need for intercultural business interactions as tourism grows in the area.

DISCUSSION QUESTIONS

1. Most everyone has been a tourist at some point in time. How do the cultural perspectives of tourist and host come into conflict and often result in incompetent intercultural communication?
2. How does culture shock affect intercultural communication? What strategies can be used by the competent intercultural communicator to assist those experiencing culture shock?
3. When planning to travel to a different country, what steps should be followed to minimize intercultural communication difficulties?

INTERCULTURAL COMMUNICATION AND HEALTH

CHAPTER 13

STUDY OBJECTIVES

After completing this chapter, you will be able to:
- Identify and describe why intercultural communication is inherent in health communication.
- Identify and explain why effective intercultural communication is essential between health care providers and patients.
- Suggest ways intercultural communication can be used in health settings.

INTRODUCTION

Imagine that your favorite sport is hockey and you absolutely love playing hockey. In the summer, you play street or roller hockey, and in the colder months you play ice hockey. While playing one day, you are checked pretty hard and injure your wrist. You now have to go to the doctor. You go to the doctor and explain what happened; the doctor then looks at your injury, tells you that your injury is a nasty sprain, and directs you to ice your wrist on and off for twenty minutes for a set number of days. You go home, do as your doctor directed and within a week, you are able to play hockey again.

Being able to communicate with your doctor made it easy for you to follow directions and to heal in a timely manner. But what if you were unable to communicate to your doctor because your doctor spoke a different language than you? What if you were unable to communicate what happened, where your injury was, and how it hurt? What if your culture prohibited the kind of treatment your doctor recommended? As the United States continues to become more and more diverse, this is an experience that is becoming common for many New Americans.

Intercultural communication in the health care industry is becoming more and more important. Doctors, nurses, and other health care professionals are daily communicating with individuals from different cultural backgrounds, different language backgrounds, and backgrounds that may affect how an individual approaches a health topic. Having knowledge of intercultural communication and being a more culturally competent communicator is essential for individuals entering the health care industry.

In this chapter, there are two readings. The first reading introduces us to why intercultural communication is important in health contexts. Although brief, the reading provides a few examples of how cultures differ from one another in rituals; and argues that with increasing probability, health care professionals will need to interact with a different culture than their own throughout their career. Our second reading comes from a research study that further highlights the need for intercultural communication to occur between physician and patient. In this study, the researchers interviewed physicians about their intercultural interactions.

At the end of the chapter, you will find an opportunity to consider the readings as answer a few discussion questions. These discussion questions will aid you in applying your knowledge about intercultural communication in health settings.

Moving Forward

Our first reading is brief and provides insight into why intercultural communication is important to health care professionals and throughout the health care industry. It highlights the United States' growing diverse-and-aging population and explains the need for culturally sensitive and culturally competent communication in the health care industry.

As you move throughout this reading, keep in mind the changing cultural landscape in the United States. As a culturally competent communicator, how might you approach a situation where your patient is from a different culture than your more culturally familiar patients? What type of intercultural communication needs to occur between a patient and health care professional? Does that responsibility solely rest on the doctor? Why or why not?

MULTICULTURAL CARE AND HEALTH

As borders continue to merge and divide, one area rich in conversation is the state of multicultural health care. When Liliana was giving birth to her daughter, the doctor was surprised that her husband, Senel, did not stand by Liliana. He did not coach her along or support her through the various stages of labor pain. In fact, he was not even in the delivery room to witness the delivery of a beautiful baby girl named Aryana. The doctor was quite perturbed and puzzled. Several months later, during a routine baby check-up, in chatting with Liliana, the doctor finally realized that Senel was not in the delivery room because of his Muslim faith and belief. For Muslims, birth comes through the "house" with a midwife in attendance, a very sacred place, and no man should be inside the room during baby delivery. Similarly, Native Indians in Belize and Panama also believe that the father should not be in the delivery room with the mother or the baby or else harm can come to both of them. If you were a trained nurse of health care professional, would you likely be aware of this religious tradition concerning childbirth?

Many immigrants and multicultural citizens have high expectations that health care workers will respect their personal beliefs and health care practices. This is not always the case. For example, Fadiman (1997) documents a case in which a Hmong child became brain-dead after doctors in Merced, California, continuously miscommunicated with the parents. The clash between traditional Hmong beliefs and the role of Western medicine resulted in a tragic incident.

Multicultural health care in this global age is an additional concern because of the aging population. Many must agonize over the rising cost of providing quality care to aging parents and grandparents. They also have to struggle with their own cultural and personal values of taking care of their aging parents at home or sending them away to a health care facility. Additionally, immigrants with limited English skills have to struggle to communicate with the hospital staff, nurses, or doctors to convey a simple message. Many immigrants also use their children as translators—which easily tips the balance between the parental role and the child's role in a status-oriented family system. Worse, even if the child speaks English fluently, she or he may not know how to translate all the medical terms or medication prescriptions for a parent.

In addition, different cultural beliefs and traditions surround the concept of "death." For many U.S. Americans, death is a taboo topic. Euphemisms are often used, such as "He is no longer with us," "She passed away peacefully," "She's in a better place," or "May he rest in peace." There are also a number of different cultural traditions in terms of burial practices. For example, the tradition among Orthodox Jews is to bury the deceased before sundown the next day and have postdeath rituals that last for several days. When Muslims approach death, they may wish to face Mecca, their holy city in Saudi Arabia, and recite passages from the Qur'an (Purnell & Paulanka, 2003). Some Mexicans hold an elaborate ceremony such as a *velorio*, which may appear like a big party; in fact, they are celebrating the person's life as she or he has actually lived it fully. Likewise, the Irish hold a *wake*, and they eat and drink and celebrate the person's bountiful life. However, if you do not subscribe to any of the foregoing rituals, you would likely find it odd that some of these groups actually laugh and sing and dance during painful periods of grieving.

Concepts such as enthnocentrism and ethnorelativism, cultural value patterns such as "doing" and "being," and intercultural conflict skills such as facework management and mindful reframing can serve as basic tools and conceptual building block for effective multicultural health care communication. Learning some of these basic concepts and skills can help professionals and service providers to launch their first steps toward practicing respectful intercultural attitudes and adaptive communication styles.

Moving Forward

Our next reading examines intercultural exchanges between physicians and their patients. Physicians often interact with a population that is very culturally diverse. Patients vary in terms of age, sex, education level, religion, race, and ethnicity, among other factors. These varying factors can often lead to frustration for both the physician and the patient.

The following reading is from a research study. In this study, researchers interviewed several physicians; they captured some interesting findings and heard experiences that may differ from how you and your family might approach health care. As you move through this reading, think about how culture can change the interaction between physician and patient. Are the described physician responses the correct way to go about interacting with their patients? If not, how as an intercultural communicator might you suggest how the physicians approach interacting with their patients differently to diffuse as much frustration as possible?

COMPARING CULTURAL DIFFERENCES IN PHYSICIAN-PATIENT COMMUNICATION

Mr. Akbar Ali, a 60-year-old Muslim from Pakistan, has been diagnosed as having insulin-dependent diabetes. Dr. Martin has prescribed insulin for him and instructed his family on how to administer it. How ever, when Mr. Ali returns for a checkup, Dr. Martin notices little improvement. Careful questioning of Mr. Ali's son reveals that Mr. Ali has not been taking his insulin, and when asked why, Mr. Ali sternly replies, "I am an Orthodox Muslim and would rather die than disobey Islam." Dr. Martin is puzzled and has no idea what Mr. Ali means. (Gropper, 1996)

Such instances are not uncommon when physicians[1] in the United States treat patients from diverse cultural backgrounds. In this case, it is likely that Mr. Ali has heard that insulin is made from the pancreas of a pig. A Muslim is expected to avoid any product of swine because it is considered unclean. Dr. Martin needs to explain that insulin can come from sheep or oxen too, and she would take care to make sure the insulin is not from a pig. This kind of problem, however, is not limited to situations in which the caregiver and the patient speak different languages and come from two different countries.

Helman (1994) aptly notes, "Physicians and patients, even if they come from the same social cultural background, view ill-health in very different ways. Their perspectives are based on very different premises, employ a different system of proof, and assess the efficacy of treatment in different way" (p.101). The following anecdote narrated by a patient named "Chris" is not uncommon even when the physician and patient perceive the other as having the same cultural background[2].

I was a sergeant in the army. I had been in the hospital, sick with fever for a week I had lost 24 pounds (15% of my body weight) and the physicians could not find the cause of the illness. The physician read the results of some blood work that had been run the day before. Without preparing me for it, he casually said, "hmm … people with your white blood count normally have leukemia" He then started walking away. When I tried to stop him to ask questions, he reprimanded me for not calling him "sir"!

In this paper, we argue that the interaction between a physician and patient is inherently an *intercultural*[8] encounter even when the two parties *perceive* they are from the same culture. The distinction between illness and disease helps explain why every encounter between a physician and patient is intercultural. Rosen, Kleinman, and Katon (1982) define disease "as the malfunctioning of biological and/or psychological processes whereas illness may be defined as the perception, evaluation, explanation, and labeling of symptoms by the patient and his family and social network" (p. 496). Traditionally, physicians focus on the disease while patients are concerned with the illness. As du Pié (2000) adds, patients are operating with feelings while physicians are addressing evidence. Thus, in our anecdote, the physician is keen to diagnose the disease (possibly leukemia), while "Chris" is dealing with the psychological implications of having leukemia. This disparity in the physicians and patient's beliefs and value structures could create miscommunication between them and lead to ineffective medical care.

Recent research on physician-patient interaction also suggests the need to study the intercultural aspects of physician—patient communication. Physician—patient research generally falls into one of two broad areas: (1) research focusing on the interpersonal communication aspects of physician—patient interactions and identifying specific interpersonal skills for physician to learn (e.g., Burgoon, Birk, & Hall, 1991, O'Hair, 1989; Ong, De Haes, Hoos, & Lammes, 1995; Roter, 2000, Sharf, 1990), and (2) scholarship focusing the cross-cultural aspects of physician—patient communication to assist caregivers in being more culturally sensitive toward their patients (e.g., Baylav, 1996; Greengold & Ault, 1996; Rosenbaum, 1995; Young & Klingle, 1996). Both of these areas of research, however, fail to bring communication and culture together; the first concentrates on communication and not culture, and the second focuses on culture, but cross-culturally rather than interculturally. Kim et al. (2000) begin the quest to create an intercultural approach to physician—patient communication by analyzing how a patient's self-construal affects his or her verbal communication with a physician. Further, Geist (2000) offers an insightful analysis of the health challenges faced in dealing with co-cultural differences in the United States. In this chapter, as part of a five-year study to develop an *intercultural* model of physician—patient communication, we offer data from our interviews with physicians in Argentina, Brazil, and India.

In this essay, we begin with a literature review on the impact of culture on physician—patient communication and summarize the key findings. After offering a brief description of our methodology (see Rao & Beckett, 2000, for further information), we offer three key findings from our interviews with 91 physicians in Argentina, Brazil, and India. Finally, we highlight our main findings and discuss the implications for future research.

Impact of Culture on Physician-Patient Communication

Traditional medical literature increasingly stresses the importance of good physician communication skills (Burgoon et al., 1991; Cegala, McGee, & McNeils, 1996; O'Hair, 1989; Ong et al., 1995; Roter, 2000). Many factors that inhibit physician—patient communication have previously been documented. Although time limitations remain the number one reason given by providers for lack of communication, some posit that the qualities that earn respect from colleagues are very different from those that earn respect from patients (Welsbacher, 1998). With the exception of several key areas (e.g., care for refugees, using interpreters), the influence of culture(s) in health-related interactions has been largely glossed over. Considering the high rates of global migration, physicians from many different sociocultural backgrounds will find themselves serving an increasingly diverse patient population. Thus, it would seem that a major gap exists within main-stream medical literature.

However, there is one notable exception within the medical arena. Researcher-practitioners within the field of nursing have long advocated that health care providers become familiar with how patients of different cultures conceptualize the notions of "health" and "care". In particular, Madeline Leininger (1991) has been at the forefront of research dedicated to extrapolating these differences. According to her Theory of Culture Care Diversity and Universality, all cultures express care but attach different meanings to health-related practices. Within the health care context, meaning is shaped by technology, religion, cultural norms, economics, and education. Her work is critical in reminding providers that there is far more to culture than simple geography.

Several themes emerge from the nursing research. We are reminded that just as diversity exists across cultures, it also exists within cultural groups (Rosenbaum, 1995). These differences can be intensified by factors such as ethnicity, religion, education, age, sex, and acculturation. As Herselman (1996) aptly states, perceptions are influenced by individual experiences as well as cultural background. Thus, there is a great danger in relying on excessive generalizations (Meleis, 1996). For example, Denham (1996) explains that medical practitioners tend to believe that rural Appalachians are fatalistic in their outlook and in their health practices. However, Denham adds that a lot of variability occurs in rural Appalachians' fatalistic beliefs and health practices. Finally, if a health care provider is to understand how these variables influence a patient's ways of thinking and behaving, he or she must first be familiar with the patient's cultural background. One must also be aware of how the patient's cultural heritage intersects with the culture of the particular health care organization.

Language can provide a major barrier to culturally appropriate care because exploring goals and expectations can become difficult (Baylav, 1996). In her thesis. "When Yes Means No," Katalanos (1994) argues convincingly that South-East Asian (SEA) patients who are recent immigrants have health beliefs that are different from those held by health care professionals in the United States, and these differences are manifested in the communication behaviors of the two parties. Katalanos's (1994. p. 31) analyses of the communication patterns (see following section) show that there is significant misunderstanding between SEA patients and U.S -trained health care providers, sometimes with serious consequences.

Physician Assistant: Are you happy here in America?
Vietnamese Patient: Oh yes, [meaning: I am not happy at all, but I do not want to hurt your feelings. After all, your country took me in.]

Further, "yes" may simply mean "I hear you, and I will answer your question." as the following exchange illustrates:

Physician Assistant: Did you take your medicine?
Vietnamese Patient: Yes. [I hear you.] No, [I did not take it.]

Physician Assistant: You did not take your medicine?
Vietnamese Patient: Yes. [I hear you] Yes, [I did not lake it. The medicine was too strong.]
Physician Assistant: Ah, so you did not take it!
Vietnamese Patient: Yes, No.

These responses leave both the health care provider and the patient frustrated, as each person is operating out of her or his own paradigm—the U.S. provider paradigm of diagnosing the specific cause of illness and providing medication, and the SEA paradigm of being polite and not wanting to hurt the provider's feelings.

Medical jargon exacerbates linguistic barriers even further. Some measures that nurses have taken to compensate for these barriers include the use of interpreters, health education sessions run in conjunction with local service providers, ethnic recruiting, alternative medical services, cultural sensitivity training, multicultural videos/fliers, and cultural health care fairs (Baylav, 1996; Kothari & Kothari, 1997).

Research in nursing has also acknowledged the importance of culture in understanding a patient's attitudes toward birth, death, sex, relationships, and ritual (Mullhall, 1996). Treatments that arc based on assumptions of how a patient regards such issues could potentially result in miscommnuniacation, if not right outright noncompliance. Spitzer et al. (1996) assert that expecting a patient to conform to a health care providers orders is simply a cultural imposition rather than a joint process of discovering the best ways to treat certain ailments. Charoko (1992) also argues that the term "noncompliant" is biased toward preserving the power of the health care provider at the expense of his or her patient. Front Charonko's perspective, it is the provider's responsibility to help patient live as productively as possible within *their* choices. Patient satisfaction, which depends heavily on communication, has been strongly correlated with compliance (Eraker, Kirscht, & Becker, 1984).

The traditional medical literature in the United sates, however, is beginning to acknowledge the increasing diversity of the United States. Between 1990 and 1996, growth in Latino, African American, and Asian American populations accounted for almost two-thirds of the increase in the U.S. population (Bureau of the Census, 1996). While the patient population in the United States is growing more diverse, little is being done to prepare our physicians to work more effectively with these patients (Baylav, 1996; Greengold & Ault, 1996; Rao & Beckett, 2000; Rosenbaum, 1995).

For example, Drake and Lowenstein (1998) hold that California is an interesting case study because "minorities" (e.g., Latinos, Asians) will soon outnumber Caucasians.[4] Texas has also attracted attention as of late because of its ranking as the fifth most culturally diverse state (Kothari & Kothari, 1997). In either case, pronounced disparities exist between ethnicity and level of access to health care. The researchers do note that education, language, and literacy are major reasons why access to health care is limited among certain populations. Studies such as this dance around the issue of culture, but stop short of providing culturally specific care based on systematic research.

One area of medical research where culture is central, however, concerns health care for refugees. Although Kang, Kahler, and Tesar (1998) assert that there are 26 million refugees in the world, the crisis in Kosovo has surely increased these numbers. And the current problems in Afghanistan are creating additional refugees. Keeping this in mind, physicians will find themselves dealing with these issues increasingly often. Similarly, Obmans, Garret, and

Treichel (1996) write that immigrants and refugees are often overrepresent in emergency room care. Interpreters are often necessary for physicians to provide care for rougees, yet many communication problem have been documented from this activity. Regardless of strategy. Obmans et al. write that negotiation and compromise will remain critical to culturally appropriate treatment.

Our succinct review suggests that culture impacts physician–patient communication in several significant ways. The key findings from research on physician—patient communication can be summarized as follows. First, most physicians follow the biomedical approach, focusing more on the disease than on the person. Roter (2000) argues, rather persuasively, that as molecular and chemistry-oriented sciences gained prominence in the 20th century, the focus on communication as a central tenet in physician—patient relationships has declined. Second, there has been considerable research emphasizing the importance of several communication skills, such as empathy and active listening, in physician—patient communication (Burgoon et al., 1991; Ong et al., 1995; Roter & Hall, 1992). Third, research in nursing and counseling has emphasized the usefulness of focusing on the patient's culture in creating more effective encounters (Leininger, 1991). Fourth, patients are most satisfied when both task and relational dimensions of the relationship are addressed effectively in the physician—patient communication (Helman, 1991; Lochman, 1983; Stewart, 1995). Fifth, while most medical students enter medical school with an idealism to save lives, they often leave with "detached concern" because of the biomedical nature of the training (Miller, 1993). Finally, some medical schools train their students to communicate more effectively with their patients, but such models still focus on general communication and not on intercultural communication (Marshall, 1993).

It can be argued, therefore, that the research on physician—patient communication has focused on how to improve a physicians interpersonal and cross-cultural skills. Since there is limited research on the intercultural nature of this encounter, we are working on a systematic research program to create an intercultural communication model of physician—patient communication. In the next section, we focus on the first phase of our research project to answer the following research question: How do physicians in different countries communicate with culturally diverse patients? We administered the Medical Provider Questionnaire (MPQ) to 29 physicians in Campinas, Brazil; 30 physicians in Madras, India; and 32 physicians in Cordoba, Argentina.[5] Each interview was tape-recorded and ranged between 45 and 90 minutes in length. The MPQ had several parts: (1) what motivated these physicians to join this profession; (2) what they liked and disliked about this profession; (3) how they communicated with culturally diverse patients; (4) the physicians response to the case study described in the first part of this atticle; (5) how physicians defined a successful encounter with a patient; and (6) what the physicians would change in the medical system if they were to go through medical school again. In this next section, we focus on the physicians' responses to questions 3 And 4. We first begin with how physicians defined cultural diversity in their context. Then, we focus on the three key findings: "half-truths," family as patient, and how physicians defined success.

Physicians Definition of Culture

Almost without exception, the physicians in Argentina, Brazil, and India saw their countries as heterogeneous. This was not surprising by itself. However, what was surprising was how physicians defined diversity in these three countries. In Brazil, a few physicians divided patients along traditional race, ethnic, and national origin lines. One of our respondents, a resident in cardiology explained:

> Oh, of course. No doubt about it because mainly the kind of settlement of people here in Brazil was in periods over these five centuries. So in the South region you have mostly a European settlement in the last century so Italians, Germans, many of these people. So in the North and Northeast mainly Portuguese and Indians and the slaves that were brought from Africa, so they are totally different.

Most of our Brazilian respondents, however, felt that their main cultural diversity was based on socioeconomic status. Brazil, according to them, had two distinctive cultures, the rich and the poor. For example, a cardiology resident summarized it rather succinctly:

> Oh, no, we have many cultures here. We have a statesman, a former minister of industry, economics, I don't know, and he always said Brazil is—was Belindia, I don't know if you ever heard of it—its part of Belgium and pan of India. You have many countries inside a country. I don't know if you have traveled for many states here. I don't know if you know the state of Mamohao. The Northeast region is the poorest region in the country. So our country is a mosaic, so if we are having problems here, you can imagine what they are having in the Northeast or the North region where we have the Amazon forest and many people don't have hospitals, don't have many roads because all of the transport system is water, its rivers and boats and all of this, so the country is extremely, it's not homogeneous like you said.

Similarly, the physicians in Argentina saw their culture as heterogeneous. One senior female cardiologist noted:

> It [Argentina] is heterogeneous. People who formed this country have different origins, different customs, different traditions, and at the same time there were people who were from here.

Most Argentinean physicians focused primarily on education and socioeconomic status to describe the diversity in their country. One internist explained:

> No, it is heterogeneous. We have people very intellectual and with a lot of knowledge and people with a complete lack of education.

An ophthalmologist described Argentina with passion:

I would say that it is heterogeneous but mainly because we have a huge difference between social classes. Instead of paying 20 dollars to go to a theater, you just think that you need food and clothing. There are many people here who are right now experiencing those kinds of problems.

Physicians in India also saw their country as diverse, but focused on different aspects of diversity—religion, language, socioeconomic status, north-south differences, and so on. A senior female general practitioner described India in the following manner:

We have patients from all spectrums of life. When the patient's language is different, it is almost like they are from a different country. Their dress is different, language is different, and habits are different. The people in the south are much more humane.

A senior oncologist, working for a large private hospital, explained:

In our setup here, we see really a cross section both geographically and culturally and even to some extent economically. It is not that only rich people come here. Here patients know that there is better treatment available. So people come here selling all their belongings. Secondly, we see a lot of patients from the northeast. At least 30% of the patients come from that region.

It is Intriguing that while Argentina, Brazil, and India have significant diversity based on immigration patterns, religion, languages, and so on, the Physicians in Argentina and Brazil focused mainly on socioeconomic status and education as the main indicators of diversity. The Indian physicians represented the various aspects of India's diversity, including language socioeconomic status, and the like. A physician in Brazil explained that because they speak Portuguese throughout the country, even though there is diversity, the common language takes care of cultural differences. This explanation is also viable in Argentina where Spanish is spoken throughout the country.

India, however, has 18 official languages, and it is difficult to ignore the cultural diversity. An Indian colleague often uses this analogy: "Think of India as a mini-Europe. You can travel 100 miles and speak a completely new language!" Thus, it is not surprising that the physicians in these cultures focused on different aspects of their country's diversity. These cultural differences also played a significant role in how they communicated with then patients.

"Half-Truths"

As part of the interview, we asked our respondents to read the following case study (cited previously) and asked them if the physician had responded appropriately:

I was a sergeant in the army. I had been in the hospital, sick with fever for a week. I had lost 24 pounds (15% of my body weight) and the physicians could not find the cause of the illness. The physician read the results of some blood work that had been run the day before. Without preparing me for it, he casually said, "hmm … people with your white blood count normally have leukemia." He then started walking away. When I tried to stop him to ask question, he reprimanded me for not calling him "sir"!

All 91 respondents indicated that the physician in this cash study had responded inappropriately. We then asked the physicians to explain what they would have done if they had to tell a patient that he or she is terminally ill. Our data suggest that 90% of the physicians in these three countries engaged in what we have termed "half-truths," where physicians did not disclose the diagnosis immediately, described the diagnosis in doses over several visits, or informed a family member of the diagnosis first before telling the patient. In all these cases, the physicians explained that hearing such life-threatening news immediately would psychologically harm patient, which, in turn, would reduce the patient's ability to fight the illness. In other words, the type of "half-truth" used was based on the psychological readiness of the patient. In 10% of the cases, the physicians insisted that they would tell the patient directly and immediately because that is what they would have liked. A cardiologist from India described his strategy:

> If I knew a patient had a terminal illness like leukemia, I would tell him that we have to do more tests before we can really be sure. If I tell him directly, he could die of the shock. If I think he is stronger, I may tell him that there are several possibilities and one could be cancer. If he is not strong, I would see which family member he has come with him and take them aside to tell them the news. We are very family oriented, and he has to get their support. So, better to tell them first. Also, they may have to make preparations.

A Brazilian physician, in response to the case study, offered a more direct example of "half-truths":

> It's completely crazy—unacceptable. First of all, because a blood exam is not enough to make a diagnosis of leukemia. It's more complicated; there are no justifications to answer this question in this way. I think the physician could hide the diagnosis in the start. If I was the physician I would try to hide my scared face. I would try not to reveal to the patient the situation and I would think more about it. I would ask for more tests, and when the diagnosis was certain, I would talk to the patient about the disease and about the treatment. Leukemia is not lethal and can be cured through chemotherapy.

A rheumatologist from Argentina described what he would do in this situation:

> One patient never comes alone, so I think that if I know the background and I recognize that the patient is unable to hear anything about himself, I firs talk with the family if the background allows me to do their. If there as no family here, in the case of leukemita, sometimes you have to wait, just one day, two days, one week until your say to the patient, to know him better to know which words to use.

One Argeritinean doctors, however, indicated that he would prefer to tell the patient directly:

> You have to tell the truth to a patient and tell what the patient wants to know. If the patient has leukernia, your have to explain to him that if you follow the treatment, you will be better. The patient knows that because you tell him about the several studies on this topic. You have to motivate the patient to do the treatment and keep on living.

In each of these cases, most of the physicians form Agrentina, Brazil, and India chose to use "half-truths" to tell a patient that he or she is terminally ill. This phenomenon can be best explained by understanding collectivism and face-saving behaviors. Argentina, Brazil, and India are collective cultures where"[a] 'we' consciousness prevails: Identity is cased on the social system; the individual is emotionally dependent on organizations and institutions, the culture emphasizes belonging to organizations: organizations invade private life and the clams to which individuals belong; and individuals trust group decisions even at the expense of individual right" (Samovar & Porter, 2001, pp. (67–68). In these three culture, the physicians are thinking of the patient's well-being within the context of his or her family and the large community.

It is common to use face-saving behaviors like "half-truths" to comfort the patient and sustain the harmony of the group. Face-saving behaviours focus less on the veracity of a statement than what is culturally appropriate for the context. In our preliminary interviews in the United States, physicians were clear that they would tell only the patient and tell him or her directly. This is consistent with the individualistic nature of the United States, where direct and explicit communication is preferred. Du Pré (2000) notes that therapeutic privilege was a practice in the United States when physicians withheld information if they thought sharing the information would hurt the patient. However, Veatch (1991) argues that if we wish for patients to be informed partners in their health care, therapeutic privilege is counterproductive. Consistent with current legal expectation in medicine, there is an expectation that physicans in the United States inform the patient as soon as the diagnosis.

Family as Patient

Our analysis of "half-truths" indicated that physicians often chose to tell a family member rather than tell the patient. Further investigation suggested that even in regular health care visits, the physician had to treat the "family as patient," rather than focus just on the patient. When a patient was ill, the family members felt ill. When a patient recovered, the family members felt better too. We had explained earlier that Argentina, Brazil, and India are collectivistic cultures. People from these cultures also tend to have an interdependent self-construal (Markus & Kitayama, 1991), in which a person's identity is intrinsically connected with his or her family's identity. A person with an interdependent self-construal often makes decisions taking into consideration the needs of his or her family members, and family members often makes decisions for him or her. Physicians described this interconnectedness in several ways. A cardiologist in India noted:

> Patients rarely come alone to the clinic. There are always two or three family members with them. I have to be careful to understand the family dynamics and understand how I should share the information. I will share certain kinds of informations with the wife,

some with the son, and may decide not to share anything with the uncle. I also know that the wife and the son feel the pain the patient is suffering from. When the patient feels better, I feel good too.

A senior cardiologist in Brazil explained how he would include the family so that they can make decisions for the patient:

If the family were there, I would tell them together. If it were just the patient, I would contact the family. Why? The patient may not need to say anything. I would try to talk to the patient's spouse or child or parents. I would say, your son, your husband, your wife has this illness and we are going to treat it. In this situation, I would tell because the family has to prepare, there is going to be therapy, days when the patient is not feeling well, his diet will change, his hair will fall out. He needs the family's help.

An obstetrician in Argentina described how he would share the news with a patient that the baby in her womb is dead:

The most common situation is to tell the news that the baby inside of the womb is dead. If I made the diagnosis, I won't tell her immediately. I will take a patient aside and, if she is alone, I will try to call the family so she begins to suspect something is wrong. I allow that to happen because it helps me. If you tell her directly her baby is dead, she will be very hurt. Now she guesses and asks if her baby is dead. So the baby is dead, but that word might come from her mouth and not mine. Then I stay with her, I hold her arms and help her cry for a little while. If the husband comes later, which happens very often, I repeat the same exercise.

In all these cases, the family is an integral part of the healing process, being constantly present, making decisions, seeking advice, and protecting the patient. Our initial conversations with physicians in the United States suggest that patients generally come alone, and if family members are present, they respect the patients space. Occasionally, the family member may seek clarification on behalf of the patient on certain issues.

Defining Success

We asked the physicians to explain when they had a successful interaction with a patient. In about two-thirds of our interviews, we asked the physician if it was a failure if their patient died. Every one of these physicians indicated that it was not a failure if the patient died, as long as they had done everything possible for the patient. Our preliminary conversations with Physicians in the United States suggest that they would see it as a failure if the patient died. It is likely that the U.S. physicians, trained in the biomedical perspective, are focusing on curing the disease If they cannot cure the patient, they have failed. Death is the ultimate failure with this perspective. Physicians in Argentina, Brazil and India focused mostly on relational issues or relational plus task issues to define success, with a limited few focusing only on task-related issues (curing the patient). An emergency room physician summarized the task-oriented perspective by saying:

> I think I am always successful because I always give them a favorable solution. I try to help them. For example, when I am in the emergency room, I am there to give all I can so that a patient can leave the hospital with a treatment or with any response to her problem.

Most physicians, however, described the importance of building trust and strengthening the relationship with a patient as a key part of being successful. A second-year nuclear resident in Brazil defined success as follows:

> When he comes back with another patient. When he brings his uncle or daughter or wife. They would come over and say, "Oh, I knew that you were here; that is why I brought my grandmother. I wanted you to take a look at her." Probably the grandmother didn't have anything, but he wanted me to look at her. That is when I know a patient likes me.

A family practice physician in Madras described how she looked at both task and relational issues to define success:

> Early diagnosis. When we are able to pick up on traits and/or behaviors that might possibly cause illness. Success is also when a patient comes to you and says that they are happy with the treatment you have given them. You are building trust with a patient that will definitely help with the cure.

A senior physician of legal medicine in Argentina summarized the need to be aware of the patients multiple needs by defining success as follows:

> In many moments, but especially when you have to transmit [to] a patient the information of an incurable disease, but not terminal. When sharing this information with the patient, if it ends up in improving the patient's wish to fight for his/her life and it has given the patient the possibility of living wonderful experiences that s/he has never lived before, I have allowed the patient a certain quality of life.

The Intercultural Journey Continues

"The doctor is mean and the patient is dumb" (du Pré, 2000, p. 48) is a common response in the United States. In this essay, we have argued that it is not fruitful to assign blame to the physician or the patient when communication fails between these two parties. While there is significant research on the interpersonal and cross-cultural aspects, there is little focus on the *intercultural* aspects of physician—Patient communication. Our overall goal is to create such an intercultural model, drawing on literature from several disciplines and from original research. Our interviews with physicians in Argentina, Brazil, and India suggest that their collective orientation influences them to use unique communication strategies to deal with culturally diverse patients. They use "half-truths" to share challenging diagnoses, treat the family as the patient, and define success mostly along relational or relational and task objectives. Our results have several significant implications for studying the role of culture in physician—patient communication.

First, as Lienenger (1991 pointed out in her work, there is more to culture than just geography. Our respondents in Argentina and Brazil defined the country's cultural diversity mainly through socioeconomic and educational differences. Many of our respondents noted that having a common language (Portuguese or Spanish) reduced the impact of other cultural differences such as gender, age, ethnicity, religion, and so on. This is a particularly important finding since Bennett (1998) points out that people from most countries generally tend to focus on race, ethnicity, religion, and language when discussing cultural diversity.

Second, it is important to understand the communication strategies used by physicians in individualistic cultures. Toward this end, we are presently interviewing physicians in the United States to understand how they communicate with patients from culturally diverse backgrounds. Finally, since there are at least two people involved in a physician—patient communication, there are at least two cultural perspectives interacting in their communication. Therefore, it is no longer sufficient to conduct research from only the physician's or the patient's perspective, rather, the physician—patient communication must be analyzed as an *intercultural* phenomena.

To achieve this goal, in addition to our interviews with physicians, we have administered our Multicultural Health Beliefs Inventory (MBHI) to 600 patients in Argentina, Brazil, India, and the United States to explicate how they define good health (Rao, Beckett, & Kandath, 2000). The MBHI assesses respondents' perceptions of good health along five dimensions of health—physical, psychological, relational, spiritual, and lifestyle/environmental. Du Pré (2000) explains how the physician and the patient bring two opposing worldviews when they interact; the physician focuses on the disease (task) only, while the patient focuses on the illness (task plus relational dimension). By combining our data from physicians and patient from several cultures, our goal is to create an intercultural model of physician—patient communication that will have both theoretical and practical lmplications.

Notes

1. In our paper, the term physicians includes only Doctors of Medicine trained in the allopathic tradition

2. We used this case study as a part of our Medical Provider Questionnaire to interview physicians.

3. Lustig and Koester (1999) explain that the term *intercultural* "denotes the presence of at least two individuals who are culturally different from each other on such important attributes as value orientations, preferred, communication codes, role expectations and perceived rules of social relationships" (p. 60).

4. Since this research was conducted, Caucasians have become a minority in California.

5. We chose these three countries to compare how physicians in collectivistic cultures treated their patients as compared to physicians in me United States, an individualistic culture. For a more detailed explanation of our methodology, see Rao and Beckett (2000).

References

Baylav, A. (1996). Overcoming culture and language barriers. *The Practitioner*, 240, 403–406.

Bennett, M. J. (1998). *Basic concepts of intercultural communication*. Yarmouth, ME: Intercultural Press.

Bureau of the Census. (1996) *Statistical abstract of the United States* (116th ed.). Washington, DC: Author.

Burgoon, M.,Birk. T. S., & Hall, J. R. (1991). Compliance and satisfaction with the physician—patient communicatioon: An expectancy theory interpretation of gender differences. *Human Communication Research*, 18, 177–208.

Cegala. D. J., McGee,. D. S., & McNeils, K. S. (1996). Component of patients and physicians perceptions of communication competence during a primary care medical interview, *Health communication*, 8, 1–27.

Charonko, C.V. (1992). Cultural influences in "noncompliant" behavior and decision making. *Holistic Nursing Practice*, 6, 73–78.

Denham, S. (1996). Family health in a rural Appalachian Ohio county. *Journal of Appalachian Studies*, 2, 299–310.

SUMMARY

As a patient, being able to communicate with your physician is important. As a health care professional, nothing can be more frustrating than a patient who does not follow your instructions about how to become healthy or heal properly. A culturally sensitive approach to health care is needed.

As we discovered in the readings for this chapter, intercultural communication is important in health contexts and patient-physician interactions. Cultures differ from one another, and as we learned in our second reading, culture is intensified by age, sex, education level, religion, ethnicity, race, and acculturation level. As the United States continues to become more diverse, health care professionals in the United States will begin to interact with people from more and more cultural backgrounds. This means that physicians will need to understand how their patients' cultures may affect their medical decisions or way of communicating. However, the readings reflected that this is not an easy task. There are several ethical issues and barriers that exist for physicians. Continue onward to the discussion questions to apply your knowledge about intercultural communication and health.

DISCUSSION QUESTIONS

1. When you get sick or injured, what is your first course of action? How did you come to approach health care in this way? Can you identify any *home remedies* that you have learned to follow in response to your health care needs?

2. Can you identify ways in which different cultural groups approach health care? How do you view these alternative ways of health care? What has influenced your thinking about alternative approaches? Have you ever had a conflict with someone who didn't agree with your remedy or the way you planned to respond to your health care need? How did you resolve the situation?

3. Should the health care industry take an ethno-centric or an ethno-relativistic approach to treating patients in need of care? Why?

4. How does paternalism and power complicate intercultural communication in physician—patient relationships?

INTERCULTURAL COMMUNICATION AND EDUCATION

CHAPTER 14

STUDY OBJECTIVES

After completing this chapter, you will be able to:
- Identify and explain why intercultural communication is needed in educational settings.
- Describe and explain how culture can affect the classroom.
- Suggest ways for students to adapt to the classroom while maintaining their culture.

INTRODUCTION

At all stages of the education system, whether it is college level or kindergarten, intercultural communication is extremely important, especially as the United States continues to experience a cultural shift in its landscape. Think back and identify a class you have taken with the largest number of enrolled students..Your largest class might be one that you are currently taking, or it could even be this class. Think about that class; think about how many cultural groups were represented and how many of those students you interacted with in your classroom. Our bet is your class was filled with an assortment of different cultures from around the United States and the world. Understanding the role culture can play in classroom communication can help you to have a more harmonious classroom experience.

You might be considering spending a semester abroad, expanding your education in another country, or even living there for a short while. Studying abroad is a wonderful experience that provides exposure to new and different cultures. Knowing and understanding how culture plays an intricate role in education is extremely helpful for those embarking on study abroad programs.

The readings for this chapter explore culture and education, and provide insight into why understanding other cultures and communicative styles is important in an educational setting. Our first reading examines the different communicative styles that may be present in a classroom setting when there are multiple cultures represented. The second reading is a brief selection from a research study observing how immigrant children understand U.S. culture through the use of literature, while attempting to maintain their own culture as well. At the end of the chapter you will find several discussion questions that will help you to apply your knowledge about intercultural communication in educational settings.

Moving Forward

Our first reading dives deep into an examination of the role culture can play in the classroom, especially when communication is occurring. Whether students are communicating with other students, with their teacher, or the teacher is communicating with the students, culture influences how the interaction happens and how it is received by everyone involved.

As you have already learned through the readings in this book, culture is dynamic, and culture influences an individual's behavior. In turn, an individual's behavior influences their communicative style. When several cultures and communicative styles are represented in the classroom, it is easy for miscommunication or frustration to occur; especially when teachers or students experience different styles than their own. Understanding the role culture can play in the classroom can ease and possibly prevent frustrations.

As you move throughout this reading, consider how individuals from different cultures may approach the act of responding to a question in class. Have you ever experienced any of the examples the reading mentions throughout your education? How might you be able to adapt your communicative style to meet the needs of your fellow classmates?

CULTURE AND COMMUNICATION IN THE CLASSROOM

Geneva Gay

A semiotic relationship exists among communication, culture, teaching, and learning, and it has profound implications for implementing culturally responsive teaching. This is so because "what we talk about; how we talk about it; what we see, attend to, or ignore; how we think; and what we think about are influenced by our culture. ... [and] help to shape, define, and perpetuate our culture" (Porter & Samovar, 1991, p. 21). Making essentially the same argument, Bruner (1996) states, "learning and thinking are always situated in a cultural setting and always dependent upon the utilization of cultural resources" (p. 4). Culture provides the tools to pursue the search for meaning and to convey our understanding to others. Consequently, communication cannot exist without culture, culture cannot be known without communication, and teaching and learning cannot occur without communication or culture.

Introduction

The discussions in this article explicate some of the critical features and pedagogical potentials of the culture—communication semiotics for different ethnic groups of color. The ideas and examples presented are composites of group members who strongly identify and affiliate with their ethnic group's cultural traditions. They are not intended to be descriptors of specific individuals within ethnic groups, or their behaviors in all circumstances. If, how, and when these cultural characteristics are expressed in actual behavior, and by whom, are influenced by many different factors. Therefore, the ethnic interactional and communication styles described in this article should be seen as *general and traditional referents of group dynamics* rather than static attributes of particular individuals.

Students of color who are most traditional in their communication styles and other aspects of culture and ethnicity are likely to encounter more obstacles to school achievement than those who think, behave, and express themselves in ways that approximate school and mainstream cultural norms. This is the case for many highly culturally and ethnically affiliated African Americans. In making this point, Dandy (1991) proposes that the language many African Americans speak "is all too often degraded or simply dismissed by individuals both inside and outside the racial group as being uneducated, illiterate, undignified or simply non-standard" (p. 2). Other groups of color are "at least given credit for having a legitimate language heritage, even if they are denied full access to American life" (p. 2).

Much of educators' decision-making on the potential and *realized* achievement of students of color is dependent on communication abilities (their own and the students'). If students are not very proficient in school communication, and teachers do not understand or accept the students' cultural communication styles, then their academic performance may be misdiagnosed or trapped in communicative mismatches. Students may know much more than they are able to communicate, or they may be communicating much more than their teachers are able to discern. As Boggs (1985, p. 301) explains, "The attitudes and behavior patterns that have the most important effect upon children … [are] those involved in communication." This communication is multidimensional and multipurposed, including verbal and nonverbal, direct and tacit, literal and symbolic, formal and informal, grammatical and discourse components.

The discussions of culture and communication in classrooms in this article are organized into two parts. The first outlines some key assertions about culture and communication in teaching and learning in general. These help to anchor communication within culturally responsive teaching. In the second part of the article, some of the major characteristics of the communication *modes* of African, Native, Latino, Asian, and European Americans are presented. The focus throughout these discussions is on discourse dynamics; that is, who participates in communicative interactions and under what conditions, how these participation patterns are affected by cultural socialization, and how they influence teaching and learning in classrooms.

Relationship Among Culture, Communication, and Education

In analyzing the routine tasks teachers perform, B. Smith (1971) declares that "teaching is, above all, a linguistic activity" and "language is at the heart of teaching" (p. 24). Whether making assignment giving directions, explaining events, interpreting words and expressions, proving positions, justifying decisions and actions, making promises, dispersing praise and criticism, or assessing capability, teachers must use language. And the quality of the performance of these tasks is a direct reflection of how well teachers can communicate with their students. Smith admonishes educators for not being more conscientious in recognizing the importance of language in the performance and effectiveness of their duties. He says, "It could be that when we have analyzed the language of teaching and investigated the effects of its various formulations, the art of teaching will show marked advancement" (p. 24). Dandy (1991) likewise places great faith in the power of communication in the classroom, declaring that "teachers have the power to shape the future, if they communicate with their students, but those who cannot communicate are powerless" (p. 10). These effects of communication skills are especially significant to improving the performance of underachieving ethnically different students.

Porter and Samovar's (1991) study of the nature of culture and communication, the tenacious reciprocity that exists between the two, and the importance of these aspects to intercultural interactions provides valuable information for culturally responsive teaching. They describe communication as "an intricate matrix of interacting social acts that occur in a complex social environment that reflects the way people live and how they come to interact with and get along in their world. This social environment is culture, and if we are to truly understand communication, we must also understand, culture" (p. 10). Communication is dynamic, interactive, irreversible; and invariably contextual. As such, it is a continuous, ever-changing activity that takes place between people who are trying to influence each other; its effects are irretrievable once it has occurred, despite efforts to modify or counteract them.

Communication is also governed by the rules of the social and physical contexts in which it occurs (Porter & Samovar, 1991). Culture is the rule-governing system that defines the forms, functions, and content of communication. It is largely responsible for the construction of our "individual repertories of communicative behaviors and meanings" (p. 10). Understanding connections between culture and communication is critical to improving intercultural interactions. This is so because "as cultures differ from one another, the communication practices and behaviors of individuals reared in those cultures will also be different," and "the degree of influence culture has on intercultural communication is a function of the dissimilarity between the cultures" (p. 12).

Communication entails much more than the content and structure of written and spoken language, and it serves purposes greater than the mere transmission of information. Sociocultural context and nuances, discourse logic and dynamics, delivery styles, social functions, role expectations, norms of interaction, and nonverbal features are as important as (if not more so than) vocabulary, grammar, lexicon, pronunciation, and other linguistic or structural dimensions of communication. This is so because the "form of exchange between child and adult and the conditions in which it occurs will affect not only what is said, but how involved the child will become" (Boggs, 1985, p. 301). Communication is the quintessential way in which humans make meaningful connections with each other, whether as caring, sharing, loving, teaching, or learning. Montague and Matson (1979, p. vii) suggest that it is "the ground of [human] meeting and the foundation of [human] community."

Communication is also indispensable to facilitating knowing and accessing knowledge. This is the central idea of the Sapir—Whorf hypothesis about the relationship among language, thought, and behavior. It says that, far from being simply a means for reporting experience, language is a way of defining experience, thinking, and knowing. In this sense, language is the semantic system of meanings and modes of conveyance that people habitually use to code, analyze, categorize, and interpret experience (Carroll, 1956; Hoijer, 1991; Mandelbaum, 1968). In characterizing this relationship, Sapir (1968) explains that "language is a guide to 'social reality' … [and] a symbolic guide to culture. … it powerfully conditions all of our thinking about social problems and processes" (p. 162). People do not live alone in an "objectified world" or negotiate social realities without the use of language. Nor is language simply a "mechanical" instrumental tool for transmitting information. Instead, human beings are "very much at the mercy of the particular language which has become the medium of expression for their society" (p. 162). The languages used in different cultural systems strongly influence how people think, know, feel, and do.

Whorf (1952, 1956; Carroll, 1956), a student of Sapir, makes a similar argument that is represented by the "principle of linguistic relativity." It contends that the structures of various languages reflect different cultural patterns and values, and, in turn, affect how people understand and respond to social phenomena. In developing these ideas further, Whorf (1952) explains that "a language is not merely a reproducing instrument for voicing ideas but rather is itself the shaper of ideas, the program and guide for the individual's mental activity, for his analysis of impressions, for his synthesis of his mental stock in trade" (p. 5). Vygotsky (1962) also recognizes the reciprocal relationship among language, culture, and thought. He declares, as "indisputable fact," that "thought development is determined by language … and the sociocultural experience of the child" (p. 51).

Moreover, the development of logic is affected by a person's socialized speech, and intellectual growth is contingent on the mastery of social means of thought, or language. According to Byers and Byers (1985), "[t]he organization of the processes of human communication in any culture is a template for the organization of knowledge or information in that culture" (p. 28). This line of argument is applied specifically to different ethnic groups by theorists, researchers, and school practitioners from a variety of disciplinary perspectives, including social and developmental psychology, sociolinguistics, ethnography, and mukicuituralism. For example, Ascher (1992) applied this reasoning to language influences on how mathematical relationships are viewed in general. Giamati and Weiland (1997) connected it to Navajo students' learning of mathematics, concluding that the performance difficulties they encounter are "a result of cultural influences on perceptions rather than a lack of ability" (p. 27). This happens because of the reciprocal interactions among language, culture, and perceptions. Consistently, when these scholars refer to "language" or "communication," they are talking more about discourse dynamics than structural forms of speaking and writing.

Thus, languages and communication styles are systems of cultural notations and the means through which thoughts and ideas are expressively embodied. Embedded within them are cultural values and ways of knowing that strongly influence how students engage with learning tasks and demonstrate mastery of them. The absence of shared communicative frames of reference, procedural protocols, rules of etiquette, and discourse systems makes it difficult for culturally diverse students and teachers to genuinely understand each other and for students to fully convey their intellectual abilities. Teachers who do not know or value these realities will not be able to fully access, facilitate, and assess most of what these students know and can do. Communication must be understood to be more than a linguistic system.

Culturally Different Discourse Structures

In conventional classroom discourse, students are expected to assume what Kochman (1985) calls a *passive-receptive* posture. They are told to listen quietly white the teacher talks. Once the teacher finishes, then the students can respond in some prearranged, stylized way—by asking or answering questions; validating or approving what was said; or taking individual, teacher-regulated turns at talking, individual students gain the right to participate in the conversation by permission of the teacher. The verbal discourse is accompanied by nonverbal attending behaviors and speech-delivery mechanisms rhat require maintaining eye contact with the speaker and using little or no physical movement. Thus, students are expected to be silent and look at teachers when they are talking and wait to be acknowledged before they take their turn at talking. Once permission is granted, they should fob low established rules of decorum, such as one person speaking at a time, being brief and to the point, and keeping emotional nuances to a minimum (Kochman, 1981; Philips, 1983).

These structural protocols governing discourse are expressed in other classroom practices as well. Among them are expecting students always to speak in complete sentences that include logical development of thought, precise information, appropriate vocabulary, and careful attention to grammatical features such as appropriate use of vocabulary and noun-verb tense agreement. Student participation in classroom interactions is often elicited by teachers asking questions that are directed to specific individuals and require a narrow range of information-giving, descriptive responses. It is important for individuals to distinguish themselves in the conversations, for student responses to be restricted to only the specific demands of questions asked, and for the role of speaker and audience to be clearly separated.

In contrast to the passive-receptive character of conventional classroom discourse, some ethnic groups have communication styles that Kochman (1985) describes as *participatory-interactive*. Speakers expect listeners to engage them actively through vocalized, motion, and movement responses as they are *speaking*. Speakers and listeners are action-provoking partners in the construction of the discourse. These communicative styles have been observed among African Americans, Latinos, and Native Hawaiians. As is the case with other cultural behaviors, they are likely to be more pronounced among individuals who strongly identify and affiliate with their ethnic groups and cultural heritages. For example, low-income and minimally educated members of ethnic groups are likely to manifest group cultural behaviors more thoroughly than those who are middle class and educated. This is so because they have fewer opportunities to interact with people different from themselves and to be affected by the cultural exchanges and adaptations that result from the intermingling of a wide variety of people from diverse ethnic groups and varted experiential backgrounds.

Ethnic Variations in Communication Styles

Among African Americans the participatory-interactive style of communicating is sometimes referred to as *call-response* (Asante, 1998; Baber, 1987; Kochman, 1972, 1981, 1985; Smitherman, 1977). It involves listeners giving encouragement, commentary, compliments, and even criticism to speakers *as they are talking*. The speaker's responsibility is to issue the "calls" (making statements), and the listeners' obligation is to respond in some expressive, and often auditory, way (e.g., smiling, vocalizing, looking about, moving around, "amening") (Dandy, 1991; Smitherman, 1977). When a speaker says something that triggers a response in them (whether positive or negative; affective or cognitive), African American listeners are likely to "talk back." This may involve a vocal or motion response, or both, sent directly to the speaker or shared with neighbors in the audience. Longstreet (1978) and Shade (1994) describe the practice as "breaking in and talking over." This mechanism is used to signal to speakers that their purposes have been accomplished or that it is time to change the direction or leadership of the conversation. Either way, there is no need for the speaker to pursue the particular discourse topic or technique further.

African Americans "gain the floor" or get participatory entry into conversations through personal assertiveness, the strength of the impulse to be involved, and the persuasive power of the point they wish to make, rather than waiting for an "authority" to grant permission. They tend to invest their participation with personality power, actions, and emotions. Consequently, African Americans are often described as verbal performers whose speech behaviors are fueled by personal advocacy, emotionalism, fluidity, and creative variety (Abrahams, 1970; Baber, 1987). These communication facilities have been attributed to the oral-aural nature of African American cultural and communal value orientation (Pasteur & Toldson, 1982; Smitherman, 1977). Many teachers view these behaviors negatively, as "rude," "inconsiderate," "disruptive," and 'speaking out of turn," and they penalize students for them.

Native Hawaiian students who maintain their traditional cultural practices use a participatory-interactive communicative style similar to the call-response of African Americans. Called "talk-story" or "co-narrative," it involves several students working collaboratively, or talking together, to create an idea, tell a story, or complete a learning task (Au, 1980, 1993; Au & Kawakami, 1985, 1991, 1994; Au fit Mason, 1981; Boggs et al., 1985). After observing these behaviors among elementary students, Au (1993) concluded that "what seems important to Hawaiian children in talk-story is not individual . . . but group performance in speaking" (p. 114). These communication preferences are consistent with the importance Native Hawaiian culture places on individuals' contributing to the well-being of family and friends instead of working only for their own betterment (Gallimore, Boggs, & Jordon, 1974; Tharp & Gallimore, 1988).

A communicative practice that has some of the same traits of call-response and talk-stojy has been observed among European American females. Tannen (1990) calls it "cooperative overlapping" and describes it as women "talking along with speakers to show participation and support" (p. 208). It occurs most often in situations where talk is casual and friendly. This *rapport-talk* is used to create community. It is complemented by other traditional women's ways of communicating, such as the following:

Being "audience" more often than "speaker" in that they are recipients of information provided by males

De-emphasizing expertise and the competitiveness it generates

Focusing on individuals in establishing friendships, networks, intimacy, and relationships more than exhibiting power, accomplishment, or control

Negotiating closeness in order to give and receive confirmation, support, and consensus

Avoiding conflict and confrontation (Belensky et al., 1986; Klein, 1982; Maltz & Borker, 1983; Tannen, 1990)

While these habits of "communal communication and interaction" are normal to the users, they can be problematic to classroom teachers. On first encounter, they may be perceived as "indistinguishable noise and chaos" or unwholesome dependency. Even after the shock of the initial encounter passes, teachers may still consider these ways of communicating socially deviant, not conducive to constructive intellectual engagement, rude, and insulting. They see them as obstructing individual initiative and preempting the right of each student to have a fair chance to participate in instructional discourse. These assessments can prompt attempts to rid students of the habits and replace them with the rules of individualistic, passive-receptive, and controlling communication styles predominant in classrooms.

Teachers may not realize that by doing this they could be causing irreversible damage to students' abilities or inclinations to engage fully in the instructional process. Hymes (1985) made this point when he suggested that rejecting ethnically different students' communication styles might be perceived by them as rejection of their personhood. Whether intentional or not, casting these kinds of aspersions on the identity and personal worth of students of color does not bode well for their academic achievement.

Problem Solving and Task Engagement

Many African American, Latino, Native American, and Asian American students use styles of inquiry and responding that are different from those employed most often in classrooms. The most common practice among teachers is to ask convergent (single-answer) questions and use deductive approaches to solving problems. Emphasis is given to details, to building the whole from the parts, to moving, from the specific to the general. Discourse tends to be didactic, involving one student with the teacher at a time (Goodlad, 1984). In comparison, students of color who are strongly affiliated with their traditional cultures tend to be more inductive, interactive, and communal in task performance. The preference for inductive problem solving is expressed as reasoning from the whole to parts, from the general to the specific. The focus is on the "big picture," the pattern, the principle (Boggs et al., 1985; Philips, 1983; Ramirez & Castañeda, 1974; Shade 1989).

Although these general patterns of task engagement prevail across ethnic groups, variations do exist. Some teachers use inductive modes of teaching, and some students within each ethnic group of color learn deductively. Many Asian American students seem to prefer questions that require specific answers but are proposed to the class as a whole. While many Latino students may be inclined toward learning in group contexts, specific individuals may find these settings distracting and obstructive to their task mastery.

In traditional African American and Latino cultures, problem solving is highly contextual. One significant feature of this contextuality is creating a "stage" or "setting" prior to the performance of a task. The stage setting is invariably social in nature. It involves establishing personal connections with others who will participate as a prelude to addressing the task. In making these connections, individuals are readying themselves for "work" by cultivating a social context. They are, in effect, activating their cultural socialization concept that an individual functions better within the context of a group. Without the group as an anchor, referent, and catalyst, the individual is set adrift, having to function alone.

These cultural inclinations may be operating when Latino adults begin their task interactions with colleagues by inquiring about the families of other participants and their own personal well-being or when African American speakers inform the audience about their present psychoemotional disposition and declare the ideology, values, and assumptions underlying the positions they will be taking in the presentation (i.e., "where they are coming from"). This "preambling" is a way for the speakers to prime the audience and themselves for the subsequent performance. Students of color may be setting the stage for their engagement with Seaming tasks in classrooms (e.g., writing an essay, doing seatwork, taking a test) when they seem to be spending unnecessary time arranging their tests, sharpening pencils, shifting their body postures (stretching, flexing their hands, arms, and legs, etc.), or socializing with peers rather than attending to the assigned task. "Preparation before performance" for these students serves a similar purpose in learning as arhcater performer doing yoga exercises before taking the stage. Both are techniques the "actors" use to focus, to get themselves in the mood and mode to perform.

For those Asian Americans who prefer to learn within the context of groups, it is accomplished through a process of *collaborative and negotiated problem solving*. Regardless of how minor or significant an issue is, they seek out opinions and proposed solutions from all members of the constituted group. Each individual's ideas are presented and critiqued. Their merits are weighed against those suggested by every other member of the group. Discussions are animated and expansive so that all parties participate and understand the various elements of the negotiations. Eventually, a solution is reached that is a compromise of several possibilities. Then more discussions follow to ensue that everyone is in agreement with the solution and understands who is responsible for what aspects of its implementation. These discussions proceed in a context of congeniality and *consensus building* among the many, not with animosity, domination, and the imposition of the will of a few.

A compelling illustration of the positive effects of this process on student achievement occurred in Treisman's (1985; Fullilove & Treisman, 1990) Mathematics Workshop Program at the University of California, Berkeley. He observed the study habits of Chinese Americans to determine why they performed so well in high-level mathematics classes and if he could use their model with Latinos and African Americans. He found what others have observed more informally—the Chinese American students always studied in groups, and they routinely explained to each other their understanding of the problems and how they arrived at solutions to them. Treisman attributed their high achievement to the time they devoted to studying and to talking through the solution with peers. When he simulated this process with African Americans and Latinos, their achievement improved radically. Treisman was convinced that "group study" made the difference. Given other evidence that compatibility between cultural habits and teaching-learning styles improves student performance, this is probably what occurred. Communal problem solving and the communicative impulse were evoked, thus producing the desired results.

These are powerful but challenging pedagogical lessons for all educators to learn and emulate in teaching students of color. Collective and situated performance styles require a distribution of resources (timing, collective efforts, procedures, attitudes) that can collide with school norms; for instance, much of how student achievement is assessed occurs in tightly scheduled arrangements, which do not accommodate stage setting or collective performance. Students of color have to learn different styles of performing, as well as the substantive content to demonstrate their achievement. This places them in potential double jeopardy—that is, failing at the level of both procedure and substance. Pedagogical reform must be cognizant of these dual needs and attend simultaneously to the content of learning and the processes for demonstrating mastery. It also must be bi-directional—that is, changing instructional practices to make them more culturally responsive to ethnic and cultural diversity, while teaching students of color how to better negotiate mainstream educational structures.

Organizing Ideas in Discourse

In addition to mode, the actual process of discourse engagement is influenced by culture and, in turn, influences the performance of students in schools. Several elements of the dynamics of discourse are discussed here to illustrate this point; they are how ideas are organized, taking positions, conveying imagery and affect through language, and gender variations in conversational styles. How ideas and thoughts are organized in written and spoken expression can be very problematic to student achievement. Two techniques are commonly identified— *topic-centered* and *topic-associative* or *topic-chaining* techniques. European Americans seem to prefer the first while Latinos, African Americans, Native Americans, and Native Hawaiians (Au, 1993; Heath, 1983) are inclined toward the second.

In *topic-centered* discourse, speakers focus on one issue at a time; arrange facts and ideas in logical, linear order; and make explicit relationships between facts and ideas. In this process, cognitive processing moves deductively from discrete parts to a cumulative whole with a discernible closure. Quality is determined by clarity of descriptive details, absence of unnecessary or flowery elaboration, and how well explanations remain focused on the essential features of the issue being analyzed. The structure, content, and delivery of this discourse style closely parallel the expository, descriptive writing, and speaking commonly used in schools. A classic example of topic-centered discourse is journalistic writing, which concentrates on giving information about who, what, when, where, why, and how as quickly as possible. Its purpose is to convey information and to keep this separate from other speech functions, such as persuasion, commentary, and critique. Another illustration is the thinking and writing associated with empirical inquiry, or critical problem solving. Again, there is a hierarchical progression in the communication sequence, beginning with identifying the problem, collecting data, identifying alternative solutions and related consequences, and selecting and defending a solution. There is a clear attempt to separate facts from opinions, information from emotions.

A *topic-associative style* of talking and writing is episodic, anecdotal, thematic, and integrative. More than one issue is addressed at once. Related explanations unfold in overlapping, intersecting loops, with one emerging out of and building on others. Relationships among segments of the discourse are assumed or inferred rather than explicitly established (Cazden, 1988; Lee & Slaughter-Defoe, 1995). Thinking and speaking appear to be circular and seamless rather than linear and clearly demarcated. For one who is unfamiliar with it, this communication style sounds rambling, disjointed, and as if the speaker never ends a thought before going to something else.

Goodwin (1990) observed topic-chaining discourse at work in a mixed-age (4- to 14-year-olds) group of African Americans in a Philadelphia neighborhood as they told stories, shared gossip, settled arguments, and negotiated relationships. She noted the ease and finesse with which a child could switch from a contested verbal exchange to an engaging story and dramatically reshape dyadic interactions into multiparty ones. Using a single utterance, the children could evoke a broad history of events, a complex web of identities and relationships that all participants understood without having elaborate details on any of the separate segments. The talk-story discourse style among Native Hawaiians operates in a similar fashion, which explains why Au (1993) characterizes it as a "joint performance, or the cooperative production of responses by two or more speakers" (p. 113).

Two other commonplace examples are indicative of a topic-chaining or associative discourse style. One is used by many African Americans who literarily try to attach or connect the sentences in a paragraph to each through the prolific use of conjunctive words and phrases; for example, frequently beginning sentences with "consequently," "therefore," "however," "thus," "moreover," "additionally," and "likewise." These sentences are in close proximity to each other—sometimes as often as four of every five or six.

The second example illuminates the storytelling aspect of topic-chaining discourse. African Americans (Kochman, 1981, 1985; Smitherman, 1997) and Native Hawaiians (Boggs, 1985) have been described as not responding directly to questions asked. Instead, they give narratives, or tell stories. This involves setting up and describing a series of events (and the participants) loosely connected to the questions asked. It is as if ideas and thoughts, like individuals, do not function or find meaning in isolation from context. A host of other actors and events are evoked to assist in constructing the "stage" upon which the individuals eventually interject their own performance (i.e., answer the question). This narrative-response style is also signaled by the attention given to "introductions" and preludes in writing. They are extensive enough to prompt such comments from teachers as, "Get to the point" or "Is this relevant?" or "More focus needed" or "Too much extraneous stuff" or "Stick to the topic." The students simply think that these preludes are necessary to setting the stage for the substantive elements of the discourse.

Moving Forward

The following reading is a short selection from a research study exploring how immigrant children understand U.S. culture through literature that is discussed in class. When immigrant children begin attending school, they are exposed to many things they find unfamiliar. In addition to their education, immigrant children must learn and adapt to a new culture while still pressured by their families to maintain their own native culture. This can be difficult. As we learned in our previous reading, culture plays a role in how students communicate in the classroom. As you move through this next selection, reverse the roles and imagine yourself in a new culture, getting an education. What might you be exposed to or experience for which you may not be culturally prepared? How might you expect to learn or communicate in your new culture?

USING LITERATURE TO EXPOSE IMMIGRANT STUDENTS TO U.S. CULTURE

Our contention is that for immigrant students, communicative interaction (as described by Kim, 2001) takes place during classroom interactions among all the individuals therein. As pointed out by Clayton (2003) and Sung (1987), school is a secondary socializer, because compulsory education laws in the United States ensure school attendance by the immigrant student "within a few days of his arrival" (Sung, 1987, p. 96). Unfortunately, and as pointed out by Sung (1987), most initial school experiences for such students are geared towards sharpening their linguistic skills (Le., providing them with "survival English") rather than addressing their cross-cultural skills, which are equally as important.

As previously mentioned, some aspects of implicit culture are less discernible. The literature reveals that integration goes beyond learning the language and adapting to food, clothing, folk dances, songs, and pastimes-what researchers like Clayton refer to as explicit or overt culture, the easiest aspects of culture to learn. More important for immigrant students, integration relates to such implicit aspects of culture as values, assumptions, and attitudes. These can encompass more covert characteristics of classroom culture, such as how teachers and students bond and act towards one another; the communication that takes place, including the rhythm and tone of the language rather than the language itself; classroom settings and organization; and the value and belief systems underpinning those characteristics. Value orientations, such as respect, sexuality, aggressiveness, demonstrations of affection, and dependency (Sung, 1987), as well as learning preferences and verbal and nonverbal communication (Clayton, 2003), are aspects of the implicit culture that immigrant students can learn about to aid their integration into the new environment.

Our second theoretical perspective relates to the use of literature in the teaching of culture to English language learners (ELLs). That viewpoint is supported by several claims and research, including the following: 1) Sandra McKay'S depiction of literature as an "ideal vehicle for ... introducing cultural assumptions" (cited in Pugh, 1989),2) Beverly McLeod's assertion that examining literary text with ELLs is an exercise in cultural relativity (cited in Gajdusek, 1988), and 3) Pugh's (1989) stance that literature provides comprehensible input for ELLs at any stage of their second language acquisition. Particularly illuminating to us was Wan's (2000) work, which illustrated how children's literature can enhance integration. She explored the kinds of books one Chinese family read aloud to their American-born toddler. Intent on ensuring that the toddler also retain her Chinese values, the family read to her what Wan (2000) referred to as Chinese storybooks with "heavily didactic themes" (p. 401), which provided good examples "of the didacticism valued within Chinese culture" (p. 401). Wan explained that the intent was to help the toddler emulate the "good kid" values in the books, such as respecting the elderly, being polite, having a sense of shame, working hard at school, and being self-disciplined. Thus, the family would often end their read-alouds with such moralistic questions as, "Would you like to respect your teacher the way the boy did in the story?" (p. 402). In this way, they tried to guide the toddler to gain Chinese values to complement the American values in which she would be socialized at her U.S. school. We believe that using literature in a similar fashion has the potential to help immigrant students assume an integrative orientation and gain access to cultural understandings in their new classrooms by exposing them to portrayals of dominant U.S. cultural content.

SUMMARY

Understanding the role that culture can play in the educational system is important, especially as the United States' cultural landscape continues to shift. Culture influences our behavior and communicative styles; when there are several cultures represented in a classroom, miscommunication or even frustration can occur. However, if we understand that people from different cultures communicate differently in a classroom context, the classroom setting can be more harmonious. Understanding culture's role can also help students who immerse themselves in another culture during a study abroad experience.

In this chapter, our first reading focused on the role that culture can play in communicative styles and behavior in the classroom. This reading provided us with an understanding of why being culturally competent communicators is important in a classroom setting; especially as many cultures are now represented in classrooms, regardless of size or grade level. Next, we focused on immigrant children and their exposure to U.S. culture through literature. This short selection introduced several elements that must be learned , as well as the need of people living in an unfamiliar culture to maintain their own culture. With this in mind, continue to the discussion questions to help apply your knowledge of intercultural communication and education.

DISCUSSION QUESTIONS

1. How has culture influenced your language, thoughts, and behavior in the educational systems you have thus far experienced? For example, how important are grades to you? Where do you think you learned to feel this way about grades?
2. In what ways does the culture of the instructor influence the communication used with students? How might this communication put some students at an advantage/ disadvantage?
3. What communication strategies should be used to enhance the interaction between individuals of different cultures sharing the same classroom or learning environment? How do you think group work enhances competent intercultural communication?

INTERCULTURAL COMMUNICATION COMPETENCE

CHAPTER 15

STUDY OBJECTIVES

After completing this chapter, you will be able to:
- Define intercultural communication competence.
- Describe the four stages of cultural communication competence.
- Identify and describe different models of intercultural communication competence.

INTRODUCTION

It should come as no surprise to you by now that cultures differ from one another. Having the ability to communicate across or alongside our differences is why intercultural communication is important to both study and practice. But what does effective intercultural communication look like? Researchers have made, and are continuously making, strides to describe and define intercultural communication competence. One widely cited model for understanding intercultural communication competence involves four stages.

The first time you interacted with someone from a different culture, you began your journey of developing into a culturally competent communicator. Reflecting on the time you have been reading selections from this book, can you identify when you might have been in one of these stages? Ultimately, the goal for an individual should be competence, where intercultural interaction becomes both effective and appropriate. If you are not yet at a point where you can say you are consciously competent in your intercultural communication, no worries. You have room to grow.

In this chapter, we explore intercultural communication competence. Our first reading provides one definition for intercultural communication competence and offers some guidelines to follow as you strive to become an effective communicator. Our second and third readings provide examples of the different models that exist in defining communication competence behaviors. These readings reveal that defining culturally competent communication behaviors is not an easy task and vary via the researcher's approach and/or the context of the communication. At the end of the chapter, you will find discussion questions that will aid you in applying your knowledge about intercultural communication competence.

STAGES OF INTERCULTURAL COMMUNICATION COMPETENCE (ICC)

Triandis (2006) identified four stages of cultural communication competence:

Unconscious incompetence—not *aware* there are problems in communicating or *knowing how* to communicate competently. Open to modifying communication behavior once problem is identified.

Conscious incompetence—the "oh-oh" stage, knowing something's not right but not knowing why or even how to mend the problem or knowing something's wrong but being unwilling to modify communication behavior.

Conscious competence—knowing something about the "other" culture, which improves communication approach, though still only with concerted effort

Unconscious competence—integrated, nearly effortless intercultural communication

---

Moving Forward

This first short reading provides our foundation for examining intercultural communication competence and provides insight into this topic by describing and defining four levels of intercultural communication competence. Offering access to essential background literature, this next selection also provides some guidelines to follow in order to be a culturally competent communicator in an intercultural setting.

As you read this next selection, think about different intercultural settings that you might experience on a daily basis, whether it is in class, on campus, or at work. Do you agree with the guidelines the authors suggest individuals should follow? Why or why not?

WHAT INTERCULTURAL COMPETENCE LOOKS LIKE

Although 50 years of conceptualizing have provided a theoretical and practical foundation for intercultural communication, it remains a fresh field. The study of intercultural communication dates back to the works of political scientists and anthropologists in the 1940s and 1950s. Whereas linguist Edward Sapir wrote about this topic in the 1920s, it took Benjamin Whorf to frame his work more fully as a communication question. As sociologists, linguists, and communication scholars have developed an interest in intercultural communication, two separate schools of thought—cultural dialogue and cultural criticism—now inform research in intercultural communication (Asante, Newmark, & Blake, 1979). Both schools have spawned significant research in intercultural communication. One of the main topics studied by the two groups is intercultural communication competence, or the effective means whereby individuals can understand cultural commonalities and move beyond cultural differences in order to reach the ideal goals advocated by cultural dialogists and cultural critics. But, we ask, What is communication competence?

Definition of Communication Competence

Two concepts have long been applied in discussions of communication competence: effectiveness and appropriateness. *Effectiveness* refers to an individual's ability to produce intended effects through interaction with the environment. This ability is treated either as a basic human skill that is obtained through learning and socialization processes (Weinstein, 1969; White, 1959) or as an acquired ability that is related neither to personal intellect nor to education (Foote & Cottrell, 1955; Holland & Baird, 1968). In either case, the ability is understood to increase as the individual's awareness of relevant factors increases (Argyris, 1965a, 1965b). In addition, ideally, competent communicators should be able to control and manipulate their environments to attain personal goals. In order to maximize such goals, individuals must be able to identify them, get relevant information about them, accurately predict others' responses, select communication strategies, implement these communication strategies, and accurately assess the interaction results (Parks, 1985, 1994).

A more systematic view of effectiveness in communication relates the concept to both interactants. To be competent in communication, a person must not only feel competent, but his or her ability should be observed and confirmed by the people with whom he or she interacts. Thus, communication competence should be judged based on individuals' abilities to formulate and achieve objectives, to collaborate effectively with others, and to adapt to situational variations (Bochner & Kelly, 1974). Rubin (1983) has further considered communication competence to be a kind of impression based on the individual's perception, an impression the individual forms of both his or her own and others' behaviors. Through this impression, a person makes guesses about the internal states of those with whom he or she is interacting.

Finally, Wiemann (1977) synthesizes the concept of communication competence from the perspective of effectiveness. He conceptualizes communicative competence as "the ability of an interactant to choose among available communicative behaviors in order that he may successfully accomplish his own interpersonal goals during an encounter while maintaining the face and line of his fellow interactants within the constraints of the situation" (p. 198). This definition argues simultaneously that competent communication is other oriented and that communicators have to accomplish their own goals.

Whereas some scholars conceive of communication competence as a function of perceived effectiveness, others look at it from the viewpoint of appropriateness. Wiemann and Backlund (1980) explain appropriateness in the communication process as follows:

> Appropriateness generally refers to the ability of an interactant to meet the basic contextual requirements of the situation—to be effective in a general sense.. .. These contextual requirements include: (1) The verbal context, that is, making sense in terms of wording, of statements, and of topic; (2) the relationship context, that is, the structuring, type and style of messages so that they are consonant with the particular relationship at hand; and (3) the environmental context, that is, the consideration of constraints imposed on message making by the symbolic and physical environments, (p. 191)

The "appropriateness of behavior" thus implicates three kinds of ability. First is the ability to recognize how context constrains communication, so that one acts and speaks appropriately by combining capabilities and social knowledge to recognize that different situations give rise to different sets of rules (Lee, 1979; Trenholm & Rose, 1981). Second is the ability to avoid inappropriate responses. An inappropriate response is defined as "one which is unnecessarily abrasive, intense, or bizarre. It is also likely to result in negative consequences that could have been averted, without sacrifice of the goal, by more appropriate actions" (Getter & Nowinski, 1981, p. 303). Third is the ability to fulfill appropriately such communication functions as controlling, sharing feelings, informing, ritualizing, and imagining (Allen & Wood, 1978). We extend Grice's (1975) recommendations concerning appropriateness in interaction to include the following:

1. Say just enough—not too little or too much.
2. Do not say something that is false—or speak about something for which you lack evidence.
3. Relate your contribution to the topic and situation.
4. Be clear about what you are saying, and say it with dispatch.

These guidelines specify the four elements of appropriate communication: quantity, quality, relevance, and manner of message sending.

To summarize, communication competence requires appropriateness, and "the fundamental criteria of appropriateness are that the interactants perceive that they understand the content of the encounter and have not had their norms and rules violated too extensively" (Spitzberg & Cupach, 1984, p. 101).

Definition of Intercultural Communication Competence

The literature treats intercultural communication competence in much the same way as it does communication competence in general (Hammer, 1988; Lustig & Koester, 1993; Martin, 1989; Ruben, 1989; Spitzberg, 1988, 1989; Wiseman & Koester, 1993). The only difference is, in addition to looking at communication competence as effective and appropriate interaction, intercultural communication scholars place more emphasis on contextual factors. They conceive of communication competence not only as effective and appropriate interaction between people, but as effective and appropriate interaction between people who identify with particular physical and symbolic environments. This orientation resembles that of communication scholars who emphasize competence as a context-specific behavior (Spitzberg & Cupach, 1984).

Although researchers conceive of communication competence as the ability to interact effectively and appropriately with others, their definitions betray greater or lesser degrees of ambiguity, confusion, and imprecision. For example, from Wiemann's (1977) synthesized definition, the question arises, What constitute "available communicative behaviors" and "constraints of the situation"? These concepts are not clear, and require definition. To alleviate the problem in defining communication competence and to apply the concept to intercultural settings, intercultural communication competence can be conceived of as the ability to negotiate cultural meanings and to execute appropriately effective communication behaviors that recognize the interactants' multiple identities in a specific environment. This definition emphasizes that competent persons must know not only how to interact effectively and appropriately with people and environment, but also how to fulfill their own communication goals by respecting and affirming the multilevel cultural identities of those with whom they interact.

Moving Forward

Intercultural communication competence is an area of research that has produced many models. The next two readings provide a snapshot of several different models that researchers have developed in an effort to explain what intercultural communication competence behaviors look like. This is by no means a comprehensive list, but we provide you with these readings to demonstrate that defining intercultural communication competence is a difficult task. As you read through these next selections, reflect on what you have learned throughout this book and in class. What does intercultural competence look like to you? What behaviors might you reflect in an intercultural interaction? We encourage you to explore these models further once you complete this chapter.

MODELS OF INTERCULTURAL COMMUNICATION COMPETENCE

Dimensions of intercultural communication effectiveness have been investigated that tested sojourners' cultural perspectives (Gudykunst, Wiseman, & Hammer, 1977), participation in workshops (Gudykunst, 1979), decision-making style (Stewart, Gudykunst, Ting-Toomey, & Nishida, 1986), and ethnocentrism (Hall & Gudykunst, 1989). Kim (1988a) offered a broad-based perspective that synthesized various disciplinary viewpoints of adaptation including anthropology, communication, psychology, sociology, and sociolinguistics. Regardless of a sojourner's motivation for being in a new culture, all people share common adaptation experiences. Accordingly, as strangers they must cope with high levels of uncertainty and unfamiliarity based on their ambivalent status in the host community. Labels such as acculturation, adjustment, assimilation, and integration emphasize different aspects of the adaptation experience. Adaptation theory assumes that individuals can and do adapt to this new, unfamiliar culture. Consequently, the focus is on how adaptation is accomplished from a General Systems perspective that regards individuals and their host environment as codeterminants engaged in communication activities. Adaptation theory proposes assumptions, axioms, and theorems that increase understanding of, and ability to make predictions of, cross-cultural adaptation.

Studies of intercultural sensitivity and competence may be found in the work of Bennett and Hammer (e.g., Bennett, 1986, 1993; Bennett & Bennett, 2004a, 2004b) on their developmental model of intercultural sensitivity (DMIS), and on measuring intercultural sensitivity through the intercultural development inventory (IDI; Hammer, 1998; Hammer, Bennett, & Wiseman, 2003). This grounded theory approach derives a theory of intercultural development (DMIS) based on observing persons' responses to cultural difference, and the organization of the observations into presumed stages of increasing sensitivity to cultural difference. Six such stages are proposed, three ethnocentric and centrally based in the observer's culture: Denial of cultural difference, defense against cultural difference, and minimization of cultural difference. And three are ethnorelative, wherein the observer's culture of origin is experienced in the context of other cultures: acceptance of other cultures, adaptation to other cultures, and integration within another culture or cultures with the ability to move readily between cultures. The extent of movement between these six stages for an individual may be measured by Hammer and Bennett's IDI, representing the first five of the six DMIS stages. The IDI consists of 60 paper and pencil items drawn from interview statements. The items are designed to measure cognitive structure indicative of a given DMIS stage. This research represents an extensive group of studies using observation, theorizing, and measurement based on those observations, with the resulting theory and measuring instrument tested and verified by multiple methods. The DIMS and resulting IDI represent an impressive line of research, well founded and useful. Discussions of cultural competence may also be found in Leigh (1998), and in Hampden-Turner (1995).

INTERCULTURAL COMMUNICATION COMPETENCE

Adding to researchers' efforts to explain intercultural communication behaviors by focusing on intrapersonal processes is an extensive amount of work devoted to the investigation of the notion of intercultural communication competence (ICC). By and large, ICC (and various similar or related concepts, such as intercultural effectiveness, intercultural communication effectiveness, perceived communication competence, linguistic competence, and relational competence) has been viewed as a culture-general phenomenon consisting of a set of factors that facilitate successful outcomes of intercultural communication (e.g., satisfaction and other positive assessments of the interaction and the interaction partner).

Given this general consensus, investigators have offered varying descriptions of ICC that emphasize different constituent elements. For example, Gudykunst's (1995) anxiety/ uncertainty management (AUM) theory explains "communication effectiveness" of individual communicators based on three core psychological variables: uncertainty, anxiety, and mindfulness. The theory further incorporates various other psychological factors (e.g., motivation and social categorization) and situational factors (e.g., informality and institutional support) that indirectly affect intercultural communication effectiveness by influencing the three core variables. A substantial amount of research evidence in social psychology and intercultural communication has been incorporated in the development of this theory, as well as in the testing of the proposed relationships among the three core variables (e.g., Gudykunst & Nishida, in press; Kimberly, Gudykunst, & Guerrero, 1999).

Other investigators from both interpretive and neopositivist perspectives have proposed ICC models that emphasize the centrality of cultural identity. Collier and Thomas (1988) offer an interpretive perspective on ICC as an individual's ability to negotiate his or her identities. Likewise, cultural identity is at the heart of neopositivists' conceptions of ICC, including that of Cupach and Imahori (1993), who highlight the ability of individuals to "manage" one another's cultural identities as essential to ICC. A broader theoretical account of ICC from the "identity negotiation" perspective is provided in Ting-Toomey's (1993) multidimensional model of communicative resourcefulness, also referred to as "facework competence" (Ting-Toomey & Kurogi, 1998). Building on her earlier theoretical work on cross-cultural differences in "facework" and "conflict styles" (Ting-Toomey, 1988), as well as on the ideas of several psychological theories, Ting-Toomey (1993) predicts "effective identity negotiation" based on cognitive, affective, and behavioral resourcefulness of communicators in intercultural encounters.

Still other researchers have offered more broadly based models that conceive ICC in terms of a range of communication abilities along cognitive (e.g., cognitive complexity, cognitive flexibility, and mindfulness), affective (e.g., positive attitude, motivation, and sensitivity), and/ or operational lines (e.g., verbal and nonverbal skills, listening skills, and interaction management skills) (see, e.g., Chen & Starosta, 1996; Hammer, 1989; Kim, 1991; Koester & Olebe, 1988; Ruben & Kealey, 1979). For example, the systems model of ICC (Kim, 1991) defines ICC as a system of interrelated cognitive, affective, and operational abilities that increase the likelihood of successful communication regardless of the particular cultural makeup of an intercultural encounter.

SUMMARY

Cultures differ from one another yet interact regularly, which makes it important to try to communicate across or alongside differences. Striving to become a competent intercultural communication is imperative as it can reduce frustration and miscommunication for both parties. In this chapter, we explored intercultural communication competence and discovered that defining and describing culturally competent communicative behaviors can be difficult and is often driven by context.

Several researchers have contributed to this topic, offering models of intercultural communication competence. These selections furthered our understanding that models of intercultural communication competence can vary depending on the researcher's approach or paradigm to intercultural communication. Regardless of any differences there may be, one thing is shared: the importance of becoming culturally competent in communicating.

In becoming a culturally competent communicator, an individual might progress, as Triandis (2006) suggested through four stages, being unconsciously incompetent, consciously incompetent, consciously competent, and unconsciously competent. The goal for any individual should focus on becoming a culturally competent communicator; understanding and practicing being effective and appropriate in intercultural interactions. Continue on to the discussion questions to test and apply your knowledge about intercultural communication competence.

DISCUSSION QUESTIONS

1. What does the term *competence* mean to you?
2. According to Triandis (2006), there are four stages of intercultural communication competence, ending with "unconscious competence," or the ability to be effective without thought. Is this stage possible? If so, would you still be engaging in "Intercultural" communication, or would this stage of competence require you to have adopted the new culture?
3. In your opinion, who measures or determines whether someone is competent? Can you measure your own competence? Can you measure someone else's?

SERVICE LEARNING

CHAPTER 16

STUDY OBJECTIVES

After completing this chapter, you will be able to:
- Define and describe service learning.
- Define and describe experiential learning.
- Explain how service learning aids in understanding cultures different than your own.

INTRODUCTION

Have you ever been in a class where your teacher assigned a service-learning project? As a student, you may or may not have experienced service learning at some point in your education. If you have experienced service learning, chances are you did not realize you really were learning until after your assignment was completed. Further, we are willing to bet that you were surprised by how much you had learned when you reflected on your experience.

Service learning is a form of experiential education. Experiential education or learning encourages nontraditional forms of educational activities that do not follow a typical traditional, lecture classroom format. As a student learning about intercultural communication, you may find that service learning will aid you in understanding cultural differences and applying class concepts to your experiences, and provide you the opportunity to experience a new culture.

In this chapter, we explore what experiential learning is and what service learning is. You will read about a service-learning experience at a college in Minnesota. At the end of the chapter, you will find a number of discussion questions that will further aid you in understanding service learning.

WHAT IS EXPERIENTIAL LEARNING?

Experiential learning is an important method for working at the analysis, synthesis, and evaluation components of Bloom's taxonomy. "Experiential" refers to a method of learning, *how* one can learn. In learning experientially one accumulates knowledge by personal involvement with people or process (Cunningham 1997). For example, one learns auto mechanics experientially by working on a car, learns chemistry by mixing elements in a lab, learns to teach by helping someone learn to read or master arithmetic concepts, and learns politics by running for office or attempting to enact and implement legislation.

Experiential learning is not what we call the "mug-and-jug" method, which considers the student's head an empty mug into which knowledge is poured from the teacher's jug. It is not rote memorization of facts that are regurgitated in the form of numbers or letters on answer sheets at test time. In experiential learning, the teacher frames the environment, offers a starting point, suggests a direction, and invites students to join the learning process.

Experiential learning requires the student to engage the world and the community, and to take in what is happening where he or she is. The experience may emphasize physical activity—as with learning auto mechanics, carpentry, and soccer—or the engagement may emphasize cerebral activity, as with learning chemistry in the lab, politics by campaigning for election, or working with residents to obtain a neighborhood playground or library. Learning is active, not passive. One probes the constraints and opportunities present in the environment, studies strengths and weaknesses of the person or group being helped, then reflects. The reflection process transitions into deciding on and implementing a course of action.

WHAT IS SERVICE LEARNING?

"Service-learning" means "serving while learning" or "learning while serving." Serving is not abstract but concrete: one serves specific others. The focus is on the act and the server in relation to another. The server provides knowledge or skills, and the other also has gifts to share, gifts that may be less obvious.

In a professional relationship, the clinician may attempt to benefit the injured or sick patient; in scientific research, the investigator may delve into the mind or behaviors of an organization or young student to push the frontiers of general scientific knowledge. A service-learner, however, listens to the concerns of the group or person, lets the "other" define the situation, and responds by trying to meet that need. In listening and learning, receiving and giving, the service-learning relationship is horizontal, lateral, parallel. It is not hierarchal.

The primary goal of service-learning is not to push the boundaries of scientific knowledge, but to work with another to attend to the other, to learn about the other in order to serve the other effectively. In the process of learning about the other, one's own knowledge expands. The service-learner offers a fresh set of eyes, seeing a situation from a different perspective. The service-learner does not follow the traditional logic of science: seeking a "one best way," then applying that fixed theory to a presumed illness or weakness (De Bono 1967). In service-learning one works with another to share and perhaps to create or expand knowledge.

The service-learner who is aware of important cultural cues and responds sensitively gains credibility with others because he or she knows how to act. The effective service-learner adapts to the culture in which he or she serves.

Understanding the concept of culture and how it unconsciously colors the way we see, talk, and act is important for building positive relationships with those whom we seek to serve. Robert Coles, a major historical force in service-learning, highlights the fact that learning may occur in unexpected places, particularly in service-learning, and shares the wisdom of important historical figures who have engaged in service. Physician and poet William Carlos Williams told Coles to learn "what you can where you can," just as Williams learned from his patients while making home visits in Paterson, New Jersey. Dorothy Day, a Catholic social activist and journalist who ran a soup kitchen in New York, told Coles that he could learn more from her guests/clients than he could from his professor friends at Harvard. Indeed, while such Harvard colleagues as Anna Freud and Erik Erikson did help shape Coles's theoretical work as a child psychiatrist, he would ultimately venture on his own to the South to learn about the children there and about civil rights. On his early trips to Alabama from Boston, Coles described rural southern children as "slow." Later, after spending more time in Alabama, Coles (1967) would change his mind, exclaiming how smart they were! Like Coles, service-learning students often cross a personal cultural divide as they begin their service-learning.

Learning about and being respectful of the culture is an important first step in building service-learning success. Most university students adopt an open learning posture, understanding that it is not "they" who must adapt to "us," but "we" who must seek to understand and adapt to "them." We must reach out, learn, break out of our mold, leave our comfort zone, and expand our understanding and appreciation of others. Then we can connect with others, serve others, and be served by others.

Moving Forward

Now that we understand a little more about what experiential and service learning are, let us explore what service learning might look like. The following reading reports on a college class that required a 15-hour service-learning experience. Students were able to choose to complete their service at one of four organizations the teacher arranged for students to work for, or with another organization approved of for the assignment. As you read this article, keep in mind the following questions: How did the students feel before and after their service-learning experience? Were there any differences in their emotions? What does a pluralist perspective mean? How can you go about developing this perspective in your own life? Some students mentioned not being exposed to diversity in their community prior to their service-learning experience. What does diversity look like in your community? Students revealed they had a better understanding of people who spoke a language other than English. If you were to participate in a service-learning experience, what cultural groups might you gain a better understanding with?

THE BENEFITS OF SERVICE LEARNING

Are college students prepared to deal with cultural diversity? Do they understand family systems, social systems, and cultural norms of immigrants? Do they understand clothing preferences and choices of immigrants? Sociocultural Aspects of Clothing, a course taught spring 2007, at The College of St. Catherine, in Saint Paul, Minnesota was a perfect place to explore responses to these questions with the intent of having each question answered "yes" at the end of the term. The course offered an opportunity to engage in actions that reciprocally benefit the common good of learning among students and immigrant individuals, families, and communities.

Service learning, a pedagogy that has many supporters, encourages learning with civic engagement (American Association of Colleges for Teacher Education, 2003; O'Grady, 2000; Robinson & Harrist, 2004). In addition, according to Department of American Studies, service learning as a required course component is beneficial because it establishes a common ground for dialogue and for synthesis of observations from the community site, and the class lecture, discussion, and readings (Service learning, n.d.). The Sociocultural Aspects of Clothing course was an ideal opportunity to incorporate service learning to enhance classroom learning and application in the community. The objectives of the service-learning component were to broaden the perspectives from which students view dress across cultures and to provide opportunities for civic engagement. It is especially imperative in the Twin Cities, which has large refugee and immigrant populations that continue to grow. Ninety percent of refugees in the state live in the Twin Cities (International Institute of Minnesota, 2002). In 2005, refugee arrivals in Minnesota accounted for 11.8% of all refugees who arrived in United States ("Record Number of," 2006).

Table 16.1 Partner Sites, Their Programs and Target Groups

LEAP INTERNATIONAL ACADEMY	JANE ADDAMS SCHOOL OF DEMOCRACY (JAS)	PROJECT REGINA	MINNESOTA INTERNSHIP CENTER (MNIC)
Provides intensive English instruction in content areas for students, ages 13 to 20 years, who are pursuing a high school diploma. Serves new arrivals to the United States or those with limited English skills. As of March 2005, students were of Asian, East African, and Latino heritages.	A community-learning and action center where everyone is a teacher and a learner with Hmong, East African, and Latino immigrants.	Part of a non-profit, Center for Asian and Pacific Islanders provides a unique 35 hour per week program combining work specific English Language Learner (ELL) instruction, training, and subsidized work experiences women.	Charter school is open to all, but seeks to enroll students who have not fared well in traditional high schools and alternative settings. College students worked with Muslim high school students.
Based on individual preference, college students were placed in English language, writing, science, and sewing classrooms.	College students joined cultural circles and participated in citizenship education and reflection sessions.	College students would have volunteered in the English classroom and sewing room.	College students volunteered in two levels of English speaking class- Levels 1A and 1B.
When? Regular daytime school hours (Monday-Friday)	When? Monday and Wednesday 6–9 PM	When? Regular daytime school hours (Monday-Friday)	When? Regular daytime school hours (Monday-Friday)
Center of Community Work and Learning, The College of St. Catherine, written communication, January 31, 2007			

This service-learning endeavor became possible because of collaboration between the Departments of Family, Consumer, and Nutritional Sciences (FCNS) and Community Work and Learning (CWL) at the College. The pedagogical model, which incorporates service learning, had been tested and implemented with one site—the Jane Addams School of Democracy (JAS) as community-based learning (Hendricks & Kari, 1999). However, based on the feedback from FCNS faculty and students who had taken the course, additional partners from the community were included to provide choice and flexibility. The partner sites (see Table 1) included LEAP International Academy, JAS, Project Regina, and Minnesota Internship Center (MNIC).

Representatives from the four organizations were invited to the classroom early in the semester for an informational session. During this session, students learned about the cultures, ethnicities, and specific needs of learners; the work environment; scheduling flexibility; and individual accommodations at each site. Students selected one of the sites for their 15-hour experience. Fourteen of 20 students chose LEAP based on the site representative's friendliness and its flexibility in accommodating their schedules. Three students chose to work at JAS, one student chose MNIC because it involved tutoring, and the other two arranged other sites, with the instructor's approval.

To keep a record of their experiences, students maintained a journal with two columns—impressions and reflections. Students also collaborated with their site representative and discussed the site's requirements and their personal objectives. Students were advised that learning is embedded in their interactions and experiences with their immigrant co-learner(s) and it was up to them to facilitate the interaction.

The service-learning component of the class culminated in a final paper. The students decided on the focus of the paper based on their experiences, class presentations, and research. The final papers were very interesting and diverse. Selected titles included "My unforgettable cultural experience," "From Laos to America: Nhia's journey," "The world of Huipil," "Muslim women and misunderstandings," and "The Somali dress and struggles of conformity. "

The CWL department requested written student feedback at three stages: pre-experience, mid-term, and end-of-term. Pre-experience feedback was guided by questions such as What excites you about your community work and service learning experience? and What concerns you about it and what do you hope to learn from it? There was initial resistance for the service project and students' pre-experience reflections expressed mixed emotions of excitement, communication challenges, and time constraints. From a learning perspective, students hoped to learn more about cultures, cultural dress, and language, as well as gain a wider perspective or worldview of immigrant individuals and their communities.

The papers and the end-of-term service- learning experience evaluations are evidence of the shift from learning about another culture to learning from other cultures and developing a pluralist perspective. A pluralist perspective is imperative to be a mature individual and work in the global economy (Damhorst, 2005). End-of-term evaluation statements included: "Overall, I would have to say I have a new respect for people trying to move to a new country and learn a different language," "I learned a little bit about their religion and daily activities. I also learned about their traditional food," and "Someone might not understand that, well, due to language barrier does not mean they are stupid. You just have to be open to learning how to get the point across."

End-of-term written feedback was based on questions about the experience. One of the questions was, Overall, how has your community work and learning experience helped broaden your understanding of the relationship of dress to the individual? To society? To other cultures and societies? Students' reflected significant changes that they attributed to their experiences. The major theme that evolved was the realization of diversity among the population within the Twin Cities and a better understanding of people who speak a language other than English. The students expressed some concerns about not being able to relate the experience more directly to clothing for these reasons: (a) many immigrants tend to dress very similarly to Americans as part of their quest to be part of the new culture, (b) clothing from their native country is not readily available, or (c) in some cases, the clothing is worn infrequently either in the country of origin or in the U.S. However, some students interacted on a one-to-one basis with learners at partner sites to learn about their dress. A student stated, "I learned from doing interviews with the Somali students about the reason why they wear the hijab—I have always wondered why they wore it and getting a chance to know about their background was good." Another wrote, "I was able to understand where people are coming from and how their dress might influence their everyday life."

Some students did not have previous experience with culturally diverse populations and this opportunity became a new experience—"I realized there is lot of diversity in the Twin Cities, both culturally and in lifestyles and backgrounds. The immigrants are not people I would normally be interacting with, and so it was intriguing to know their stories of change in their life."

In addition to end-of-semester written feedback, representatives from CWL were invited to the last class of the semester. A class discussion brought out key emotions representing students "before" and "after" responses. Students indicated that the before experience was characterized by apprehension, confusion, excitement, nervousness, and concern about the time-consuming nature of the activity. After the experience, students indicated that they were curious to know more, felt appreciated by people of diverse backgrounds, had new insights, and, in some cases, were still somewhat confused. This transformation clearly identifies with the definition of service learning as stated on the website of Learn and Serve America's National Service-Learning Clearinghouse, "Service-learning is a teaching and learning strategy that integrates meaningful community service with instruction and reflection to enrich the learning experience, teach civic responsibility, and strengthen communities" (nd, ¶1).

According to Hendricks and Kari, "This course challenged students to understand the role that clothing plays as part of the broad social context of a culture" (1999, p. 63). Based on student feedback through their reflections and a discussion with a colleague, it was suggested that the experience be called a cultural experience instead of service learning. The term *cultural experience* better communicates the underlying purpose of the service-learning component.

Based on qualitative interpretation of student papers, reflections, and feedback, it is evident that this venture improved the student understanding of diverse cultures with reference to family, social, and cultural systems promoting pluralism. Some students were able to make connections of clothing choices with these systems. In addition, the community sites benefited from the volunteer time of the students. During their volunteer time, students helped the immigrant students to learn English and American culture, fostering common good of learning among students and immigrant individuals, families, and their communities.

SUMMARY

In this chapter, we learned about experiential learning and discovered that the classroom is not the only place for us to learn. Sometimes, our teacher may assign a service-learning experience that requires us to step outside our comfort zone and experience a new culture. Studying intercultural communication can help us adapt more easily in a new culture and help us gain credibility during our experience. Continue on to the discussion questions to test your knowledge about service learning and intercultural communication.

DISCUSSION QUESTIONS

1. Just as there is cultural diversity, there is also diversity in learning styles. In what ways do you learn most effectively? How might YOU benefit from service learning?
2. Sometimes, in order to complete a service learning assignment, we have step outside our comfort zones. Have you ever interacted in a setting that was initially uncomfortable? How did that impact your experience?
3. One thing that experiential and service-learning assignments provide for you is insight into another culture or co-culture in your community. What kinds of co-cultures exist where you live? How might you be able to serve them?

APPENDIX

SERVICE LEARNING MATERIALS

In Chapter 16, you were introduced to service learning. Service learning enables you to apply the course content you learn throughout the semester to an experience outside of the classroom. This assignment provides you the opportunity to engage in service learning as a component of your intercultural communication class.

In this assignment, each student will provide fifteen hours of service to a community organization throughout the semester. Provided service may be concentrated during one month, or it may be spread across several months throughout the semester.

Students should find service opportunities in places where they will meet and interact with people from various cultures, including cultures that differ from the student's culture. Concepts drawn from this textbook and lecture can be used to help students communicate effectively in face-to-face situations. While serving the needs of the community organization or group, students will be able to practice their intercultural communication skills.

This assignment has six parts:

1. Service Learning Checklist
2. Service Learning Contract
3. Mid-Semester Service Learning Report
4. Mid-Semester Record of Service
5. Final Service Learning Report
6. Final Record of Service

The following pages include the materials needed to complete this assignment. Make sure to pay attention to due dates throughout the semester and to the number of service hours that must be completed prior to turning in each part of the assignment. Further, check with your instructor if your university requires a participation waiver to be included with these materials.

SERVICE LEARNING CHECKLIST

DUE DATE: _____

NAME: _____

AGENCY: _____

Directions: *Use the following checklist in choosing an organization or group for which you will be providing service this semester. You will turn this checklist in along with your service learning contract. This must be turned in BEFORE you begin your first volunteer session OR by the date that your instructor assigns. Service completed before the contract and checklist are turned in will not count towards the required fifteen hours of service.*

Am I interacting with other people representing a different culture than mine?	Y / N
Am I able to complete at least 7.5 hours with this organization before my mid-semester report is due?	Y / N
Am I able to complete at least fifteen hours with this organization throughout the semester?	Y / N
Do I foresee myself learning from this experience with this organization?	Y / N
Do I understand what the purpose of this organization is?	Y / N
Has this organization responded to my request in a timely manner?	Y / N
Out of all the organizations for which I considered completing my service, is this organization the best organization for me?	Y / N
Will I be able to contribute to this organization's needs?	Y / N
Am I aware of what my duties will be at this organization?	Y / N

Signature of Student_____

Date Submitted to Instructor_____

SERVICE LEARNING CONTRACT

DUE DATE: _____

NAME: _____

Directions: *Planning a schedule in advance will help you stay on track throughout the semester. Complete the following information and hand in to your professor BEFORE you begin your first volunteer session OR by the date that your instructor assigns. Service completed before the contract and checklist are turned in will not count towards the required fifteen hours of service. Please note that animal shelters will not be approved organizations.*

Name of Student_____

Agency Selected_____

Name of Agency Contact Person_____

Telephone/Contact Information for Agency Contact Person_____

Date of Initial Contact with Agency Contact Person_____

Agreed Upon Schedule of Volunteer Sessions:

Date_____   Time_____

Date_____   Time_____

Date_____   Time_____

Date_____   Time_____

Date_____   Time_____

Date_____   Time_____

Date_____   Time_____

Date_____   Time_____

Date_____   Time_____

Date_____   Time_____

Date_____   Time_____

Date_____   Time_____

Date_____   Time_____

Date_____   Time_____

Signature of Student_____

Date Submitted to Instructor_____

MID-SEMESTER SERVICE LEARNING REPORT

DUE DATE: _____

NAME: _____

AGENCY: _____

HOURS COMPLETED: _____

Directions: *This report should be completed when you have finished at least SEVEN hours of your service learning experience with your chosen organization. The service learning checklist and service learning contract must be turned in prior to turning in this report. Reports will not be accepted for credit until the checklist and contract are turned in.*

Using the following questions, reflect on what you have been doing during your service learning opportunities. You should type the question and your response (at least three–five sentences per question) to each item on a separate sheet of paper and hand it in when due.

1. Describe the work you have done thus far with your agency.
2. Describe any fears or concerns you have had about working with this agency as part of this class.
   a. Have the fears/concerns been resolved?
   b. Explain how any fears/concerns were resolved.
3. Describe what you have learned about the culture of your agency and the people you have served.
4. What changes, if any, have you made in the way you communicate with clients at the agency?
5. What have you found to be the most challenging part of this service learning experience thus far?
6. What have you found to be the most rewarding part of this service learning experience thus far?

Signature of Student_____

Date Submitted to Instructor_____

MID-SEMESTER

RECORD OF SERVICE

DUE DATE: _____

NAME: _____

AGENCY: _____

Directions: *Keep an ongoing log of your service throughout the semester. Make sure that an authority figure at your chosen organization signs this log after each time you complete your service. This record needs to be turned in with the mid-semester service learning report.*

DATE OF SERVICE	HOURS OF SERVICE	SIGNATURE/VERIFICATION OF SERVICE

FINAL SERVICE LEARNING REPORT

DUE DATE: _____

NAME: _____

AGENCY: _____

HOURS COMPLETED: _____

Directions: *This report should be completed when you have completed fifteen hours of your service learning experience with your chosen organization, and should be accompanied by the record of service form. Reports will not be accepted for credit until all required service learning documents are turned in.*

Using the following questions, reflect on your experiences and write out your answers. Type the questions and your answers (at least three–five sentences per answer) on a separate sheet and hand in when it is due. There are three content sections: learning, service, and process. Make sure to answer all questions completely.

Learning

1. What information did you learn in the class that helped you communicate while doing the service?
2. What communication skills did you develop through your service activities?
3. How did this service experience help you to better understand ideas or subjects we studied in class?
4. Through this service learning project, what did you learn about:
    a. Yourself?
    b. Working/communicating with others, including people in the class?
    c. Your community?
5. How will you use what you learned in this experience?

Service

1. What was the need for your service effort?
2. What contribution did you make?
3. What was the effect of your efforts on the agency?
4. How did your service affect the community?

Process

1. Were there any differences between the initial project plans and what you actually did?
2. What ideas do you have for improving any part of the project/course?

Signature of Student_____

DateSubmittedtoInstructor_____

FINAL RECORD OF SERVICE

DUE DATE: _____

NAME: _____
AGENCY: _____

Directions: *Keep an ongoing log of your service throughout the semester. Make sure that an authority figure at your chosen organization signs this log after each time you complete your service. This record needs to be turned in with the final service learning report.*

DATE OF SERVICE	HOURS OF SERVICE	SIGNATURE/VERIFICATION OF SERVICE

DATE OF SERVICE	HOURS OF SERVICE	SIGNATURE/VERIFICATION OF SERVICE

Signature of Student Volunteer _____

Date Submitted to Instructor _____

SERVICE LEARNING & ICC ACTIVITY

Directions: *Throughout the semester, you and your teammates have been working with different organizations to fulfill the service learning assignment requirements.*

In your own terms, define Intercultural Communication Competence. What does Intercultural Communication Competence look like to you?

Now, take a few moments and share your service learning experience with your teammates and complete the following questions:

Can you recall a time in your service that you experienced competent intercultural communication? Explain.

Can you recall a time in your service that you experienced incompetent intercultural communication? Explain.

PERSONAL REPORT OF INTERCULTURAL COMMUNICATION APPREHENSION (PRICA)

NAME: _____

DUE DATE: _____

Directions: *Complete the following assignment at the beginning of the semester. The fourteen statements below are comments frequently made by people with regard to communication with people from other cultures. Please indicate how much you agree with these statements by marking a number representing your response to each statement, using the following choices:*

1 = Strongly Disagree	2 = Disagree	3 = Neutral	4 = Agree	5 = Strongly Agree

_____ 1. Generally, I am comfortable interacting with a group of people from different cultures.

_____ 2. I am tense and nervous while interacting with people from different cultures.

_____ 3. I like to get involved in group discussions with others who are from different cultures.

_____ 4. Engaging in a group discussion with people from different cultures makes me nervous.

_____ 5. I am calm and relaxed with interacting with a group of people who are from different cultures.

_____ 6. While participating in a conversation with a person from a different culture, I get nervous.

_____ 7. I have no fear of speaking up in a conversation with a person from a different culture.

_____ 8. Ordinarily I am very tense and nervous in a conversation with a person from a different culture.

_____ 9. Ordinarily I am very calm and relaxed in a conversation with a person from a different culture.

_____ 10. While conversing with a person from a different culture, I feel very relaxed.

_____ 11. I am afraid to speak up in conversations with a person from a different culture.

_____ 12. I face the prospect of interacting with people from different cultures with confidence.

_____ 13. My thoughts become confused and jumbled when interacting with people from different cultures.

_____ 14. Communicating with people from different cultures makes me feel uncomfortable.

James W. Neuliep and James C. McCroskey, Excerpt from: "The Development of Intercultural and Interethnic Communication Apprehension Scales," *Communication Research Reports*, vol. 14, issue 2. Copyright © 1997 by Taylor & Francis Group.

HISTORY AND INTERCULTURAL COMMUNICATION ACTIVITY

Directions: *Prioritize the following contexts based upon* **which one your team believes has the greatest influence on how American students understand and communicate about history.** *Discuss the different contexts listed below,* **select** *the one your group believes has the greatest influence,* **prioritize** *the contexts, and* **provide your reasons** *supporting your team's decision.*

If you have students from other countries on your team, or if you have experienced other cultures before, how might you prioritize the following contexts?

Political context—Students know about the past because they are taught about politicians and their decisions that shaped history (e.g., decision of George W. Bush to attack Saddam Hussein after 9/11 and the start of the Iraqi war).

Intellectual context—Students know about the past because they are taught about broad concepts and how these ideas are developed, transmitted, and enacted in society (e.g., history of capitalism or Marxism and how these concepts shaped economic policies that affect our way of living).

Social context—Students know about the past because they are taught by observing the everyday lives of people and their cultural attitudes, beliefs, and values (e.g., origins of social interaction patterns, courting rituals, standards of cleanliness).

Family context—Students know about the past because they are taught through oral history, passed along from one generation to the next (e.g., genealogy, family heirlooms).

National context—Students know about the past because they are taught stories, verging on myths, that give life to events and figures important to the people of the nation (e.g., arrival of Europeans in North America, stories of the Founding Fathers, the California gold rush, Abraham Lincoln freeing the slaves).

CONTEXT	PRIORITY RANKING
Political	
Intellectual	
Social	
Family	
National	

Reason(s) for ranking order:

Directions: *When traveling abroad, Americans sometimes are not treated well by non-Americans. Which of the following contexts does your team believe to be the reason for this animosity (ill will)? Sometimes international students are not treated well by Americans. What might be some reasons for this animosity (ill will)? Discuss the different contexts listed below, select the one your group believes is the most significant reason for the animosity, prioritize the contexts, and provide your reasons supporting your decision.*

CONTEXT	PRIORITY RANKING
Political	
Intellectual	
Social	
Family	
National	

Reason(s) for ranking order:

NONVERBAL ACTIVITY

This activity is meant to help you apply the knowledge you have gained from learning about nonverbal communication. There is no correct answer to these questions/scenarios. As a team, you should discuss the problem and the options listed below, deciding together which choice makes the most sense. **In order to earn full points for this activity**, you must write a justification for each of your team's answers in the space provided below the scenario. Please be prepared to share your justifications with the rest of the class.

Concerning the idea of attraction in nonverbal communication, we often associate good qualities with people we find attractive and negative qualities with people we find unattractive. We often refer to this as the "halo" and "horn" effects of perception. For people we perceive as good, we place halos over their heads, and we place horns on the heads of those we perceive as bad. Take a look at the pictures on the screen and tell me what you think of these people. They are probably pretty average-looking, but do you think they are good or bad based on physical appearance?

A. Individual #1
B. Individual #2
C. Individual #3
D. Individual #4
E. Individual #5

****If you happen to recognize any of these people, keep it to yourself until after we've discussed this as a large group.****

1. Based on what you see, which one(s) seem like good people?

_____

_____

_____

_____

_____

_____

What about them gives you this impression?

_____

_____

_____

_____

_____

_____

2. Based on what you see, which one(s) seem like bad people?

_____

_____

_____

_____

_____

_____

What about them gives you this impression?

_____

_____

_____

_____

_____

_____

_____

_____

3. According to some communication scholars, 93 percent of all meaning in our communication is derived from our nonverbal communication, which makes these messages incredibly powerful. Despite the fact that our nonverbal behaviors speak so loudly, we are rarely conscious of them (or in control of them). In the following two scenes from the movie *Crash*, you will see two situations filled with prejudice, stereotyping, and discrimination. Some of what you will see is very obvious/overt, while some of what is presented is very subtle/covert. If we believe that the nonverbal messages, as some scholars argue, are more important than the words spoken, which kind of nonverbal behavior do you think speaks loudest in these scenes?

**Please be aware that there is a fairly significant amount of swear words used in this R- rated movie clip. If you would like to leave the room while it is played, please do, and your team or I can fill you in on the gist of the scenes afterwards.

A. Eye Contact
B. Proxemics
C. Paralinguistics
D. Facial Expression
E. Gestures

Answer: _____

Why do you believe these kinds of nonverbal messages are so powerful?

_____

_____

_____

_____

_____

_____

_____

_____

LEARNING APA ACTIVITY

Directions: *One of the goals in this class is to learn APA style. The following five references have errors. Identify the errors in each reference and provide the correct citation at the end.*

A.)
Littlefield, R. S., Currie-Mueller, J., Vevea, N., and Ghazal-Aswad, N. (Eds.) *Intercultural Competency: Learning, Communicating, and Serving*. San Diego, CA: Cognella Academic Publishing.

Errors:

B.)
Littlefield, R.S., Currie-Mueller, J., Vevea, N., & Ghazal-Aswad, N. (2014). Intercultural competency: Learning, communicating, and serving. CA: Cognella Academic Publishing.

Errors:

C.)
R. S. Littlefield, J. Currie-Mueller, N. Vevea, and N. Ghazal-Aswad. (Eds.) (2014). Intercultural competency: Learning, communicating, and serving. San Diego, CA: Cognella Academic Publishing.

Errors:

D.)
Littlefield, R. S., Currie-Mueller, J., Vevea, N., and Ghazal-Aswad, N. (2014). *Intercultural competency.* San Diego, CA: Cognella Academic Publishing.

Errors:

E.)
Littlefield, R. S., Currie-Mueller, J., Vevea, N., & Ghazal-Aswad, N. (Eds.) (2014). Intercultural competency: Learning, communicating, and serving. Cognella Academic Publishing.

Errors:

Correct citation:

CLASSROOM CULTURE ACTIVITY

Description of Activity

How is the classroom an extension of mainstream culture?

A. Individualism—concern for self, independent, competitive

B. Collectivism—concern for group, dependent, noncompetitive, relationship-focused

C. Power distance—in-class and out-of-class student and teacher behavior and relationships kept separate, rules are made and followed, classroom setting places teacher and student in fixed locations

D. Uncertainty avoidance—desire to seek information, discomfort with ambiguity

E. Masculinity/femininity—roles clearly defined, relationships defined

Each team should spend some time talking about the different educational experiences of its members. Every member should share an experience pertaining to each of the five items. Consider situations where students from different cultural backgrounds have been part of the experience. It is likely that you have been in many situations where students and teachers have behaved in ways that demonstrated their cultural differences.

Select one of these situations that the group decides was most memorable and create a short skit involving a student(s) and a teacher to demonstrate one of the five concepts listed above.

You will have an opportunity to present your skit to the class. The goal is to see if your classmates can recognize the concept based upon your performance of the skit.

CREATE A SCRIPT FOR YOUR GROUP BELOW

Identify the concept:

_____

Provide a brief description of the situation:

_____

Identify the characters:

_____

Write the script:

POPULAR CULTURE ACTIVITY

Part 1: Your instructor will show you a series of video clips in class.

    A. Video Clip #1   Rank:_____
       Reasons for resistance:

    B. Video Clip #2   Rank:_____
       Reasons for resistance:

    C. Video Clip #3   Rank:_____
       Reasons for resistance:

    D. Video Clip #4   Rank:_____
       Reasons for resistance:

    E. Video Clip #5   Rank:_____
       Reasons for resistance:

Part 2: Each of the videos you watched represents a culture text to consume. People often resist particular forms of popular culture by refusing to engage in or respond to them. For each of the cultural texts portrayed in the videos, provide reasons why people might resist it.

Part 3: After you have identified the sources of resistance for each cultural text, rank them 1-2-3-4-5 based upon which you believe should be most resisted. Provide a rationale for your ranking of 1.

RELATIONSHIPS ACTIVITY

Internet Relationships

Due to the expanding social networking systems available to the public, internet dating and relationships are a growing trend. However, despite the positive aspects of this phenomenon, several problems or barriers to effective communication exist. In your opinion, which of the following problems is the greatest problem or barrier? Rank the problems from 1 to 5 and provide your reasons why you ranked #1 and #5 as you did.

PROBLEM	RANK FROM GREATEST TO LEAST 1 = GREATEST 5 = LEAST	EXPLAIN WHY YOU RANKED #1 AND #5 AS YOU DID.
A. Written messages can be misunderstood, particularly humor, irony, and sarcasm. Example: You write a message that you intend to be a joke, and your friend or date misinterprets it. The message results in a conflict.		
B. The absence of nonverbal cues makes clarification of messages difficult. Example: You write a message telling your friend or date you are sorry about what happened; your friend or date perceives the message as being too short, putting your sincerity in question.		
C. Hierarchy is impossible to determine, complicating messages with supervisors/ subordinates. Example: You get your first e-mail from your new place of employment telling you when to be at work, and you are asked to respond. You are unsure about the status of the sender and don't know how to respond.		
D. The online medium makes it difficult to decode high- and low-context messages. Example: You might be comfortable being straightforward about your feelings, while your partner might prefer to be more ambiguous. You want commitment, but your partner might want more time.		
E. The ability to mask one's true identity increases the likelihood of deception and dishonesty. Example: You visit a chat room and meet a person who seems to be your ideal partner. You hit it off, but can you be sure the person you met online is the real person you'd meet if you were to take the relationship offline?		

Intercultural Dating

The following example is developed based on a real-life relationship.

My girlfriend and I are both Mexican. She (and her family) is religious, while I am not at all, nor is my family. At times the religion difference has been a cause for some complications. For instance, she did not want to let her family know that I am an atheist when we began dating because she thought they would dislike me without getting to know me. Not ever having given much thought to religion, I thought it would not matter. But to my surprise, one of the first times I met her grandmother I was asked about my religion, which church I attended, and when I was baptized. I could see the look on my girlfriend's face as I calmly answered that I was not religious. Almost instantly, I could see the looks of her family change, and I quickly understood why she was so worried. While I do not believe her family hates me, I know that they remember that conversation. Now the family insists that my girlfriend stop seeing me.

Consider the following options the couple might take to resolve this situation.

OPTION	ADVANTAGES	DISADVANTAGES
A The couple should continue seeing each other. They should do nothing overt.		
B She should confront her family when he is not around and ask them to accept him, even though they do not approve.		
C He should ask the grandmother for her blessing and explain that he will not stop her from practicing her religious beliefs.		
D They should attend mass occasionally, even if he doesn't believe, so the family will see him in that context.		
E Perhaps he should consider joining her church if she insists.		
F They should discontinue their relationship.		

Which is the best option for this situation?_____

Explain your reason why you picked the option you did:

IDENTITY ACTIVITY

Directions: *Read the following scenario. Discuss the different identities Yamir and his friends may have reflected by their words and actions. Decide which identity was the reason for the confrontation and explain your reasoning in the space provided.*

TASK #1

Yamir is a freshman at Red River State University. He is one of several young men from his country who have come to study construction and mechanical engineering at RRSU. New to the university and newly arrived in the United States, Yamir and his friends are in the process of meeting people and adjusting to the city and their new surroundings. Yamir is Muslim and strives to follow the teachings of the Koran in his daily life. He and his friends have enjoyed walking the streets of the city and often hold hands as they walk, remembering their homeland and talking about their plans for the future. One night, they decided to go out to enjoy some of the local culture. They saw other young people going into what looked like a restaurant, so they decided to go in. The restaurant turned out to be a bar and grill with a local band playing on a stage. They decided to stay and were invited by a group of single American women to join them around a table. Soon Yamir and his friends were up dancing and having what appeared to be quite a good time. Yamir and his friends appeared equally comfortable dancing with the women and sometimes danced with each other. During one of the dances, a group of local patrons who had been watching the American women confronted Yamir and his friends and told them they should leave the bar and go back to where they came from. Yamir and his friends decided not to put up a fight and left.

Discuss each of the following identities and arrive at a consensus about what each identity involves.

Decide which identity was the reason for the confrontation.

  A. Gender identity
  B. Sexual identity
  C. Age identity
  D. Racial/ethnic identity
  E. Religious identity

Provide a reason for your choice:

TASK #2

We know that Majority Identity Development is a process that members of the dominant group in a society experience as they come to know how they fit in. Majority Identity Development has four stages. Discuss the four stages and arrive at a consensus about what each stage involves. Write your explanation for each below:

Stage 1—Unexamined Identity

Stage 2—Acceptance

Stage 3—Resistance

Stage 4—Redefinition and Reintegration

Spend a few minutes deciding how you would characterize the following groups in American society:

    A. Upper class
    B. Middle class
    C. Working class
    D. Lower class
    E. Impoverished class

Given what you know about the four stages of Majority Identity Development, which of these groups would have the most difficulty recognizing the need for resistance, redefinition, and reintegration?

    A.   People in the upper class
    B.   People in the middle class
    C.   People in the working class
    D.   People in the lower class
    E.   People who are indigent

Provide a reason for your choice:

Conflict in the Workplace

The following individuals work in the same office at a major research university:

Fahryah

Fahryah is a 45-year-old African woman who sought refugee status in the United States due to a drawn-out religious conflict in her home country. She is a practicing Muslim and wears traditional clothing, including a hijab. She is multilingual, used to high-context situations, and tends to assertively separate herself from those around her whenever she does not like or approve of what they are doing. She is very direct when she wants something. This has gotten her into trouble with her coworkers, who think she is rude and uncooperative. However, she always completes the tasks assigned to her and receives compliments from her supervisors on the quality of her work.

Tim

Tim is a young, 25-year-old sojourner—a global nomad—whose parents were executives in an international corporation. He is multilingual and non-assertively assimilates to the situation whenever anything is asked of him. This has gotten him into trouble with his coworkers, who think he is only looking out for himself. However, his ethno-relative approach to everything often makes him a culture broker in his work environment, and as a result he can often move projects forward in spite of opposition.

Carlos

Carlos is a Hispanic/Latino man who migrated from Brazil to the US nearly twenty years ago. He speaks Spanish and English and uses an elaborate communication style when he describes his projects. This often irritates his coworkers because, as they say, "he likes to talk, talk, talk instead of getting things done." He prefers close contact when working with colleagues and credits his ability "to figure things out without being told" as a strength. He relies on assertive accommodation when communicating with his coworkers. Carlos is well-liked because he spends time with everyone asking them about their families and circumstances, sends cards and gifts to coworkers when he perceives they are having a bad day, and makes everyone feel like their opinions matter.

Steven

Steven is a 38-year-old white male, born in Alabama. He speaks only English, and his aggressively accommodating style and reliance on paralanguage reflects his ability to function in a high-context environment. He'd like to be the supervisor one day, but he rarely confronts anyone, often using an indirect communication style. Some of his coworkers think he has trouble making decisions. However, his intuition, willingness to take risks, and his tolerance for ambiguity has helped him develop some very exciting programs for the university.

Melinda

Melinda is a 40-year-old English-speaking woman from Nebraska. She is very conscious of deadlines and prefers everything to be spelled out before she starts a project. Her colleagues are often impatient with her when she does not allow them to move more quickly into the activities associated with their work projects. She is understated in her communication style and relies on nonassertive accommodation to get along in the office. However, the differences between how she communicates with others and how she understands what should be done causes problems for her with her coworkers. She is very good at keeping track of tasks and budgets, and her supervisors have identified her as a promising candidate for an Associate Dean of Finance position that is opening up in the near future.

Last summer, this team of individuals was given the task of organizing a parents' weekend for incoming freshmen. Now it is November, and the event hasn't happened. There has been a lot of conflict on the committee. The upper-level administrators are wondering why. Your team has been hired to get to the bottom of the problem and help this group do what it was asked to do. Here is what you found out:

- Steven is comfortable with a relaxed schedule where freshmen and their parents explore the campus together, with only meals and some social activities being structured events.
- Melinda wants structure, thinking that a relaxed schedule will not be much of a draw for parents coming from a great distance. After all, when people come to campus, they want to have a schedule and do things with their children.
- Fahryah thinks the weekend is a waste of resources, as most of the freshmen students had their parents with them when they did summer orientation. Personally, she has also shared her impatience with freshmen and thinks that if we are going to have parents on campus, their activity should be very structured. She believes that "feel-good" activities costing a lot of money and that have not proven to be that successful in the past are a bad idea at this time of economic uncertainty.
- Carlos often shares stories of past parents' weekends that were successful and unsuccessful.
- Tim has said little at the meetings thus far.

You have decided that the team needs a leader if it is going to get the Parents' Weekend scheduled for spring semester. Based upon their identities, verbal and nonverbal preferences, and adaptation skills, who do you think should be the leader of the team?

Each individual has strengths and weaknesses. Discuss the pros and cons of each choice. Record your comments in the table below.

INDIVIDUAL	PROS	CONS

Which individual would be your first choice as leader?

_____

Explain your recommended choice:

TOURISM ACTIVITY

Step 1: Watch the video clip about Istanbul. Your instructor will play the video in class.

Consider the following: There are several challenges for tourists who visit Istanbul, including the following:

A. Search for authenticity
   List examples:

B. Social norms
   List examples:

C. Social expectations
   List examples:

D. Culture shock
   List examples:

E. Language differences
   List examples:

Step 2: As a team, prioritize the challenges and provide reasons for each of your decisions.

CHALLENGE	RANK 1 TO 5 (1 = GREATEST, 5 = LEAST)	JUSTIFICATION FOR YOUR RANKING
Search for authenticity—finding the real culture		
Social norms—the spoken and unspoken rules of behavior governing communication and actions		
Social expectations—perceptions of what is anticipated of others		
Culture shock—the disorientation that occurs upon entering a new culture		
Language differences—unfamiliarity with code systems (words and meaning) used by people in social systems		

PERSONAL REPORT OF INTERCULTURAL COMMUNICATION APPREHENSION (PRICA)

Directions *Complete the following assignment at the end of the semester. The fourteen statements below are comments frequently made by people with regard to communication with people from other cultures. Please indicate how much you agree with these statements by marking a number representing your response to each statement, using the following choices:*

1 = Strongly Disagree   2 = Disagree   3 = Neutral   4 = Agree   5 = Strongly Agree

_____   1.   Generally, I am comfortable interacting with a group of people from different cultures.

_____   2.   I am tense and nervous while interacting with people from different cultures.

_____   3.   I like to get involved in group discussions with others who are from different cultures.

_____   4.   Engaging in a group discussion with people from different cultures makes me nervous.

_____   5.   I am calm and relaxed with interacting with a group of people who are from different cultures.

_____   6.   While participating in a conversation with a person from a different culture, I get nervous.

_____   7.   I have no fear of speaking up in a conversation with a person from a different culture.

_____   8.   Ordinarily I am very tense and nervous in a conversation with a person from a different culture.

_____   9.   Ordinarily I am very calm and relaxed in a conversation with a person from a different culture.

_____ 10.   While conversing with a person from a different culture, I feel very relaxed.

_____ 11.   I am afraid to speak up in conversations with a person from a different culture.

_____ 12.   I face the prospect of interacting with people from different cultures with confidence.

_____ 13.   My thoughts become confused and jumbled when interacting with people from different cultures.

_____ 14.   Communicating with people from different cultures makes me feel uncomfortable.

James W. Neuliep and James C. McCroskey, Excerpt from: "The Development of Intercultural and Interethnic Communication Apprehension Scales," *Communication Research Reports,* vol. 14, issue 2. Copyright © 1997 by Taylor & Francis Group.

SUPPLEMENTAL MATERIAL ACTIVITIES

DEATH OF JOSSELINE
BY MARGARET REGAN

Directions: *The following questions refer to the book, The Death of Josseline. This activity is designed to discuss some of the experiences that Margaret Regan shares in the book. Make sure to think critically about each question and discuss thoroughly with your team. These questions will aid in connecting class concepts to this specific book and your upcoming paper. Provide rationale for your answers; there are no wrong or right answers.*

Activity #1—Discussion

1. *The Death of Josseline* is a collection of stories representing many people in different roles along the border of Arizona and Mexico. In our culture and pop culture unit, we learned about stereotypes and the power of media. Does the portrayal of migrants in popular films and other media align with the stories told in *The Death of Josseline*? If so, how are they similar? If not, how do they differ?

2. Immigration affects both the Mexico and the United States side of the border. What are some of the impacts that migrants have had on Mexican cities? What are some of the impacts that migrants have had on US cities? Are these impacts similar or different?

3. Josseline's mother, Sonia, arranged for her 10-year-old son and 14-year-old daughter to travel from El Salvador to Los Angeles via a coyote. What are some dialectical tensions that Sonia may have experienced in choosing to hire a coyote?

4. Refer to the Arizona–Sonora Borderlands map located in the beginning of the book, noting the size of the Tohono O'odham Nation. Within this nation, Mike Wilson carried out his water ministry, leaving water for migrants traveling from Mexico to the United States. Wilson experienced opposition and support for his ministry. What are some reasons members of the Tohono O'odham Nation might support Wilson's efforts? What are some reasons members might oppose his efforts? Would your team support or oppose Wilson? Why?

5. Why is Café Justo so significant? Should this business model be implemented elsewhere? Why or why not?

6. Margaret Regan offers a variety of perspectives pertaining to the construction of the wall between Mexico and the United States. What symbolic description of the wall offered in *The Death of Josseline* is the most appropriate? Why?

NEITHER WOLF NOR DOG

BY KENT NERBURN

Activity #1: Drunk on Jesus

Dan thought that Jesus, the centerpiece of Christianity, should have been an Indian. So let's imagine that the Indians believed what the Christian missionaries told them: that Jesus came to earth as an Indian and would come again to save them.

   Which of the following characteristics about Jesus coming to earth as an Indian would have been the most troubling to the US government of the time?

A—He didn't own anything.
B—He slept outside on the earth.
C—He moved around all the time.
D—He shared everything he got.
E—He talked with the Great Spirit as his father.

Which of the following would have made the government **most** angry if Jesus had came back as an Indian?

A—Jesus would have persuaded the Indians to fight the government.
B—The white people would have been exposed as not living like Jesus had told them.
C—The white people would have been afraid Jesus was coming to help the Indians, not them.
D—It would have shown the Indians that if they were united they could regain their land.
E—The white people were afraid Jesus would give them the Indians hope.

For Dan, how were the contradictions between the message of Christianity and the practices of the US government regarding the treatment of native peoples reconciled, if at all?

Activity #2: Ethnic identity

Ethnic identity means having a sense of belonging to a particular group and knowing something about the shared experiences of group members. When the dominant coalition of whites came to America, they began to identify the peoples they found in ways that were different from how they had previously been identified, causing confusion and conflict. These identifiers have changed over time. However, the confusion and conflict remains.

Part I: As a team, clarify the meaning and the basis for using the following ethnic identifiers. For example, why would you call someone one of these particular labels?

A—American Indian
B—Native American
C—Native People
D—First People
E—Aboriginal People

Part II: Which of the following would Dan prefer that you use if you were to meet him and introduce him to others?

A—American Indian
B—Native American
C—Native People
D—First People
E—Aboriginal People

Provide a reason for your first choice.

Which of the following would you think Dan would least prefer?

A—American Indian
B—Native American
C—Native People
D—First People
E—Aboriginal People

Provide a reason for your first choice.

Activity #3: The Land

White people and native people have differing perspectives that reflect dialectical tensions about which position should prevail. Consider each of the following tensions and complete the following items:

Decide which position is dominant.
Provide a reason supporting your decision.

Tension 1: The land is something to be shared vs. the land is property to be owned.

Dominant position:

Reason:

Tension 2: Receiving tobacco is a sacred gift vs. picking up a pack of cigarettes at a store is a common act.

Dominant position:

Reason:

Tension 3: The true native story should be told vs. the native story should reflect what the dominant coalition believes it should be told.

Dominant position:

Reason:

Tension 4: Indians feel sadness about what happened to their elders and people vs. white people feel guilt about what the dominant culture did to the people who first inhabited the continent.

Dominant position:

Reason:

Tension 5: Silence and waiting should precede speaking and taking action vs. speaking and taking action should precede silence and waiting.

Dominant position:

Reason:

Which of these five dialectical tensions listed above (1-2-3-4-5) is the most difficult to determine? Why?

Which of the five dialectical tensions is the least difficult to determine? Why?

THE SPIRIT CATCHES YOU AND YOU FALL DOWN

BY ANNE FADIMAN

There are three tasks to this activity.

Lia Lee died on August 31, 2012. She was thirty years old and had been in a vegetative state since the age of four. Until the day of her death, her family cared for her lovingly at home. Now, years after her story was written, some have questioned whether Anne Fadiman was evenhanded in her presentation of Hmong culture and medical culture. Thus, the question for you to consider today is, "How might this book have been different if it had been written by a team of authors?"

To consider this question, the publishers of the book have brought together the following group of individuals to consider whether the story of Lia and her family should be rewritten. These individuals include:

A. A member of the Hmong community

B. A doctor

C. An anthropologist

D. An intercultural communication specialist

E. A journalist

Your first task is to consider the perspective each of these individuals might have coming into the discussion.

INDIVIDUAL	PERSPECTIVE
A member of the Hmong community	
A doctor	
An anthropologist	
An intercultural communication specialist	
A journalist	